"She had picked up a
small flat piece of wood

Charles Demuth : Behind a Laughing Mask

University of Oklahoma Press : Norman

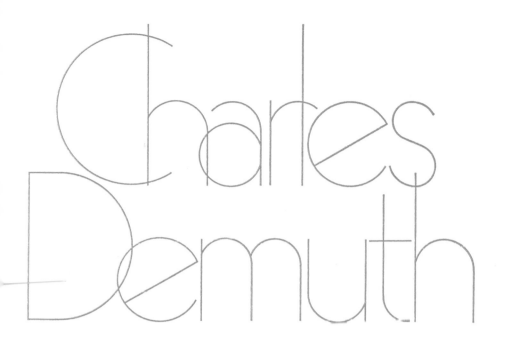

Charles Demuth

Behind a Laughing Mask

By Emily Farnham

INTERNATIONAL STANDARD BOOK NUMBER: 0–8061–0913–0

LIBRARY OF CONGRESS CATALOG CARD NUMBER: 70–108804

Copyright 1971 by the University of Oklahoma Press, Publishing Division of the University. Composed and printed at Norman, Oklahoma, U.S.A., by the University of Oklahoma Press. First edition.

To the memory of my mother,
METTA LAKE FARNUM,
a ninth-generation American who
loved music, art, and books;
and who, at eighty-nine,
looked forward to this par-
ticular book

Acknowledgments

This volume is the result of the generous co-operation of many individuals and institutions over the fourteen-year period during which it has been in the process of emerging. Among the legion of contributors to this emergence I wish to mention gratefully and thank formally the following (some of whom are deceased):

For encouragement and constructive criticism at the inception of the study—Dr. Frank Seiberling and Dr. Sidney Kaplan.

For kindness in granting interviews—Louetta Bowman, Charles Daniel, Stuart Davis, Christopher Demuth, Marcel Duchamp, Elsie (Mrs. Frank J.) Everts, Edith Gregor (Mrs. Samuel) Halpert, Darrell Larsen, Robert Locher, Henry McBride, Susan Watts Street, Carl Van Vechten, Richard W. C. Weyand, William Carlos Williams.

For courtesy in replying to Demuth questionnaires—George Biddle, Marcel Duchamp, Henry McBride, Abraham Walkowitz, William Carlos Williams.

For generous research assistance and help in obtaining photographs and reproductions—Donald Gallop and his assistant, Anne (Mrs. H.) Whelpley of the Yale University Library; also, the Yale University Art Gallery, and Herbert S. Levy.

For outright gifts of photographs or color transparencies for use as illustrations—Leo Castelli, Elsie (Mrs. Frank J.) Everts, Robert Indiana, William H. Lane of the William H. Lane Foundation, Darrell Larsen, Robert Locher, Mr. and Mrs. Arthur Magill, Dorothy Norman, The Norton Gallery and School of Art, Georgia O'Keeffe, Mr. and Mrs. Robert C. Scull, Richard W. C. Weyand.

For permission to use as illustrations reproductions of works which they own—The Art Institute of Chicago, David G. Ashton, Jr., The Baltimore Museum of Art, The Barnes Foundation, The Boston Museum of Fine Arts, The Brooklyn Museum, The Columbus Gallery of Fine Arts, Edith Gregor (Mrs. Samuel) Halpert, Richard H. Hopf, The Los Angeles County Museum of Art, Violette de Mazia, The Metropolitan Museum of Art, The Museum of Modern Art, The Philadelphia Museum of Art, Mrs. Stanley R. Resor, James Thrall Soby, Mr. and Mrs. Burton Tremaine, The Whitney Museum of American Art, The Wichita Art Museum, Yale University Art Gallery, Yale Library.

For permission to quote from the following copyrighted works —George Biddle (*Adolphe Borie* and *An American Artist's Story*); Marcel Duchamp (Charles Demuth, "For Richard Mutt," *The Blind Man*); Charles H. Hapgood (Hutchins Hapgood, *A Victorian in the Modern World*); Georgia O'Keeffe (Charles Demuth, "Between Four and Five," *Camera Work*; Charles Demuth, Introduction to 1926 catalogue "Georgia O'Keeffe Paintings," The Intimate Gallery; Charles Demuth, foreword to catalogue "Peggy Bacon," The Intimate Gallery; Charles Demuth, Introduction to 1929 catalogue for Georgia O'Keeffe exhibition, The Intimate Gallery).

Also *Art in America* (Lloyd Goodrich, "The Decade of the Armory Show"); *The Art Journal* (Emily Farnham, "Charles Demuth's Bermuda Landscapes"); *Art News* (David Antin, "Warhol: the Silver Tenement," and David Bourdon, "E=MC² à Go-Go"); Bollingen Foundation (André Malraux, *Museum Without Walls* Vol. I of *The Psychology of Art*); Doubleday & Company (From *Part of a Long Story*, by Agnes Boulton. Copyright © 1958 by Agnes Boulton Kaufman. Reprinted by permission of Doubleday & Company, Inc.); Harcourt, Brace &

World (Sidney Janis, *Abstract and Surrealist Art in America*); Harvard University Press (Sigfried Giedion, *Space, Time and Architecture*).

Also the John Day Company, Inc. (Copyright © 1937 by the John Day Company, Inc. Reprinted from *The Importance of Living*, by Lin Yutang by permission of The John Day Company, Inc., publisher); The Literary Guild of America (*America and Alfred Stieglitz, a Collective Portrait*, edited by Waldo Frank and others); The Museum of Modern Art (Andrew Carnduff Ritchie, *Charles Demuth*); New Directions Publishing Corporation (William Carlos Williams, *The Autobiography of William Carlos Williams*. Copyright 1948, 1949, 1951 by William Carlos Williams. Reprinted by permission of New Directions Publishing Corporation; William Carlos Williams, *Collected Earlier Poems*. Copyright 1921, 1938 by William Carlos Williams. Reprinted by permission of New Directions Publishing Corporation); The Pennsylvania Academy of the Fine Arts (1955 catalogue for 150th Anniversary Exhibition).

Also the Pennsylvania State University Press (Emily Genauer, text for 1966 catalogue "Charles Demuth of Lancaster," William Penn Memorial Museum); Random House, Inc. (Gertrude Stein, *The Autobiography of Alice B. Toklas*, Copyright 1933, 1960 by Gertrude Stein); Time-Life Library of Art (Calvin Tomkins and the Editors of Time-Life Books, *The World of Marcel Duchamp*); W. W. Norton & Company, Inc. (*The New Caravan*, Copyright 1936 by W. W. Norton & Company, Inc., Copyright Renewed 1964 by Lewis Mumford. Ed. by Alfred Kreymborg, Lewis Mumford, and Paul Rosenfeld).

For intelligent, expert typing of the text performed with the utmost integrity—Jane (Mrs. Norman) Keller.

Most remarkable of all, for reading the text and making suggestions preceding publication—Georgia O'Keeffe.

EMILY FARNHAM

Greenville, North Carolina
June 22, 1970

ix

Picture Sources and Credits

END PAPERS: Philadelphia Museum of Art photograph by A. J. Wyatt, Staff Photographer.

PHOTOS INSERTED IN THE TEXT: Pp. 33, 35—Jack Long. 113, 114, 115, 118, 119, 120—New York Public Library. 152, 154—Kelly Adams (material provided by Yale University Library). 159, 161, 164, 165—Yale University Library.

BLACK AND WHITE PLATES: Plate 1—Jack Long. Plates 2, 3 (a, b, c, d)—Photographs presented to the author by Robert Locher and Richard Weyand. Plate 4 (a, b, c)—Alfred Stieglitz. Plate 5—Photograph presented to the author by Locher and Weyand. Plate 6—Alfred Stieglitz. Plate 7—Photograph presented to the author by Locher and Weyand. Plate 8 (a, b)—Carl Van Vechten. Plate 9—Dorothy Norman. Plate 10-a—Museum of Modern Art photograph by Soichi Sunami; 10-b—Leo Castelli Gallery photograph by Rudolph Burckhardt. Plate 11—Phillips Studio of Philadelphia. Plate 12—Barnes Foundation photograph. Plate 13—Negative for photograph presented to the author by Elsie (Mrs. Frank J.) Everts. Plate 14—Columbus Gallery of Fine Arts photograph. Plate 15-a—Parke-Bernet photograph by Taylor and Dull, Inc.; 15-b—Metropolitan Museum of Art photograph. Plate 16—Baltimore Museum of Art photograph. Plate 17—Los Angeles County Museum of Art photograph. Plate 18—Jack Long. Plate 19-a—

Barnes Foundation photograph; 19–b—Museum of Modern Art photograph by Rudolph Burckhardt. Plates 20, 21, 22—Barnes Foundation photographs. Plate 23—Philadelphia Museum of Art photograph. Plate 24—Columbus Gallery of Fine Arts photograph. Plate 25–a—Art Institute of Chicago photograph; 25–b—Museum of Modern Art photograph. Plate 26—Columbus Gallery of Fine Arts photograph. Plate 27—Yale University Art Gallery photograph. Plate 28—Oliver Baker. Plate 29—Museum of Modern Art photograph. Plate 30–a—Downtown Gallery photograph by Oliver Baker; 30–b—Kelly Adams. Plate 31–a—Metropolitan Museum of Art photograph; 31–b—Rudolph Burckhardt. Plate 32–a —Art Gallery of Ontario photograph; 32–b—Whitney Museum of American Art photograph by Eric Pollitzer; 32–c—Eric Pollitzer; 32–d—Eric Pollitzer; 32–e—Kelly Adams, from a Frederick Teuscher (Portable Gallery Press) color slide.

COLOR PLATES: Color Plate I—Sandak, Inc., New York. Color Plate II—Museum of Modern Art. Color Plate III—Brooklyn Museum. Color Plate IV—Yale University Art Gallery. Color Plate V–a—Yale University Art Gallery; V–b—Kelly Adams. Color Plate VI—William H. Lane Foundation. Color Plate VII—Whitney Museum of American Art photograph by G. Clements. Color Plate VIII—Norton Gallery and School of Art.

Contents

Illustrations

xv

xvi

COLOR PLATES

Charles Demuth : Behind a Laughing Mask

Introduction

~~~ A young man (to call him a genius would have flattered him) was painting in a garden. It was in the forenoon, a summer afternoon, and the light which flooded the landscape was that of the sun as it first touches the line of the tree tops when it's going on its way to light the other side of the world. All the objects in the garden took from the light, for the moment, some of its color and quality . . . . When the young man began to paint, all things seemed to him to glitter and to float in golden liquid so dazzling was the scene.[1]

~~~ But I love Broadway and—well, and vulgarity, and gin. In fact, I love my country.[2]

Every life holds contrasts—between the dream and the reality, the lie and truth, the spiritual and the carnal. But Demuth's life remains endlessly fascinating because the "dazzling," "golden" "glitter" of his talent contrasts so absolutely with the dross of his perversity.

Both sides of his nature come together in many of his works, most shockingly in the delicate flower paintings. William Carlos Williams said: "In my painting of orchids which Charlie did— the one called *Pink Lady Slippers* [1918]—he was interested in

---

[1] Charles Demuth, "In Black and White," unpublished MS.
[2] Charles Demuth, "You Must Come Over," unpublished MS.

the similarity between the forms of the flowers and the phallic symbol, the male genitals. Charlie was like that."[3] A flower blossom—fresh, perfect, beautiful beyond compare—has the most sublime spiritual meanings. Yet, although Demuth understood this fact better than most, since he passionately loved flowers, in his art the beauty of the blossoms and his perverted sex life merged.

One is reminded of Leonardo da Vinci's *La Gioconda*, beneath whose quiescence, serenity, and ambiguous smile resides an endlessly intriguing, disturbing element that causes us to sense in her a waiting serpent, a Lucrezia Borgia. The enigmatic, sinister content which converges with exquisite beauty in many Demuth works presents a comparable phenomenon. And since both artists are known to have been homosexual (though the Italian is believed to have been nonovertly so), it can be assumed that the hypnotic quality common to their art is the expression of a sublimated abnormal sexual pattern.

Demuth's life involved a vital inner existence dependent upon intuition and feeling, while the surface of his life was comparatively uneventful. It is hoped that in this biography the recording of a plethora of factual details may, in summation, bring him to life. He would have been pleased by such an effort, since, like Henry James, this was the way he himself worked in his illustrations—employing a multitude of details to evoke a sensation.

Edward Alden Jewell, when he was art critic for the *New York Times*, wrote:

Demuth comes closest to "naturalism" in some of his flower watercolors, although there is nearly always even here, a kind of tell-tale introspective, shy, etherealized loveliness.

Charles Demuth was like Kipling's cat that "walked by himself." And perhaps his garden adjoined an ivory tower.[4]

[3] Interview with William Carlos Williams.
[4] Quoted by Lettie (Mrs. John E.) Malone, in "Charles Demuth," 16.

1

Enigmatic Personality

Charles Demuth's long friendship with William Carlos Williams, the doctor-poet, began when they were young students together in Philadelphia. Demuth, who was from nearby Lancaster and attended Drexel Institute from 1901 to 1905, enrolled at the Pennsylvania Academy of the Fine Arts in 1905. Williams, who was from Rutherford, New Jersey, graduated in medicine at the University of Pennsylvania in 1906. Long afterward, Dr. Williams wrote in his *Autobiography:*

During these days I met Ezra Pound in my room in the dormitories. I met Hilda Doolittle and must have brushed against Marianne Moore also, without meeting her, at Bryn Mawr. I met Charles Demuth over a dish of prunes at Mrs. Chain's boarding house on Locust Street and formed a lifelong friendship on the spot with dear Charlie. . . .

In spring among the back streets, when supper would be over . . . , Charlie Demuth used to take long walks with me in West Philadelphia. . . . There was a high brick wall along the south side of Locust Street, just west of Thirty-sixth, inside of which there must have been an old garden, long neglected. The thought of it fascinated me. Charlie laughed when I spoke of it. "Not many could enjoy such a thing as that," he said, "by merely looking at the outside of the wall."[1]

Both Williams and Demuth were able to sense the magic waiting to be discovered behind garden walls. Demuth especially loved

[1] William Carlos Williams, *The Autobiography of William Carlos Williams,* 51–53. Hereafter cited as *Autobiography.*

the barrier behind which lies obscurely hidden, but at the same time somehow revealed, that rare treasure which men call beauty.

In the foreword of the catalogue for a 1928 Peggy Bacon exhibition presented at Alfred Stieglitz' Intimate Gallery, Demuth wrote: "All this work comes only out of the American scene, it could come from no other. All of it is covered, glazed with our own wit. One feels in it something very funny, very sharp and bright, and always an after touch of the pathetic. I think Peggy Bacon finds comedy and tragedy both qualities to be smiled at."[2]

And in his short story "The Voyage Was Almost Over," which described the last evening aboard ship when he sailed to Europe in 1921, Demuth reported the festive after-dinner donning of paper hats by fellow passengers thus:

The professor of Greek wore the hat of a Watteau shepherdess, the oldest woman that of a Harlequin and the infant prodigy a doctor's hood. As they ascended the stairs the light from above, touching their fantastic headgear, gave the effect of a beautiful Masque.[3]

Recalling a costume ball where masks were worn, which both he and Demuth attended, Marcel Duchamp said:

There was no night-club in the Village in 1915, the year that I came over. The Brevoort Café in the hotel of that name was the rendezvous of the artists. There was a lot of drinking. . . .

I remember the Webster Hall Ball—it was a masquerade ball. Webster Hall was located at about East 11th Street between Second and Third Avenues.[4]

In Demuth's watercolor *At Marshall's* (1917) (Plate 12) the leaping central figure wears what appears to be a cat mask. And a masked ball is the theme of two of Demuth's most fascinating,

[2] Charles Demuth, "Peggy Bacon," foreword to catalogue.
[3] Charles Demuth, "The Voyage Was Almost Over," unpublished MS. Hereafter cited as "Voyage."
[4] Interview with Marcel Duchamp.

sophisticated figure pieces: *Costume Sketch (Bal Masque) #1: La Rose Noire (Costume for Black and White Ball)* (1928) and *Costume Sketch (Bal Masque) #2: Costume after Beardsley (for Black and White Ball)* (1928). In the latter work a woman is shown wearing a bouffant white skirt, black hose, black gloves which extend above the elbow, and a décolleté white top with beaded straps. In true Beardsley manner, the design of the white top in *Costume Sketch #2* is a sinister, leering mask the cutout sections of which occur at the level of the woman's breasts.

Demuth made important use of the mask as symbol in two of his *hommages*, the poster portraits he produced late in life as tributes to friends. In *Love, Love, Love* (1928) (Plate 32–a), his *hommage* to Gertrude Stein, a white mask functions as the central motif; while in *Longhi on Broadway* (1927) (Color Plate VI),[5] his *hommage* to Eugene O'Neill, two masks (one red, one blue) appear. Behind the mask which overlaps the large whisky bottle in the latter work Demuth painted a suggestion of the bleary eyes of O'Neill himself; while behind the mask in the former work he indicated pupils and irises in such a way that the viewer feels he is looking into the mystical eyes of the formidable Miss Stein.

A careful survey of Demuth's total production reveals more than the usual interest the artist traditionally has in penetrating beneath false façades in search for reality and truth. He entertained a passionate obsession for all that was "covered, glazed with . . . wit"—for, in short, all that was veiled or masked. Similarly, he understood the kind of distinction resident in delicate surfaces, particularly when those surfaces masked implied profundities. In the aforementioned written tribute Demuth prepared in connection with a Peggy Bacon exhibition, he deplored the fact that "lightness is seldom understood and never forgiven!" This feeling for lightness was allied in his nature to a deep love

[5] Note that the foreword to the Peggy Bacon catalogue and four of the Demuth paintings referred to here in connection with the theme of a masquerade or mask belong to the years 1927–28, when the artist appears to have been deeply interested in this subject.

for anything obliquely stated or half-revealed. Demuth's fellow artist Marsden Hartley understood this when he wrote that his friend "liked nacreous whisperings such as are to be found in the delicate work of that other hyper-sensitive Charles, in the English esthetic world, Charles Conder, whose deepest wonder brought forth . . . fine touches on silk." According to Hartley, Demuth "rubbed his hands, so to speak, if he came close enough to the . . . secrets of life."[6]

The mask which Demuth himself wore was, most of the time, a smiling, witty one. Usually it was a sweet and gentle mask, often it was genial, less frequently it was caustic, bitter, angry, or despondent. Whatever its expression, it was always there, protecting the artist from a too curious world, maintaining what Duchamp called Demuth's "curtain of mental privacy" and what Dr. Williams described as the artist's habit of hiding his thoughts, so that even his close friends scarcely knew him.[7]

Demuth spoke with a strong Lancaster accent in a high, squeaky voice. Like the Spanish, he had "a high giggle that sounded like the whinny of a horse." According to Duchamp, he possessed "kind of a drawn face with piercing eyes. And a wonderful sense of humor. . . . He was very sweet."[8]

In addition, we have been told that Demuth was urbane, shy, cosmopolitan, dandified, and charming. He was all of these things. But he was also stubborn by nature and possessed a quick, violent temper. During the early years of his life, before diabetes was diagnosed, he drank a good deal, living the life of a *débauché*. He was spoiled in the sense that, as is often the way with an only child who is frail, his parents habitually gave him his own way; so that "always having his own way as a child, he had it in manhood."[9] And he was inverted—the typical retiring, sensitive son of an aggressive, dominating mother.

[6] Marsden Hartley, "Farewell, Charles, an Outline in Portraiture of Charles Demuth—Painter," 559–61. Hereafter cited as "Farewell, Charles."
[7] Interviews with Duchamp and Dr. Williams.
[8] Interview with Duchamp.

8

As all of this implies, Demuth possessed a complex, enigmatic personality which, like his art, was replete with contradictions and subterranean subtleties. And this complexity was rendered more impenetrable by the artist's natural aloofness. Dr. Williams said: "Charlie never spilled over to his friends but kept a tight-lipped and well-groomed appearance always. . . . He gave nothing [about himself] away." Also, "due to his being cross-eyed, one eye sometimes looked at his nose, and he never looked right at you. You never knew what he was thinking."[10]

According to Dr. Williams, physically Demuth was "a wisp of a man." His "lower jaw stuck out. His ears stuck out. And he was very lame [owing to a childhood illness which had left him with a bad hip and one leg shorter than the other]."[11] Like his father, he was born with a cast in one eye. Yet the artist possessed beautiful, expressive hands which were said to have a life of their own, to be alive. Alfred Stieglitz photographed them and Hartley wrote about them saying: "How the Chinese would have fêted them, even Charles's whole appearance was at times permeated with Oriental stillness. . . ."[12]

Except for his height Demuth looked something like a Spanish bullfighter. With his long face, olive skin, very black eyes, raven-black hair, and slender figure, he would have looked in character in the pink and blue costume of a toreador. Only his limp would have betrayed the role.

The artist was very vain, as his self-portrait in the nude attests. And he was a great dandy who invariably appeared looking like a fashion plate. When he was in Provincetown, Massachusetts, where the most casual kind of dress prevailed, Demuth would appear wearing "a black shirt, white slacks, a plum-colored scarf tied around his waist, and black-laced shoes, highly polished."[13] He habitually wore English- and Irish-made clothes, and custom-

9 Elsie (Mrs. Frank J.) Everts to the author, May 28, 1956.
10 Interview with Dr. Williams.
11 Interview with Miss Susan Watts Street.
12 Hartley, "Farewell, Charles," 560.
13 Interview with Miss Street.

built shoes. His friends recall that he sometimes wore an especially handsome Donegal tweed jacket, and that he owned the most beautiful neckties in New York. His dealer Charles Daniel said: "He must have the tie that he liked, and he liked the best. That was Demuth. It came out of his sensitivity. It had to be good."[14] The artist was always concerned with quality, liking things which were simultaneously unusual and conservative. One of his favorite sayings was: "It's the last word in that kind of thing."

Further evidence of Demuth's vanity is found in the letter he wrote Stieglitz soon after first seeing the famous Stieglitz photograph of himself garbed in overcoat and scarf, standing before a matted Picasso drawing in a gallery. This letter, dated May 2, 1923, was mailed from the Physiatric Institute in Morristown, New Jersey, where the artist was being treated for diabetes.

DEAR STIEGLITZ:

You have me in a fix. Shall I remain ill retaining that look, die, considering "that moment," the climax of my "looks," or live and change. I think the head is one of the most beautiful things that I have ever known in the world of art. A strange way,—to write of one's own portrait,—but, well, I'm a, perhaps, frank person. I send it this morning to my mother.

The artist practiced certain characteristic mannerisms. One person who knew him recalled that "he always had a white handkerchief in his hand, and often held his hand to his face,"[15] a mannerism conceivably connected with his health. Occasionally he would glance at another person with a look of hurt ferocity. "He had an evasive way of looking aslant at the ground or up at the ceiling when addressing you, followed by short, intense looks of inquiry."[16] One of his acquaintances said that he "never saw Demuth when he wasn't smiling,"[17] and Duchamp wrote: "He had a

[14] Interview with Charles Daniel.
[15] Interview with Carl Van Vechten.
[16] Williams, *Autobiography*, 151.
[17] Interview with Van Vechten.

curious smile reflecting an incessant curiosity for every manifestation life offered."[18] The artist often sat with one arm resting on the arm of a chair or sofa, expressive hand drooping from the wrist.

Lettie Malone, Lancaster woman artist, recalled her home-town friend with affection in a paper she read before the Lancaster County Historical Society in 1948:

Socially he was delightful, with his wit, fine sense of humor, and always sympathetic understanding. Mr. Hammond[19] says of him that he never disparaged a fellow artist. . . . He was extremely modest about his work, showing real appreciation when anyone admired it, never saying unpleasant things about others' work, simply making no comment when he could not like it. His tact and quiet manner made for him many friends in the art world, and outside of it.[20]

Demuth was naturally kind and liberal toward others. Hartley wrote that Demuth "liked to be admired, and certainly, himself, enjoyed and admired avidly."[21] As Mrs. Malone wrote, John Marin was Demuth's natural rival because early in the century the Rutherford man was the only other watercolor painter who approached him. Yet Demuth would see a Marin painting which he especially liked at the Daniel Gallery and say to Daniel: "That Marin down there—it's out of this world."[22] His letters to Stieglitz were studded with words of appreciation for Marin's work and with messages saying that he was forwarding various sums of money in payment for his Marin, Martin, and Lachaise purchases. In a letter to Stieglitz dated March 12, 1923, Demuth wrote:

I have written and talked to Barnes.[23] . . . I hope that he

18 Andrew Carnduff Ritchie, *Charles Demuth*, 17. Quotation from "A Tribute to the Artist" by Marcel Duchamp (hereafter cited as "Tribute").
19 Frederick W. Hammond was a Lancaster picture-framer who did odd jobs around the Demuth home. He once retrieved from a fireplace the four extant letters which Demuth wrote to his mother.
20 Mrs. Malone, "Charles Demuth," 4.
21 Hartley, "Farewell, Charles," 561.
22 Interview with Daniel.
23 Dr. Albert C. Barnes, the physician who made a fortune through the sale of Argyrol, formed one of the finest private art collections in the Western world. It is housed in the Barnes Foundation Museum at Merion, Pennsylvania.

takes those sea things [by Marin]. They are the only really great marines since Courbet. . . .

In similar vein he wrote to the same correspondent on June 18, 1928:

⟿ Well, I've talked Marin for (can it be, now) twenty-five years—anyway, some years before I ever saw him and long before I [first] knew you which was in 1913; and, some years before water-colour came into my own life.

Writing appreciatively concerning Duchamp in a letter to Stieglitz dated February 5, 1928, Demuth noted:

⟿ Marcel . . . is stranger than any of us—and that's writing a lot! But a great painter. The big glass thing, I think, is still the great picture of our time.

And revealing a refreshing attitude toward fame, Demuth wrote in his unpublished play "You Must Come Over":

⟿ If what I like happens to have a famous name attached, it doesn't worry me. I go on liking it. I like Picasso's work—still like it.

Appreciation for fellow artists and their work was characteristic of American artists early in the twentieth century. They were cultured persons within William James's definition of culture—capable of entertaining "sympathies and admirations" as opposed to "dislikes and disdains." Duchamp praised Demuth as having possessed "a marvelous sense of esthetics" and as having been "without the pettiness which afflicts most artists; worshiping his inner self without the usual eagerness to be right."[24] Hartley set up the great Ryder, his contemporary, as his personal god and,

[24] Ritchie, *Charles Demuth*, 17. Quotation from Duchamp, "Tribute."

following Demuth's early death, wrote a ten-page eulogy in which he eloquently praised his late friend's virtues as he saw them, saying: "Charles was, as we all know, a fine painter, he had a true painter's cultivation, he had a real feeling for esthetic values."[25]

Demuth lived through the post–World War I era of disillusionment and the years of depression which followed. Yet he always remained essentially *fin de siècle*. His interest in negative, degenerate aspects of life, the way in which he became an habitué of night clubs and cafés, his "wistful apprehension of what many a too tender soul has called infectious sin,"[26] and his immense respect for his fellow man were all aspects of the *art nouveau* mentality.

The artist could be derisive and caustic, but usually toward anonymous persons. He once quoted Poe, in the above-mentioned foreword for the catalogue of a Peggy Bacon exhibition, as follows:

"Yet we have heard discoursing of carpets, with the air *d'un mouton qui rêve*, fellows who should not and could not be entrusted with the management of their own moustaches. Every one knows that a large floor may have a covering of large figures, and that a small one must have a covering of small—yet this is not all the knowledge in the world."

If Peggy Bacon were a critic, she would belong to the same school of criticism as the person who wrote the preceding lines. "*D'un mouton qui rêve*" . . . covers certain characters, lightly and completely. She, in her portraits . . . covers lightly all the material which is considered related to the giving of the subject—but, how completely![27]

And in a letter to Stieglitz dated October 16, 1929, Demuth complained:

Some one in Boston must have a drawing, it seems, of that

25 Hartley, "Farewell, Charles," 556.
26 *Ibid.*, 554.
27 Demuth, "Peggy Bacon."

13

vintage—the result of [Henry] McBride *chez Creative Art*, you know. "If there were only an acrobat drawing, I'd take that." And if there were an acrobat drawing they'd want peaches. What most of them really need is a banana.

Demuth's wit was a bitter wit, that of a lame, ill person who was courageous. It emerged from a base of perverse contrariness. When he was asked, "What do you look forward to?" he replied "The past." When asked "What do you consider your strongest characteristics?" he answered "Lack of ambition."[28] In the inverted man, humor became a matter of inversion, also.

Dr. Williams, who believed Demuth to have been tubercular as well as diabetic, said: "The heat which burned inside him is a hectic, diabolic heat. It warms up the body and the brain. Knowing the source of it must make a person cynical. This is the reason for the intensification of talent and the cynical wit which occur in such people."[29]

Yet to dismiss Demuth's wit thus is to ignore some of its healthy manifestations. In the artist's figure pieces, for instance, the quality of the wit is positively delightful, akin to the more lusty, vigorous wittiness present in Picasso and his art. Demuth's is a subtle wit, now cynical, now playful, now risqué. Often it manages to capture what Hartley called "the comic insinuation which lies within and behind so much average experience."[30] To have been aware of this "comic insinuation" in routine living, to have impaled it and expressed it palpably—therein lay genius.

Not only was the artist witty, his nature was habitually merry. Advancing and receding according to the condition of his health, there was alive in him to the end a joyous attitude toward life. He loved life and was a happy playmate to his friends.

Demuth was gifted with a capacity for friendship, "believed

---

[28] Charles Demuth, "Confessions: Replies to a Questionnaire," *The Little Review*, Vol. XII, No. 2 (May, 1929), 30–31.

[29] Interview with Dr. Williams.

[30] Hartley, "Farewell, Charles," 561.

PLATE I   The Demuth houses at 120, 118, 116, and 114 East King Street, Lancaster, Pennsylvania, photographed in 1968 after the house at 120–118 had been sold to an insurance firm. The steeple of the Lutheran Church of the Holy Trinity can be seen above the roofs.

PLATE 2   The boy Charles in the Demuth family parlor.

PLATE 3-A Charles with his mother in her garden.

3–B
Ferdinand A.
Demuth,
Charles's father.

3–C
The steeple of the
Lutheran Church of
the Holy Trinity.

3–D
Augusta Wills
Buckius Demuth,
Charles's mother.

 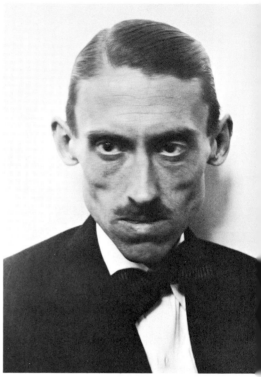

PLATE 4–A, 4–B   Two photographs made by Alfred Stieglitz of the ill Demuth when he was en route to the Morristown sanitarium, spring, 1922.

4–C   Demuth's hands as photographed by Alfred Stieglitz, March, 1923.

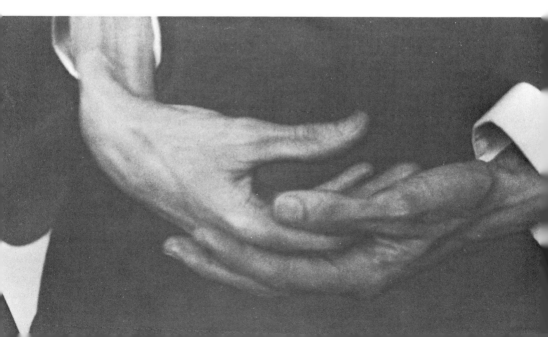

PLATE 5 Sculpture of Demuth by Arnold Rönnebeck, c. 1921.

PLATE 6   Demuth after he had begun to take insulin, as photographed by Alfred Stieglitz, March, 1923.

PLATE 7   Robert Locher.

PLATE 8–A, 8–B Two photographs of Demuth conversing with Georgia O'Keeffe in front of the old Museum of Modern Art, May 3, 1932. Photographs by Carl Van Vechten.

in friends and was amply supplied with them."[31] Duchamp said he was "one of the few artists whom all other artists liked as a real friend, a rare case indeed."[32] And he was popular with both men and women—so much so that he was obliged to resort to special methods for fending off friends and acquaintances when he wanted to work. In New York City he was lionized. "Mabel Dodge would want him at one soirée and Louise Norton Verèse, at another."[33] Demuth would go off to Lancaster to get away from the pressures of the outside world. Because he was financially independent, he could associate with only those he liked, simply avoiding people who bored him or whom he actively disliked— for a sensitive person, a luxurious way of life, indeed.

Although he was popular, Demuth was eccentric, aloof, and something of a snob; a mental snob, according to his fellow artist George Biddle.[34] Having no sympathy for average people engaged in everyday occupations or for the poverty-stricken, squalid, or those who were in any way underdogs on the face of the earth, Demuth was also something of a social snob, an individual less humanist than hedonist. He loved the life and pose of cultivated leisure, of the *flâneur*, and all that goes with this rare segment of existence. Because of this aspect of his character, and because he was a finished person of breeding and good manners, he was naturally attracted to persons belonging to the upper income brackets (such as the Stettheimer sisters and Susan Watts

---

[31] *Ibid.*

[32] Ritchie, *Charles Demuth*, 17. Quotation from Duchamp, "Tribute."

[33] Interview with Miss Street.

[34] From the answers given to a Demuth questionnaire by George Biddle. For years, books on art have slavishly repeated an alleged statement by Demuth which first appeared on p. 216 of Biddle's book *An American Artist's Story*. This statement reads: "One recalls the charming *bon mot* of Charlie Demuth. 'All of us drew our inspiration from the spring of French modernism. John Marin pulled his up in bucketfuls but he spilled much along the way. I had only a teaspoon in which to carry mine; but I never spilled a drop.'"

Robert Locher, who knew Demuth well, said: "Charles never said that. It wouldn't have been like him to say that." To anyone who knows Demuth's mind, this so-called *bon mot* seems the last thing he would have said about himself. Surely in this perhaps mistakenly recalled statement, Biddle may be trying to laugh last.

15

Street of New York) and to such individuals as Duchamp who, like himself, enjoyed the leisurely way of life. At one point in his life, probably when he was very young, Demuth wrote:

➤ I always hope for the grand manner. If one does not acquire this, or have it—there is no success in the purely social.[35]

From the above it could be concluded that Demuth took society, and his place in it, seriously. Yet he was not a social climber. According to Duchamp: "It was fun to be with Demuth because he didn't care where he belonged or was in the social scale."[36] Essentially, this is an aristocratic or highbrow attitude, since it is only the middlebrow who climbs. As Demuth himself would have expressed it, he *was*; that is, he was fundamentally akin to the Stettheimers, Streets, and Duchamps of the world.

On the surface Demuth appeared to be (and may have wished to appear to be) almost a dilettante, with what Hartley called "a flair for the frivolities, but they had to be of elegant tone, a little precious in their import, swift in their results, he spent hours chasing phantoms of an aristocratic nature, and was often overcome by the highly defined appearance of things." He found things interesting "only by the degree of excitement they held" for him; being "a bit proustian in this, he liked fragile gossip . . . the flair of à la mode creations . . . superficialities."[37]

Demuth loved elegance. He and a Lancaster friend, New York decorator Robert Locher, furnished the Demuth home in a Victorian manner consistent with the character of the beautiful old structure. Everything the artist touched gained an elegant, unpretentious quality. Even the titles of his paintings, though he was never really at home with words, possess quality—such titles as *End of the Parade—Coatesville, Pa.* (1920), *Incense of a New Church* (1921) (Plate 26), and *My Egypt* (1927). The artist tried constantly to avoid the commonplace and the banal (now the chosen precinct of Pop art).

[35] Weyand Scrapbook No. I, 93.
[36] Interview with Duchamp.   [37] Hartley, "Farewell, Charles," 559.

Fortunately, it was never necessary for Demuth to earn a living. During his early years he managed to get along on the modest allowance provided by his mother. And before he died, his paintings had sold so well he was able to leave a modest estate of his own earning, along with unsold paintings worth a potential fortune. Financial independence was a blessing, particularly since Demuth was lame. Because of this independence, he was able to paint, paint slowly as was his natural way, achieve a real fruition of his talent, and keep his paintings off the market until he felt that he was ready to submit them—all advantages which might have been denied him had he been obliged to earn a living.

The artist's attitude toward his paintings was hardheaded. Demuth did not resent negative criticism of his work, but learned from it—a sign of intellectual maturity. Toward the mundane matter of selling his works he maintained an aristocratic attitude of nonchalance, even while selling at high prices, compatible with the *art nouveau* attitude of Art for Art's Sake. His letters to Stieglitz reveal that he wanted very much to sell, however. In a letter dated January 29, 1923, Demuth said he wanted the entrepreneur at 291 Fifth Avenue to take his watercolors "as Daniel has sold one or two—well, below the 'thousands.' " In a letter dated January 28, 1930, Stieglitz wrote Demuth saying: "Several people have been after your 'Green Pears,' but have balked at $2,500.00 saying that at Kraushaar's, etc., etc.—Always the same old story." And on September 10, 1931, Demuth wrote complainingly to Stieglitz: "If I were only as well off as they think—I'd give them away. At that I almost, it seems, do!"

The artist kept careful watch over the building of his prestige and the maturing of his talent, guided by a mysterious lifelong knowledge of who he was and where he was headed. His numerous letters to Stieglitz court professional favors from the dealer who was sympathetic with and knew so well how to promote the avant-garde artist in America during the early decades of the century. Demuth needed a Stieglitz to make him famous as one of the Stieglitz Group of Five, just as at an earlier time he had needed a Daniel to sponsor him as a neophyte in New York.

Yet in spite of the patronage of these two dealers and the colorful aspects of his personality, Demuth was so retiring by nature and so loath to advertise himself that many Americans did not discover him until the Whitney Museum's memorial exhibition of 1937–38, more than two years after the artist's death. In Lancaster at the middle of the century the man in the street still had not heard of Charles Demuth, partly because—in spite of his considerable success in New York—the artist had never made any attempt to become known in his home town; indeed he was actually hostile to any kind of local publicity. In addition, much of Demuth's work lies hidden away in private collections, so that only a few persons realize the quality and scope of his total production. Ironically, the man who loved what was half-hidden, half-revealed, is himself obscure.

Someone has written that with less eccentricity and more aggressiveness Demuth could have been the Guys of his time, a twentieth-century version of Baudelaire's dandy. But Demuth was himself, and seldom has so refined a native product graced the American scene.

In 1929 Demuth wrote in the *Little Review* article "Confessions: Replies to a Questionnaire": "If I could write and believed in having a cause—well, certainly I would write about the paintings which are being done, at the moment, in my country." And to the question, "What things do you really dislike?" he once replied, "Anything concealing a 'cause.'" Because he was firm and stubborn in his beliefs, however, many of the artist's likes and dislikes could be called causes, and Demuth himself could be said to have carried aloft the banner of a credo.

One of the things the artist distrusted was the written or spoken word, in regard to which he once wrote in his published essay "Across a Greco Is Written":

Colour and line can say quite a bit, unaided by words, when used by one for whom they are a means of expression. Words are not to me a means. I can only paint. . . . To me words explain too much and say too little. . . .

Across a Greco, across a Blake, across a Rubens, across a Watteau, across a Beardsley is written in larger letters than any printed page will ever dare to hold, or Broadway façade or roof support, what its creator had to say about it. To translate these painted sentences into words—well, try it. With the best of luck the "sea changes" will be great. Or, granting a translation of this kind were successful what would you have but what was there already, and as readable— and perhaps, on repetition, a trifle boring.[38]

Yet, like Hartley, Demuth never got over trying to write, though apparently he arrived at a realization that the literary art was not his forte.

Demuth disliked talk about art. And in connection with this antipathy it is interesting to realize that more than one of his close friends was an inveterate talker. Stieglitz, who dominated any conversation he engaged in, would "talk by the hour about 'life,' as it manifests . . . itself in all human relations—marriage, politics, morality."[39] Miss Street, New York society girl whom the artist first met in Provincetown in 1914, was also an inces- sant talker whose conversation Locher once unkindly described as: "Trivia, trivia, trivia."[40] Hartley was an excessively wordy man, with regard to both the spoken and the written word, but even he would attempt to escape from Hutchins Hapgood and George Cram Cook in Provincetown when they would begin conversing about the universe. Hartley wrote:

There was the customary inflowing at Mary's down along, or at Jack's up along, and in between this area Hutchins, or Hutch, and Jig (Cook) could be found interminably talking about the universe which never ended, and they would be talking about it now quite likely, if they were together—and as it wore some of us down so, if we saw Hutch and Jig coming up along, Demuth and myself would

[38] Charles Demuth, "Across a Greco Is Written," *Creative Art*, Vol. V (Sep- tember 29, 1929), 629 and 634. Hereafter cited as "Across a Greco."
[39] Hutchins Hapgood, *A Victorian in the Modern World*, 337. Hereafter cited as *A Victorian*.
[40] Interview with Robert Locher.

say—let's scoot, here come Hutch and Jig talking about the universe, and it always seemed so odd that they could find so much of it to talk about, and nobody knows if they ever came to perfect and definite conclusions.[41]

Demuth did not dislike talk in general—only serious conversation. He liked light social chatter, harmless gossip, badinage. From this one could draw the inference, as George Biddle did, that Demuth was not a true intellectual, only "intellectually sophisticated."[42]

Actually, both Demuth and Duchamp entertained distaste for the serious artist, and in this attitude the two friends shared an entire philosophy. It is a philosophy more Eastern than Western (reminding one that "Charles's whole appearance was at times permeated with Oriental stillness"[43]), one which says: Let us relax and meditate on the enjoyment of living and the importance of leisure, let us sit in the shade drinking sweet wine while we watch our industrious neighbor fall off his roof. Demuth's personal philosophy was, in fact, strikingly close to the teachings of Lao-tse, which dwell upon "the wisom of the foolish, the advantage of camouflage, the strength of weakness, and the simplicity of the truly sophisticated."[44]

> What is in the end to be shrunk
> Must first be stretched.
> Whatever is to be weakened
> Must begin by being made strong.
> What is to be overthrown
> Must begin by being set up.
> He who would be a taker
> Must begin as a giver.
> This is called "dimming" one's light.
> It is thus that the soft overcomes the hard

[41] Hartley, "Farewell, Charles," 557.
[42] From the answers given to a Demuth questionnaire by George Biddle.
[43] Quoted at greater length previously in connection with a description of the artist's hands, p. 9.
[44] Lin Yutang, *The Importance of Living*, 105.

And the weak, the strong.
"It is best to leave the fish down in his pool;
Best to leave the State's sharpest weapons
where none can see them."[45]

Calling Chinese philosophy a "gay science," Lin Yutang has suggested that the world "has need of a wise and merry philosophy. . . . After all, only a gay philosophy is profound philosophy; the serious philosophies of the West haven't even begun to understand what life is." In a passage which closely parallels the thinking of Demuth and Duchamp, he has written: "The modern man takes life far too seriously, and because he is too serious, the world is full of troubles."[46] Conjuring up the specter of all of Demuth's burdens (lameness, tuberculosis, diabetes, homosexuality, and social disapproval), Lin Yutang has written: "I call no man wise until he has made the progress from the wisdom of knowledge to the wisdom of foolishness, and become a laughing philosopher, feeling first life's tragedy and then life's comedy. For we must weep before we can laugh."[47]

But can such a philosophy bear fruit? Duchamp did not become "too lazy to play chess, for besides the pawns there are other stakes"; and Demuth did not become "too lazy to look at the hills and streams, for there is a painting within my heart's portals."[48] Demuth was deceptively a lounger or dilettante. During the long periods when he isolated himself in his upstairs studio at the rear of the Demuth home in Lancaster, he worked hard, to the limit of his physical capacity; and at these times his philosophy did bear fruit. Demuth's cheerful philosophy was a mature one which emerged from the tragic circumstances of his life. Behind his playboy façade, he worked.

In addition to a distaste for words and seriousness, Demuth enjoyed other "causes." He entertained a restrained attitude

[45] *Ibid.*, 107. This is a quotation from Lao-tse (604?–531 B.C., after 518 B.C.), Chinese philosopher and moralist who became the founder of Taoism.
[46] *Ibid.*, 13.
[47] *Ibid.*
[48] *Ibid.*, 154.

toward the academic in art, the stale parrotlike school product as opposed to the truly creative object. He once wrote that a Homer Martin landscape was "all very quiet, all almost of the academy—but, all removed by him into his created world."[49] In "Across a Greco Is Written" Demuth noted that he was able to enjoy a painting even when it had been produced by a famous artist: "Some day, when before a painting, you will see it without thought of the name of its author, or amount paid. You will see it in its glory in the world of paint. You will have received the stigmata."[50]

And in "You Must Come Over" he referred to a quality in Washington Allston's self-portrait in the Boston Museum, one "which creates between itself and the beholder an understanding, a sympathy—call it what you like if you know what I'm talking about—otherwise, ask Dr. Barnes."[51]

Demuth wrote frequently to Stieglitz in sorrowing disappointment at the regrettable lack of understanding about art in a Philistine America. Writing to the New York dealer from London on August 13, 1921, he said:

The National Gallery has been rearranged by some rare hands—and one wonderful Greco added.

I wonder if it will ever happen in the land of the free? Or—is it happening? I never knew . . . not so surely, that New York, if not the country, has something not found here. It makes me feel almost like running back and doing something about it—but what does that come to? So few understand love and work. I think if a few do we may not have lived entirely without point.

Six years later, in a letter to Stieglitz dated August 15, 1927, Demuth wrote that Washington Allston's self-portrait, with which he was greatly impressed, "is able to say: 'America doesn't really care—still, if one is really an artist and at the same time

---

[49] Demuth, "You Must Come Over."
[50] Demuth, "Across a Greco," *Creative Art*, Vol. V (September 29, 1929), 634.
[51] Demuth, "You Must Come Over."

an American, just this not caring, even though it drives one mad, can be artistic material.' "

As indicated above, Demuth rarely condemned another artist, being instead genuinely appreciative of the work of other men. Yet, according to Hartley, he "never could abide the vulgarities in the world of flower painting produced by a powerful painter like Courbet, who has no trace of feeling for them at all."[52] (He admired Courbet's paintings of the sea.) In "You Must Come Over," Demuth expressed his disdain for Arthur B. Davies and Ernest Hemingway, the latter of whom he must have known in Provincetown:

Washington Allston. No, you've never heard of him—so many American painters have never been heard of. Well, he's not a discovery of mine. Henry James wrote about him. James used him as proof that America is no land for the artist. Allston went mad after returning to America from years spent in Europe. Perhaps James was right—I know America is only for the very strong. Hemingway—yes, he lives in Europe. . . .

Yes, Homer Martin. I always think of Coleridge when I see a Homer Martin. I, too, now wonder why. "I looked upon the nothingness of the sea." I wonder? No, he painted a country which seemed to be all sand dunes. . . . He seems to have suffered in the grand manner. Now they only talk about it, if they can afford to, to Freud. After these talks they paint something in the manner of Arthur B. Davies.[53]

Far outnumbering the few antipathies which Demuth entertained were his many enthusiasms in the arts. Those artists and writers whom he admired he named in his literary works: in "Across a Greco Is Written" he mentioned El Greco, Blake, Rubens, Watteau, Beardsley, Pater, and Joyce; in "You Must Come Over," Picasso, Allston, Henry James, Fuller, Martin,

52 Hartley, "Farewell, Charles," 561.
53 Demuth, "You Must Come Over."

Hawthorne, and Coleridge; in his 1928 foreword to the Peggy Bacon exhibition catalogue mentioned earlier, Marin, Joyce, Proust, Michelangelo, O'Keeffe, Florine Stettheimer, Cranach, Brueghel,[54] and Sharaku. To these names should be added those of Cézanne, Toulouse-Lautrec, Rodin, Nolde, and Kandinsky, all of whom influenced Demuth, and Fragonard (Demuth is reported to have once told McBride, art critic on the staff of the *New York Evening Sun*, that Fragonard "was, and had been, the maddest passion of his *vie intellectuelle*"[55]). In addition, Demuth enjoyed the work of such of his contemporaries as Rivera, Duchamp, Man Ray, Hartley, Dove, Spencer, Pascin, Lachaise, and "all of the French modernists," including Matisse, Braque, Gris, Metzinger, Léger, Picabia, and Gleizes. And in a letter he once wrote Stieglitz, Demuth revealed a deep appreciation for Twachtman.

Four small drawings, quaintly hung in front of the wall of bookshelves in the upstairs parlor of the Demuth home in Lancaster, included one by Pascin depicting figures on a busy street; two drawings of human heads by Matisse, executed in this artist's economical, calligraphic manner; and a pen-and-ink work by Aubrey Beardsley which had been given to Demuth by Schofield Thayer, an English collector of Beardsleyana. The last named *art nouveau* drawing, rendered in Beardsley's typically exquisite, stylized technique, depicted overlapping Medusa-headed female figures enveloped in long-sleeved cloaks.

Demuth was an omnivorous reader who owned a fair-sized library of his own and subscribed to the art magazines and the *New York Times*. As is indicated by the Zola, Wedekind, Henry James, Poe, Pater, and Balzac works he chose to illustrate, he

[54] Probably Lucas Cranach the Elder (1472–1553) and Pieter Brueghel the Elder (1525/30–1569), patriarch of the Brueghel family of painters.

[55] Demuth may have mentioned Watteau to McBride instead of Fragonard. This seems more likely in view of the facts: that Demuth is known to have been deeply interested in Watteau, that there is no mention of Fragonard in the American's writings, and that Watteau was one of the great masters of pictorial form (the aspect of painting in which Demuth became progressively absorbed as he developed).

24

enjoyed reading general literature more than art criticism. Some
of the best authors of his time were his personal friends. These
included Miss Stein, Miss Moore, Edith Sitwell, Dr. Williams,
Wallace Stevens, Pound, O'Neill, Robert McAlmon, and Djuna
Barnes. Miss Street said:

> Demuth liked Pater's things, especially his imaginary portraits. He
> was delighted by Jane Austen and Maeterlinck, though I think that
> the latter author bored him a little. Once he gave me a Jane Austen
> book; and I had to read a little Maeterlinck, was told that I should.
> The *fin de siècle* was the period of Baudelaire and Verlaine. . . . De-
> muth also gave me a copy of Huysmans' *A Rebours*, which consti-
> tutes a negation of natural life and is somewhat decadent.[56]

Late in life Demuth read Proust's *Remembrance of Things Past.*
His affinity for both Proust and Henry James is of great interest
for the reason that all three were masters of the art of richly
evoking a time and place while reporting an accumulation of
everyday detail. All three were notably patient, unhurried artists
who worked in an expanding spirallike manner, and whose individual lives unfolded and expanded to a further extent than
those of most. All three examined their inner selves in a painfully
exhaustive manner, becoming absorbed in their personal sensations, and illuminating those sensations in their art. And it was
characteristic of all three, as it is said to have been of James, that
their "only demand on life, in childhood and long after . . . was
'somehow to receive an impression or an accession, feel a relation
or a vibration.' "[57]

When Demuth was in Paris for the last time, in 1921, he made
an effort to see Proust and was rebuffed. Proust was indifferent,
either because of his natural tendency to be disinclined or because
of his health. The French author, who was twelve years older
than the American, died in 1922 at fifty-one, only a few months
after Demuth had tried to see him. The American was to die
at the same age, in 1935.

[56] Interview with Miss Street.
[57] Newton Arvin, "Henry James: Autobiography," *New York Times.*

25

Demuth did not begin to read Proust until the summer of 1927, when he was forty-three. Writing to Stieglitz the following fall, in a letter dated October 30, 1927, he said:

⁓ Over the summer have read Proust. So, I've joined the others—not without reservations, however. He's too much like myself for me to be able to get a great thrill out of it all—marvelous, but eight volumes about one personal headache is almost unreadable, especially when you have your own headache most of the time.

In his Peggy Bacon tribute, Demuth mentioned *À la Recherche du Temps Perdu*. And ten years after he had tried to see Proust in Paris, four years after he had begun to read this author and four years preceding his own death, he wrote in a letter to Stieglitz dated September 10, 1931:

⁓ I've finished reading the final book of the Proust sufferings. Most of it is like my big Marin water-colour—it doesn't quite happen but, the idea being so grand, well, you are quite satisfied with what is there. Of course the pages which do "happen" are quite like the water-colours where they "happen,"—in and beyond Time.

In the realm of music Demuth is said to have enjoyed Ravel, Stravinsky, and symphony orchestras, not opera. Yet it is also said that he did not understand classical music, that he much preferred popular compositions. Probably he enjoyed both categories, classical and non-classical. Certainly the artist's vaudeville and night-club paintings reveal a genuine enthusiasm for Negro music and jazz. In this connection Miss Street recalled:

I remember that he [Demuth] used to come to my apartment at the same time as some of *Les Six* musicians. As well as Demuth and Locher there would be Darius Milhaud and Erik Satie at my apartment. And Jean Cocteau and Man Ray. I recall that once (there was

26

no such thing as a *glacière* or refrigerator in apartments then) we bought some champagne at the shop next door, wrapped it in wet bath towels, and put it on the balcony to chill.[58]

Miss Street also stated:

My sister played the piano very well. I remember that once she played the *Pavane pour Une Infante Défunte* by Ravel when Demuth was there. He was crazy about this piece. Sister had a clavichord (a copy of an antique) the top of which was always raised. The inside of the instrument and of the top was painted lacquer red. When Demuth first saw it he was delighted, saying: "Where did you get the baby lobster?" It had a delicate tone like the buzzing of bees.[59]

As his figure paintings vividly attest, Demuth loved the circus, vaudeville, and musical comedy. In his play "You Must Come Over" (the title of which, though used by Demuth in the sense of an American speaking to a European, was actually a by-line stolen from the routine of the female impersonator Bert Savoy) he wrote:

Couldn't we talk about American musical shows, revues —the people who act in them, have acted in them, and dance. They are our "stuff." They are our time. Yes, in that sense our paintings are—well, what you do not call great. You could say the same, and not hurt my feelings, about our writers for the stage. The world has called some of these—at least one of these, I'm led to believe—great. A child of the church, Longfellow and Freud— say if those three were not too much of a crowd.[60]

As pointed out earlier, intellectually Demuth entertained a passion for ambiguity, the riddle, and veiled insinuation. When he wrote a tribute to Stieglitz, he wrote about lighthouses and fog—"a lighthouse and many fogs."[61] And when he wrote in praise of Peggy Bacon, in order to illuminate this artist's unique

[58] Interview with Miss Street.
[59] *Ibid.*
[60] Demuth, "You Must Come Over."
[61] Charles Demuth, "Lighthouses and Fog."

capacity for achieving a complete statement in her paintings, he called attention to interior designers whose knowledge "is not all the knowledge in the world."

Similarly, Demuth loved the symbol and the simile, and seems to have thought in terms of symbols and similes much of the time. It was his way of getting at life obliquely, of avoiding the directness which to him appeared to be simple and crude. He loved indirectness in a way which was not superficial, or casual, or acquired, but emergent from his basic psychology.

In his strange, autobiographical story "The Voyage Was Almost Over" Demuth wrote:

Sometimes, stopping by the rail and looking at the moonlit sea, he would think: it is like beautiful placid flesh seen through webs of blue and silver. Or again, as the moonbeams danced more merrily for a moment on its surface, how it resembled a huge purple fish caught in a gilded net. No, after all, it was more like a gigantic blue flower seen through the spray of a waterfall, he decided, and would continue his walk. All the pauses in his wanderings around and around the deck and the wandering, too, were full of these ideas: how like the ocean is to that and how like the golden moon in her turquoise sky is to this.[62]

This is, of course, the classical attitude toward life of the poet, as demonstrated in the famous conversation between the sensitive, imaginative Hamlet and a pragmatic Polonius:

HAMLET:	Do you see that cloud, that's almost in shape like a camel?
POLONIUS:	By the mass, and 'tis like a camel, indeed.
HAMLET:	Methinks, it it like a weasel.
POLONIUS:	It is backed like a weasel.
HAMLET:	Or, like a whale?

[62] Demuth, "Voyage."

POLONIUS: Very like a whale.
HAMLET: Then will I come to my mother by and by.

[Act 3, Scene 2]

In his tastes Demuth literally bridged two centuries. Because his imagination embraced the past as well as the future, he belonged intellectually and emotionally to several centuries. He felt affinity for the elegant, dynamic Mannerism of the sixteenth century and El Greco; and for the civilized, refined eighteenth century of Wren, Watteau, and Blake. Perhaps more than anything else he was *fin de siècle*, a Victorian allied in his sensibilities to the rarefied climate of nineteenth-century *art nouveau*. Demuth also pioneered in modern painting during the first decades of the twentieth century, intuitively allying himself to the most radical trends of the time in Paris, and serving as an important agent for the carrying of Cubist theory to America.

2

Family Background

The first recorded Demuth name[1] (the name is correctly pronounced Dee'muth, with the accent on the first syllable) appears to have been that of one Christoph Demuth of Moravia, Charles Demuth's ancestor seven generations removed, who was born between the years 1653 and 1658. Whether the name appeared on a military roll, church register, tax list, or guild list is not clear.

It is known that this Christoph had four sons, and that in the year 1726 three of these sons, because of the persecution of Hussite Protestants by the Catholic church, fled across the Moravian border from central Czechoslovakia into German Saxony where they settled on the estate of Count Nicholas Ludwig von Zinzendorf (1700–60). The estate of Count Zinzendorf, founder of the Moravian sect, who established several Moravian missions in North America, was located near the Moravia-Saxony border

---

[1] The meanings associated etymologically with the root of the name "Demuth" are of considerable interest in connection with the life and character of Charles Demuth. The German word *mutter* (meaning mother, matron, or womb) is the source of the word *muth*. *Muth* means mood, disposition, character, or frame of mind; spirit, courage, and mettle.

Zu muthe sein means to feel; *zu muthe werben*, to come to feel; *muth machen*, to encourage; *muth sassen*, to take courage or take heart; *guten muthes sein*, to be of good cheer; and *muthwoll* (adjective), courageous or full of courage.

Charles, who was devoted to a mother who ruled his life psychologically, and who was by nature an individual charged with feeling, lived a life marked by high courage. Though beset by psychological and physical ills, he was a cheerful, smiling person who possessed spiritual strength.

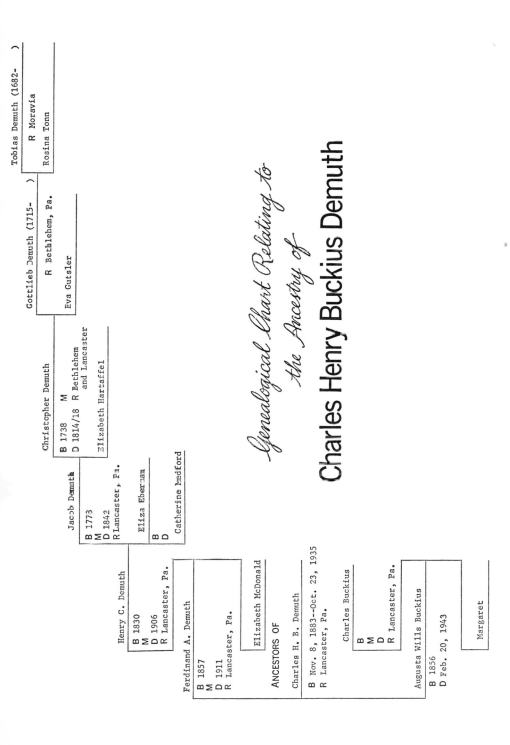

Tobias Demuth (1682–)
R Moravia
Rosina Tonn

Gottlieb Demuth (1715–)
R Bethlehem, Pa.
Eva Gutsler

Christopher Demuth
B 1738   M
D 1814/18   R Bethlehem
            and Lancaster
Elizabeth Hartaffel

Jacob Demuth
B 1773
M
D 1842
R Lancaster, Pa.
Eliza Eberman
B
D
Catherine Medford

Henry C. Demuth
B 1830
M
D 1906
R Lancaster, Pa.

Ferdinand A. Demuth
B 1857
M
D 1911
R Lancaster, Pa.
Elizabeth McDonald

ANCESTORS OF

Charles H. B. Demuth
B Nov. 8, 1883--Oct. 23, 1935
R Lancaster, Pa.

Charles Buckius
B
M
D
R Lancaster, Pa.

Augusta Wills Buckius
B 1856
D Feb. 20, 1943
Margaret

Genealogical Chart Relating to
the Ancestry of

Charles Henry Buckius Demuth

in the town of Herrnhut. There the three Demuth brothers were soon joined by their sister-in-law Rosina Tonn Demuth (widow of Tobias [b. 1682], Christoph's oldest son) and her four children, Joseph, Gottlieb (b. 1715), Anna Maria, and another daughter.

A second major resettlement of the Demuth family occurred nine years after the flight to Herrnhut. In 1735 Gotthard,[2] one of the three brothers who had originally fled to Saxony, emigrated along with his nephew Gottlieb, son of Tobias, to Savannah, Georgia. The two men sailed to America on the same vessel that carried General James Edward Oglethorpe on his way to assume his duties as royal governor of the British colony of Georgia.

Soon after their arrival in the New World, Gotthard and Gottlieb Demuth traveled northward, where they helped establish the town of Bethlehem, Pennsylvania, there to be joined by Anna Maria. Joseph Demuth, who went directly to Pennsylvania from Herrnhut, served in the armed forces of the colonies during the Revolution. Gottlieb, a carpenter by trade, married Eva Gutsler and served subsequent to the Revolutionary War in the Battalion of Northampton County, Pennsylvania.

Gottlieb's son Christopher (1738–1814/18), who was born in Bethlehem, settled in Lancaster, Pennsylvania, where he married Elizabeth Hartaffel and started a small tobacco shop. Situated at 114 East King Street, this shop was established five years before the War of Independence began. Christopher eventually purchased the fine brick residence at 114–116 East King Street, possibly from his father-in-law, and constructed a small brick snuff factory at the rear of the lot, facing Mifflin Street. Still functioning, the Demuth tobacco shop on East King Street is the oldest store of its kind in the United States.

When one enters the Demuth tobacco shop today, one sees prominently displayed near the front of the store a plaque bear-

---

[2] In all likelihood the given names—Rosina, Gotthard, Gottlieb, Joseph—and such later names in the Demuth family as Jacob, Samuel, and Emmanuel, form the basis for the rumor that Charles, who looked very Spanish, may have been descended from a Spanish Jew.

DEMUTH'S

The Oldest Tobacco Shop in the United States

SELLING SNUFF, CIGARS AND TOBACCOS

Founded by Christopher Demuth in 1770
    and kept by him until 1814
By Jacob son of Christopher until 1842
By Emanuel son of Jacob until 1843
By Lawrence son of Jacob until 1853
Again by Emanuel until 1864
By Henry son of Jacob until 1906
By Ferdinand & Henry sons of Henry until 1911
By Henry son of Henry until 1937
Since 1937 by Christopher son of Henry

Plaque listing proprietors of Demuth's Tobacco Shop.

ing the names of the shop's proprietors—all male descendants of the Christopher who founded the business.

As the plaque shows, Christopher's son Jacob (1779–1842) succeeded his father as proprietor of the tobacco shop and remained in charge of the family business until his death. He married three times, the maiden names of his wives being Eliza Eberman, Catherine Medford and Anna Frances Hurst, in that order, and Jacob is noteworthy for fathering twenty children. It wasn't long before the house at 114–116, though a capacious dwelling, seemed inadequate; so Jacob purchased the double-width house next door at 118–120 East King street, where his sons lived dormitory-style, while his daughters remained in the original home at 116.

Among Jacob Demuth's twenty children, who were Charles Demuth's great-aunts and great-uncles (except for his grandfather Henry C.), there were several amateur artists of talent. Caroline Suzanne and Samuel Christopher left sketchbooks; Louisa Elizabeth, a watercolor painting of a bouquet of flowers. Caroline Suzanne's sketchbook contains black-and-white drawings and watercolors, including a painting of lilies. Samuel Christopher's sketchbook, which consists of "designs for a barn, outline drawings of toadstools, mushrooms, and curiously enough, of Chinese pagodas," is dated 1829, the year that he was twelve. Charles (after whom the famous painter may have been named) left behind a watercolor painting of parrots and a pencil-drawn mourning sketch.

Sarah married Aaron Eshleman, a Lancaster painter; Emmanuel married Margaret Eichholtz, daughter of the artist Jacob Eichholtz, who must have contributed to the Demuth family's already pronounced artistic tendencies; and Elizabeth married a man named Cooper and bore children all of whom were musical.

In addition, Jacob's brother John, uncle of the twenty children with the musical names, made a reputation as a sculptor and painter. His painted wooden sculpture *The Snuff Taker of Revolutionary Days*, depicting an elegant gentleman in eighteenth-century American colonial costume holding a hank of tobacco in

Painted wooden sculpture *The Snuff Taker of Revolutionary Days* by John Demuth, originally used as a sign in front of De-muth's Tobacco Shop.

his left hand and a snuffbox in his right, occupies a place of honor today in the Demuth tobacco shop. Originally this carving served on the outside of the shop as its first sign. John Demuth also painted family portraits, including one of his niece, Anne E.

Ferdinand A. Demuth (1857–1911), Charles's father, was an excellent amateur photographer. One of his photographs of the steeple of Lancaster's Lutheran Church of the Holy Trinity, which towered over the Demuth garden, is well known.

That Charles Demuth was half Buckius appears to have escaped researchers into his family history. For one thing, the Demuths counted for more in Lancaster than the Buckius family, which was well-to-do but of lower class than the family into which Augusta Wills Buckius married. Although the paternal side of the artist's family can be traced back seven generations, the maternal side can be traced back only two.[3]

The city of Lancaster was settled more than half a century before the Revolution, and was at one time the largest inland city of the thirteen colonies. At the center of the town where King and Queen Streets meet is the town square, and the city which spreads out from this focus is unique in the land.

Facing the square on one side stands the City Hall, a finely proportioned red-brick colonial structure with elegant white detail. A bronze plaque on its façade reads in part:

LANCASTER
PENNSYLVANIA

First settled about 1717 and known as Hickorytown and Gibson's Pasture. County seat of the County of Lancaster est. 1729. Laid out as a town and named Lancaster by James Hamilton—1730 when it became a trading center. Site of Indian treaty with the six nations—1744. Important supply base during the Revolution. Capital of the United Colonies when the Continental Congress met in the Courthouse in the center of this square September 27, 1777. Capital of Pennsylvania 1799–1812. Chartered a city March 20, 1818.

[3] Apparently the artist was named for his two grandfathers, Charles Buckius and Henry Demuth, with the somewhat awkward result: Charles Henry Buckius Demuth.

Lancaster's houses excel in architectural integrity. Substantial-appearing, modest buildings, they are constructed of brick and abut the sidewalks, so that there are few front yards in Lancaster. Typically they display regularly spaced shuttered windows, shallow ridgepole roofs, and a noticeable lack of overhang at the eaves. The shutters and trim are customarily painted blue, black, or some other subdued color, giving an effect of severity and understatement.

In Demuth's day the community and its environs were devoted to agriculture. And out in the countryside may still be seen the thriving farms of the Plain religious sects whose land excels in the production of milk, wheat, and corn, and the raising of chickens and cattle. The farms of Lancaster County produce a greater tonnage of tobacco than those of any other county in the nation. Beside the green fields of large-leaved tobacco plants rise huge, neat barns, decorated with the protective hex signs common to the area. They are built of wood combined with fieldstone or brick, and like the Pennsylvania German houses in the towns possess shallow ridgepole roofs with little emphasis at the eaves.

In many ways Lancaster expresses the restraint implicit in its religious orientation:

People almost never cross streets against traffic signals. No doubt, ever since . . . the town was founded, they rigidly observed similar regulations because there is a right way to do things so why not do them that way. A large number of townspeople stem from one of the plain religious sects.[4] Those who kicked over the traces and became something outlandish like Lutherans or Presbyterians still maintained their quiet attitude toward life and they did not find the bonnet and shawl and the horse and buggy so insufferable as to move away. Both town and country Lancastrians like things neat. Their farms and houses are unbelievably spruce. Social problems do not exist or, at least, are not recognized; there is only human perversity.[5]

[4] Plain religious sects which exist in Lancaster County in great numbers include the Amish, Mennonites, Dunkards, Moravians, and Quakers.
[5] Ruth Brightbill, "Wine of the Country," unpublished term paper.

37

A Marin, a Pollock, or a Rauschenberg could not have emerged from such a town, but in relation to Lancaster the art of a Demuth appears utterly logical. For though he is reported to have loathed and been "bored to death with Lancaster and the Pennsylvania Dutch,"[6] to which group he belonged, Demuth bore the authentic stamp of the area. The precise patterns of the fields in the surrounding countryside punctuated by trim, monumental barns; the reticence and integrity of the black- and blue-costumed Plain people; the exquisite taste, essential modesty, and pervasive exclusiveness resident in the understated domestic architecture; even the high quality of the flowers, fruit, and other foodstuffs in the two Central Markets—all are accurately mirrored in the artist's works.

S. Lane Faison, Jr., made a valuable contribution to our understanding of Demuth when he had certain Lancaster scenes, some of them corresponding to the artist's paintings, photographed. In one of these photographs, an incidental view of a segment of the city's sky line, there can be identified two Wren-like steeples with weather vanes at their summits, a Renaissance dome resting on a columned base, two square Italian Romanesque towers, two smokestacks, and two water towers. Lancaster burgeoned with painting material for a Demuth. "In the town, chimneys and smoke disfigured the sky," Jerome Mellquist wrote, and everywhere appeared "the straight lines, the rectilinear shapes, the water towers and brick façades and Egyptian visages"[7] which the artist depicted in his work. Demuth loathed Lancaster? He may have loathed the city's people, but to him the city's landscape was endlessly beautiful, so that he was always going home from Paris or elsewhere to paint.

The wealth of architectural forms thrusting into the sky above the city reminds one of Italy, where every rise of land displays its tower pointing like a Leonardoesque forefinger toward God. Italian also is the decoration on Lancaster's most beautiful steeple, that of the Lutheran Church of the Holy Trinity which stands

---

[6] From the answers given to a Demuth questionnaire by George Biddle.
[7] Jerome Mellquist, *The Emergence of an American Art*, 339.

beside the Demuth snuff factory on East Mifflin Street. At the corners of the steeple's base are situated four free-standing sculptured figures representing the Evangelists Matthew, Mark, Luke, and John. The present sculptures are replicas, but in Demuth's time the original pieces, carved by William Rush of Philadelphia, stood at the level where the main part of the wooden steeple joins the square brick tower. One of the largest steeples in America, so large it dominates the city for blocks around, it towers over the old Demuth houses and once cast its shadow onto the red-brick paths of Augusta Demuth's garden.

Charles painted a curvilinear, eight-pointed star, light against a dark oval ground, onto the ceiling of the lantern located at the center of the steeple. As a boy he must have been fascinated by the structure's interior, which contained a painter's basket and a colonial chime console. One of the bells in the tower functioned for years as Lancaster's only fire alarm.

Ferdinand photographed the steeple. Augusta, a devout church member, willed the church a sum of money ($16,984.28) on condition that a window be installed in memory of her parents and two sisters, the income from the residue to be used for the regular painting of the steeple. And Charles painted Wren-like steeples all his life, as though they were naturally entwined with his existence. He painted them in other places than Lancaster, but for him there must have existed only one. It was an Eternal Presence of refined proportions and precise detail, white against a blue-gray sky, with a whirling brass weather vane at its summit and the figure of Saint Matthew, protector of corporeal matters, looking down upon a lame boy and his parents in their secluded garden.

Sometime in 1887, when Charles was four, he suffered a hip injury the exact nature of which was never known, after which it was necessary for him to wear a built-up shoe. The injury may have resulted from an attack of poliomyelitis, then called "hip disease." It may have been the outcome of a fall suffered, conceivably, when the child Demuth was being tossed into the air

39

by his elders in the family tobacco shop. Or the hip difficulty may have resulted from an unrecognized tubercular condition. The last theory was the one held by Dr. Williams, who said, "We always thought that he [Demuth] had had tuberculosis of the hip when he was a child, that he had a tuberculous hip. In spite of his hip, he used to do a lot of walking, though he was not athletic."[8]

As a child and young man Charles is reported to have hiked and swum determinedly with the most accomplished of his fellows. Locher said that Demuth was an excellent swimmer and also danced well, but could not ride.[9]

In her group painting *Cathedrals of Fifth Avenue* (1931), Florine Stettheimer (whom Demuth beaued around, at least once escorted to an O'Neill play in the Village) depicted her Lancaster friend sporting a white flower in the buttonhole of his lapel, wearing a mustache, and carrying a cane. Hartley wrote that on the occasion of the particular luncheon at the Restaurant Thomas in Paris when he and Demuth first met, the artist had "ambled up to our table"; that "because of a hip infirmity he had invented a special sort of ambling walk which was so expressive of him." Hartley informed us, further, that Demuth carried a cane "elegantly and for service, not for show, as he had always the need of a cane."[10] On the other hand, Miss Street said that although Demuth was "*very* lame . . . he didn't always carry a cane, by any means. He always sat crooked, sideways on the chair or sofa . . . with one shoulder *much* higher than the other, and with his neck strained into a funny position because of where his shoulders were."[11]

It was characteristic of Demuth to invent an expressive way of walking and to carry his cane elegantly, with distinction. Always clever and courageous, he carried off his infirmity so successfully that his friends forgot about it and, on the surface of his life, at least, his lameness became an asset. Undoubtedly the fact that he

[8] Interview with Dr. Williams.
[9] Interview with Locher.
[10] Hartley, "Farewell, Charles," 554–55.
[11] Interview with Miss Street.

was halt contributed to his special kind of bitter charm, lent a romantic note to what was already an intriguing personality.

A man halt in more ways than one, Demuth understood better than most the many ways in which an individual can be crippled; just as, by his own testimony, he understood perfection better than most.[12] He dealt gallantly with the fact that he was lame, never, even in childhood, permitting his infirmity to relegate his existence to the special realm of the handicapped, but choosing to live in the world of the physically uncrippled.

But Demuth's life was nonetheless influenced by his lameness. It was difficult for him to carry oil-painting equipment to the beach at Provincetown and elsewhere, as a result of which he once confided to a friend: "I'd much rather do watercolors. Oil paints are so messy!"[13] The fact that he worked mostly on small formats was a direct result of his physical condition. And when he was a boy, his frailty must have influenced his parents to sympathize with his desire for a career as an artist rather than as a merchant in the family tobacco business.

The building at Nos. 118–120 East King Street, constructed in the year 1750, was originally an inn called William Pitt, the Earl of Chatham. As mentioned earlier Christopher established the tobacco business at No. 114 and purchased the double-width house at Nos. 114–116 in 1770, and his son Jacob bought the companion residence next door at Nos. 118–120 about the year 1800 in order to provide lodging for his numerous sons. So from about 1800 forward there were two contiguous double-width Demuth residences on East King Street—Nos. 114, 116, 118, and 120.

Like the tobacco shop at No. 114, No. 120 was meant to function as a store, as it consisted of a large front room opening directly onto the sidewalk and a small back room designed for use as a

12 In Demuth's "Voyage" the following lines appear:
◀━━ Why, why was everything wonderfully made, perfectly made, and I given the power, above many, to appreciate this wonder and perfection? And yet denied the one thing which would perfect me, truly?

13 Interview with Miss Street.

41

storage place or office. Augusta Demuth rented No. 120 as a store; and after Locher inherited her property in 1943,[14] he and his associate Richard Weyand used the rooms for an antique shop which they called 120 Antiquities.

Constructed directly on the sidewalk and abutting one another so that they possessed common walls, the houses were built of dull-hued, handmade brick which Charles used to mention in a reverent way as though he were speaking of the Demuth jewels. Against the uneven coloring of the blue-violet brick the mat black trim imparted an incomparably rich effect. Since they are situated only a short distance from the old town square, the Demuth houses today have assumed the displaced mien old homes acquire when surrounded by houses of commerce. One has to imagine how they looked in September, 1777, when the Continental Congress, driven out of Philadelphia by the British, made Lancaster its capital for a day.

When Charles was six, Ferdinand moved his small family from 109 North Lime Street in Lancaster, where Charles had been born, to the old Demuth home at 118 East King Street next door to the tobacco shop. The house had recently been vacated by Charles's only remaining great-aunt, one of Jacob's twenty children. Here in this spacious old home Charles was to grow to manhood. He was to spend the remainder of his life in this house, producing most of his paintings in the little upstairs studio, and returning to it again

[14] After Locher's death on June 10, 1956, Weyand inherited the Demuth home. He died shortly after Locher did, on November 13, 1956, and following Weyand's death, his four brothers and sisters had the old home sold at auction. The Lancaster newspaper *New Era* carried the following notice regarding the sale of the home in its March 28, 1957, issue:

"One of Lancaster's oldest buildings, the former home of internationally famous painter Charles Demuth at 118–120 E. King St., was purchased by S. Nissley Gingrich, Inc., 12 S. Duke St. for $48,000 at public sale yesterday.

"In recent years the building was the home of the late Robert E. Locher and the late Richard Weyand. Locher, lifelong friend of Demuth, was a nationally known theatrical and interior designer and architect. . . .

"The dwelling was built in 1750. . . . About 60 persons attended the sale, which was marked by spirited bidding."

and again following sporadic visits to the Bohemian corners of the world. It was in this house the artist died.

The imposing entrance to No. 118 consisted of a small vestibule separated from the front hall by a door. This hall, from which a stairway led to the second story, connnected with a large dining room which occupied most of the first floor. At the far end of the dining room was an old-fashioned fireplace, on the left of which a door led to the kitchen. The dining room's only windows, also on the left, opened onto the private Demuth garden.

Augusta Demuth's garden, a famous one in the region, was paved with red bricks in plain and chevron patterns, and red bricks edged the raised plots of planted earth arranged between the paths. There were several trees in the garden, including a white birch, but it was a small city garden, only about twenty by eighty feet in size. Surrounded on the north and west by the rented shop and dining room and on the south and east by a high board fence, it extended the length of the block, all the way to Mifflin Street.

The stairs leading up from the right side of the front hall led first to an intermediate landing from which one stepped into a delightfully intimate upstairs living room, then turned to the left and continued to a third level on which were situated a large hall (which Locher used for an exhibition gallery) and three bedrooms. The upstairs living room was situated directly over the dining room, and duplicated both the downstairs fireplace at the far end of the room and the single wall of windows overlooking the garden. However, here the door at the left of the fireplace led through a white-tiled bathroom to a small room at the back of the house connected with the kitchen by a rear stairway. It was this little upstairs room far from any outside door or street, located near the middle of the block high up like a nest in a tree, isolated even from the rest of the house by the bathroom and rear stairway, which was Demuth's studio.

[It was a workshop variety of studio,] the same room which was fled to one day when the small Charles decided he wanted to be alone in order to put down on a sheet of drawing paper what he wanted to

43

remember about a flower he had picked in his mother's garden. (His mother has that magic with flowers which belongs to a few rare individuals.) His mother's sewing machine was in it then. . . .

Edward Hopper should paint it some day—this storeroom of discarded things, the white-washed walls, the camp bed, the Lautrec lithograph—and he should put Charles Demuth sitting in a corner huddled over a drawing, catch him as he looks up with that expression of his, as of a kind of hurt ferocity.[15]

On the walls of the studio were hung at various times, in addition to the Lautrec lithograph, a Marin watercolor, an O'Keeffe work, an early Bouché drawing, and Man Ray's photographs of Robert and Beatrice Locher.

The entire complex of house and garden was effectively set apart from the world, creating "a secure retreat and all the more so with Demuth there—against his proper background,"[16] according to McBride. Three doors, two entrance halls, and the shop with its bufferlike back room separated the dining room from the street. And most of the windows in the house opened onto the walled garden, as in a cloister or a Spanish dwelling.

The exclusiveness, charm, and substantial quality of the old residence became part of the character of Demuth. His home stabilized him, afforded him a sense of security and inner peace, functioned as a dear known place toward which he need not react and in which he could be his best creative self. Given the conditions of this permanent home and the means for livelihood his family provided, Demuth was able to create an art which was relaxed, calm, and assured. While his friend Hartley, who had no stable source of income and no fixed home, was breathlessly and unhappily charging between Provincetown and Gloucester in New England, Maine, New York, Paris, Berlin, Bermuda, New Mexico, California, Austria, Italy, London, New Hampshire, Mexico, Bavaria, and Nova Scotia in search of a congenial environment, Demuth was painting in his mother's garden.

[15] Rita Wellman, "Pen Portraits: Charles Demuth, Artist," Vol. IX (December, 1931), 484. Hereafter cited as "Pen Portraits."
[16] Henry McBride, "Charles Demuth, Artist," foreword to catalogue.

Hartley has told us that Demuth, who "had a talent for decoration," spent much of his time making his Lancaster home into "all but a deluxe affair inside." Hartley wrote:

Report records its charm and the exactitude of detail, for the kind of house that it is. It belongs to the era of shell flowers, wax fruit, painted velvet, bead-encrusted antimacassars, and the usual complement of horsehair, bell pulls, opaque glass, silver lustre, and all the lavish profusion of accessory of such periods.[17]

Mrs. Demuth (to whom Charles sometimes referred as "Augusta the Iron-Clad," at other times as "a ship under full sail") was a perfectionist housekeeper. According to Hartley, ever since Charles could remember she had arrived at the Mennonite market "among the earliest, never later than six in the morning, because she wanted the dew on those fresh greens," proceeding to buy her provisions "with the manner of a lady who can trust no servant for qualities." Hartley wrote.

She bought this or that of her special Mennonite ... and the greens were so precious looking they seemed more like corsages than edibles, and a basket of them would have set a chef of the Cordon Bleu to gloating with culinary glee. ...

In the midst of this rich domestic milieu Charles was reared, and when he was at home he liked it thoroughly, as when he was abroad he liked the usual variations of such character.[18]

[17] Hartley, "Farewell Charles," 555.
[18] Ibid.

45

3

The Pennsylvania Academy of the Fine Arts and Philadelphia

While he was still attending public school, Demuth took private lessons in art from Miss Martha Bowman of Lancaster, who had studied at the Sorbonne and painted on Martha's Vineyard off the coast of Massachusetts. Charles would go to the Bowman house on East Chestnut Street for his lessons, entering the cavernous depths of the large, richly furnished house where years later a small Demuth still life of apples, willed to Miss Martha by the artist, hung on the sitting-room wall. Miss Martha's sister, Miss Louetta (who inherited the still-life painting from her sister but did not believe in ownership), met visitors at the door wearing the gray-blue cotton dress and delicate white organdy cap of one of the Plain sects. The boy Charles sketched the countryside surrounding Lancaster under Miss Martha's direction.

Before he was seventeen Demuth had tried his hand at pyrography, china painting, and needle point—all *fin de siècle* enthusiasms. He was ten when he was taught by Miss Letty Purple of Columbia, Pennsylvania, to decorate "teacups, saucers and plates with flowers, ladies' heads with hats on, and so forth."[1] When he was a man, Demuth gave a number of these china pieces to the Stettheimer sisters of New York, and in her old age Ettie Stettheimer, who survived her sisters, divided what she owned of these objects between Locher and Carl Van Vechten.

1 Interview with Van Vechten.

46

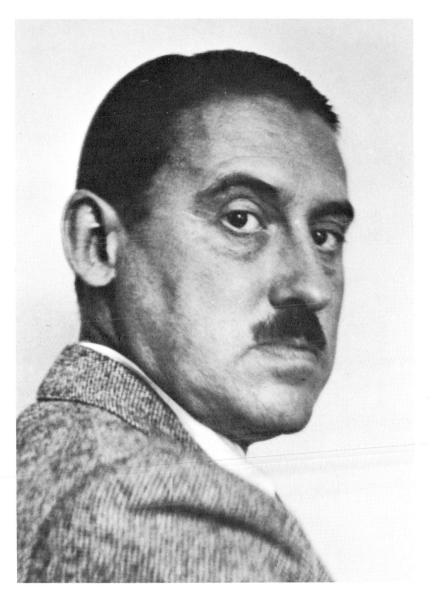

PLATE 9 Demuth as photographed by Dorothy Norman, 1932.

PLATE 10–A   *Pansies #1.* 1915.
Watercolor, 10¼ x 7¹¹⁄₁₆ in.
Collection of Mrs. Stanley R.
Resor, New York. The area
outlined above is said to have
inspired the Warhol painting
at right.

10–B   Andy Warhol, *Flowers.*
1964. Acrylic and silk-screen
enamel on canvas, 48 x 48 in.
Collection of Mr. Leo Castelli,
New York.

PLATE 11 *Horses*. 1916. Watercolor, 8 x 11 in. The Philadelphia Museum of Art: The Samuel S. White, 3rd and Vera White Collection.

PLATE 12 *At Marshall's* (or *Negro Dancing*). 1917. Watercolor, c. 12 x 8 in. (sight). Copyright (1970) by the Barnes Foundation, Merion, Pennsylvania.

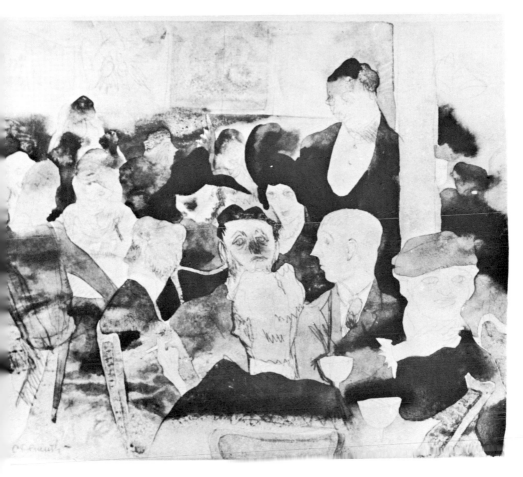

PLATE 13 *Café Scene #1: The Purple Pup.* c. 1917. Watercolor, 8 x 10⅜ in. Collection of the Museum of Fine Arts, Boston: Charles Henry Hayden Fund.

PLATE 14 *Still Life No. 3*. c. 1917. Watercolor and pencil, 13½ x 9⅝ in. The Columbus Gallery of Fine Arts, Columbus, Ohio: The Ferdinand Howald Collection.

PLATE 15–A *Fish*. c. 1917. Watercolor, 8 x 10 in. Collection of
Mr. David G. Ashton, Jr., New York.

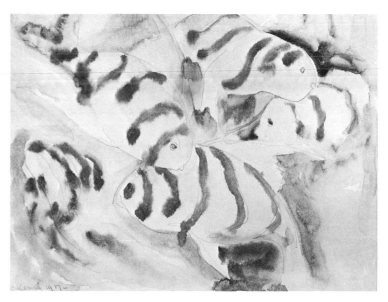

PLATE 15–B *Fish Series No. 3*. 1917. Watercolor, $7\,{}^{15}\!/_{16}$ x $9\,{}^{7}\!/_{8}$
in. The Metropolitan Museum of Art, New York: The Alfred
Stieglitz Collection, 1949.

PLATE 16 *Abstract Trees and Barns, Bermuda* (or *Landscape with Tree*). 1917. Watercolor, 9¾ x 13⅝ in. (mat opening). Collection of the Baltimore Museum of Art: Charlotte G. Paul Bequest Fund.

It must have been about this time, while he was attending Franklin and Marshall Academy in Lancaster, that the artist produced the needlepoint or *gros point* articles he is reputed to have stitched; though the famous Cubist-inspired needlepoint must have been accomplished at a considerably later date. Charles and his mother collaborated on this work, Augusta Demuth laboriously filling in the backgrounds around central motifs already completed by her son.

The September that he was sixteen Demuth entered Franklin and Marshall Academy, the local two-year preparatory school founded in 1787 with a gift from Benjamin Franklin. He attended this school two regular years, graduating in June, 1901. Demuth's record at Franklin and Marshall was not excellent, but above average. He did his best work in history and languages, his poorest in mathematics and other sciences. Following graduation from the Lancaster academy he went to school in nearby Philadelphia, attending one school or another in the Quaker City between 1901 and 1911—the period of a decade.

Demuth began his formal training in art in the fall of 1901 when he enrolled at Drexel Institute, and he continued at Drexel until sometime in 1905. It was during these early years in Philadelphia that he first met Williams, then studying medicine at the University of Pennsylvania. As has been mentioned, the two men met at Mrs. Chain's boardinghouse on Locust Street. When he was an old man, Dr. Williams recalled: "We just looked at each other and were friends instantly. . . . Charlie always called me Carlos—the only person in my life to do so. He liked the name."[2]

A handsome, brilliant young man, Williams was of Dutch, Basque, English, and Jewish extraction. An alert, sensitive individual endowed with feeling for the arts, he was destined to become one of the twentieth century's significant poets, "more experimental [than Frost], and less accessible . . . a true avant-garde poet and master of the spare, stripped-down image."[3]

[2] Interview with Dr. Williams.
[3] Alwyn Lee, "Poets: The Second Chance," *Time*, Vol. LXXXIX, No. 22 (June 2, 1967), 67.

During the period of their student days in Philadelphia Demuth and Williams went for long walks together and "had great talks." It was a time in world history when the future appeared challenging and hopeful, and both young men looked forward eagerly to success. During these years Demuth was entertaining thoughts of becoming a writer, while Williams was trying to decide whether or not to become a painter. Dr. Williams wrote later in his *Autobiography* that he "coldly recalculated all the chances."[4]

The warm spirit of communion and mutual encouragement which developed between the two men can be felt in the letter Demuth wrote Williams on September 17, 1907, just before setting sail for his second visit to Paris:

Carlos, Carlos, how good your letter did sound. I want to answer it before I sail & know if I let it go much longer it will be impossible. . . .

But getting back to your affairs; you have no idea how your letter affects me. I have always felt that it would happen to you some day—that you would simply *have to* write. However, hearing that it would happen this winter was grand news. . . .

I will not be able to see you before I go—yes—*it is* too bad. Still, Carlos, when I come back—*when I come back*, well, we may both have a start in a small way then. . . .

And Carlos even though nothing happens after your six months' work in Boston, don't give up, will you? It's worth all the worry & tears, after all. To feel the joy of creating for a single moment seems to repay one for a year's work. Of course, I know, so do you, that at times it's hell. When you feel like giving it all up & then you think: what *would* become of me if I *really* were made to give it up forever. Heaven be praised neither one of us will meet such a fate—I hope. . . .

Good-bye—good-bye, with the very best wishes.

DEMUTH

[4] Williams, *Autobiography*, 52.

48

When Drexel Institute dropped some of its painting classes in an effort to lay greater emphasis on architecture and the applied arts, Charles and a group of his friends decided to enroll at the Pennsylvania Academy of the Fine Arts. Demuth registered at the Academy for the first time in the spring of 1905 and returned the following fall for a daytime life class. In the spring of 1906 he simultaneously attended a life class at the Academy and a course in drawing from plaster casts at Drexel Institute. During his second year at the Academy (1906–1907), Demuth studied oil and water-color painting with Thomas Pollock Anshutz, Henry McCarter, Hugh Breckenridge, and William Merritt Chase. During the summer of 1907 he continued to work under the direction of Anshutz and Breckenridge at Darby School, the Pennsylvania Academy's summer camp located at Fort Washington, Pennsylvania. Altogether, Demuth attended the Pennsylvania Academy for a period of approximately five years between 1905 and 1911.

Founded in 1805 largely through the efforts of Charles Willson Peale, the Pennsylvania Academy of the Fine Arts is the oldest art school in the United States. The school still occupies the Gothic Revival (General Grant) building constructed on the corner of Broad and Cherry streets in 1876, seven years before Demuth was born in nearby Lancaster. It is an imposing structure, a fitting home for the extraordinary American collection it houses and for the parade of distinguished students who have passed through its doors.

On the left and right of the inner doorway, decorating the entrance just as they must have in Demuth's day, two immense paintings face one another—Washington Allston's *Dead Man Restored to Life by Touching the Bones of the Prophet Elisha* and Benjamin West's *Paul and Barnabas at Lystra*.

The principal feature of the interior is not the entranceway, however, but a large two-story well surrounded on the ground floor by passageways created by marble pillars. The passageways expand on three sides into offices and classrooms. Two wide stairways lead up beside rich coffered walls to the second-floor

49

galleries where the permanent American collection and temporary exhibitions are displayed.

During the five years he was at the Academy, Demuth must have become familiar with not only the two large paintings in the foyer and the two murals by West (*Death on a Pale Horse* and *Christ Rejected*) situated vis-à-vis across the stairwell. He must also have come to know John Vanderlyn's *Ariadne of Naxos*, Gilbert Stuart's Lansdowne portrait of Washington, Henry Inman's self-portrait, William Mount's *Landscape with Figures*, Thomas Couture's *Roman Youth*, various portraits by Robert Feke, John Neagle, Thomas Sully, and the Peales, and (perhaps most important for Demuth) two small still lifes by Raphaelle Peale entitled *Apples and Fox-grapes* and *Fox-grapes and Peaches*.

Demuth habitually examined with great care those paintings he saw which he considered worthy of study. In this connection he once wrote:

Paintings are; and, I call complete drawings paintings too, to be looked at. If the "inner eye" does not glitter . . . added physical words will not cause it to glitter—even though spoken or written by Pater or Joyce. Your choice—ladies! . . .

Paintings must be looked at and looked at and looked at—they, I think, the good ones, like it. They must be understood, and that's not the word, either, through the eyes. No writing, no talking, no singing, no dancing will explain them. They are the final, the 'nth whoopee of sight. A watermelon, a kiss may be fair, but after all have other uses. "Look at that!" is all that can be said before a great painting, at least, by those who really see it.[5]

In 1955, the catalogue of the Pennsylvania Academy's 150th Anniversary Exhibition listed twenty-five glittering names, the pride and joy of the century-and-a-half-old institution. Of this number, seventeen had been students at the Academy, seven, members of its faculty, and three, associated with the school as director or, as in the case of West, sympathizer with its beginnings. The list included:

[5] Charles Demuth, "Across a Greco," *Creative Art*, Vol. V (September 29, 1929), 634.

Benjamin West (b. 1738)
Charles Willson Peale (b. 1741)
William Rush (b. 1756)
Thomas Birch (b. 1779)
Thomas Sully (b. 1783)
John Neagle (b. 1796)
George Caleb Bingham (b. 1811)
Mary Cassatt (b. 1844)
Thomas Cowperthwait Eakins (b. 1844)
William Michael Harnett (b. 1848)
William Merritt Chase (b. 1849)
Thomas Pollock Anshutz (b. 1851)

John Frederick Peto (b. 1854)
Charles Grafly (b. 1862)
Cecilia Beaux (b. 1863)
Henry McCarter (b. 1864)
Robert Henri (b. 1865)
George Luks (b. 1867)
Alexander Stirling Calder (b. 1870)
William James Glackens (b. 1870)
John Marin (b. 1870)
John Sloan (b. 1871)
Everett Shinn (b. 1876)
Arthur B. Carles (b. 1882)
Charles Demuth (b. 1883).[6]

Implied in the above list is the Philadelphia climate, that characteristic leaning toward the right (toward sanity, respectability, conservatism, and realism) which has always been and continues to be the Academy's and Philadelphia's hallmark. This realistic tradition (begun by Charles Willson Peale, who was enamored of objects as they exist in nature, and continued through the thoroughly American realism of Eakins and magic realism or *trompe-l'oeil* of Harnett down through the Ashcan School of Henri, Luks, Sloan, Shinn, and Glackens to the contemporary realism of Franklin Watkins, Francis Speight, and Walter Stuempfig) apparently constitutes for Philadelphians an irresistible attitude toward art which Demuth, with his tenacious hold on recognizability, emphatically shared.

Eakins rubbed this properly curried fur the wrong way long before Demuth appeared at the corner of Broad and Cherry streets, when he insisted on having Academy students draw from the nude. Henri and the Ashcan School were also rebels in their day who managed to disturb the status quo of the provincial mind. Demuth, another rebel in the sense that he rejected the past and

[6] The Pennsylvania Academy of the Fine Arts, 150th Anniversary Exhibition, catalogue, 1955, Index to Artists and Authors, 10-11. Listed alphabetically in the catalogue, the names are given here in chronological order.

embraced the new, did not fit comfortably into the Philadelphia environment, the building with the pseudo-Gothic arches so pretentious when compared to the modest architecture of Lancaster County. He belonged to Philadelphia to the extent that his spirit was in accord with the city's sober Quaker origins; yet he did not belong. Fundamentally, Demuth was a bohemian who felt most at home in Greenwich Village, Provincetown, and Paris.

Even in the art-school environment, always a milieu abounding in colorful personalities, Demuth seemed an iconoclast. Very early he displayed a high degree of self-assurance and individuality, and a sure sense of direction. According to Helen W. Henderson, a fellow student at the Academy, Demuth's peers "understood him and knew him at once for a genius, but the professors, with the exception of Anshutz, who knew and understood everything, mistrusted his exoticism, his individualistic pose. . . ."

Miss Henderson, who served for several years as art critic on the *Philadelphia Inquirer*, wrote forty years later a remarkable description of Demuth as he appeared when he was at the Academy:

I wish that I could make you see him as he was in those earliest days of his appearance as an art student in Philadelphia. Slender and of medium height, he walked with a limp which he never allowed to hamper his activities. He walked, danced, swam, did all those athletic things as well or better than the other boys. His bearing was distinguished; he was always dressed in perfect taste. He had the richest of coloring—a clear, olive skin, strange, very black eyes, the pupil indistinguishable from the iris—thick, glossy, raven black hair—hands like no one else—thin, nervous, instinct with character.

In short, he was a genius and he looked it—but on the other hand, he was of the most charming simplicity. He never threw his weight about in later years when he had reason for self-satisfaction, but was affectionate and sweet.[7]

Of the four men who were his principal teachers at the Academy, Demuth himself gave highest praise to and was most in-

[7] Helen W. Henderson, "Charles Demuth," in "Art and Artists Pass in Review," *Philadelphia Inquirer*.

fluenced by Anshutz, who had been a member of the instructional staff since 1881 and was dean of the faculty. By the time Demuth arrived, Anshutz was fifty-four, a "tall, slender, elegantly made" man, with long legs, well-shaped hands, and "a fine head" punctuated by "penetrating blue" eyes, who "carried one shoulder higher than the other" and "dressed usually in gray" with a derby hat. He was one of a group of Philadelphia artists whose talents had matured under Eakins' regime.[8] Possessed of "a magnetic personality" and intolerant of dishonesty and superficiality in art and life, he attracted a coterie of fervent student admirers who paid him a wholesome kind of homage. Anshutz's approach to teaching was not so much a matter of giving of himself and his ideas as the discovery and nourishment of what already existed in his students' minds and hearts. More than one report asserts that Anshutz was a great teacher who, according to Miss Henderson, could "see into the minds of his students and he criticized their work from their mental attitude towards it."[9]

The personality of the famous painter Chase was in direct contrast to that of Anshutz. According to Rita Wellman, who attended the Academy at the same time Demuth did, Chase was a spectacular figure with pince-nez, goatee, white spats, and red four-in-hand tie who resembled "a little French banker." In Rita's and Charles's day, he was the current giant of the faculty, just as Eakins had been at an earlier time. But Chase's ostentatious personality and the superficial, exuberant Munich-inspired technique he used in painting did not impress the sensitive, perceptive Demuth.

Instead, next to Anshutz, the instructor who exerted the greatest influence on Demuth was McCarter. A fascinating man of imagination who was forty-one in 1905 when Demuth first became acquainted with him, McCarter "had seen Van Gogh in life, had watched Corot paint, spoken with Toulouse-Lautrec and studied

---

[8] Helen W. Henderson, "Thomas Pollock Anshutz," in the Pennsylvania Academy of the Fine Arts catalogue, 105.

[9] *Ibid.*, 106.

in the atelier of Puvis."[10] Following five years of study at the Pennsylvania Academy, at the age of twenty-three, he had gone to Paris, where he remained for another five-year period. Before returning to Philadelphia in 1902 to teach at the Academy, he had worked as an illustrator in New York for *Scribner's, Collier's,* and *Century.* The following incident related by McCarter to his students reveals this teacher's instructional methods:

At Ancourt's lithograph establishment . . . Mr. Arsène Alexandre came in asking Lautrec to color a proof key plate for a frontispiece for "Le Rire." M. Alexandre explained . . . "it was urgent,—and— since the colors to be used were quite simple,—Chocolat [a Negro clown of the Nouveau Cirque] in white, wearing his white gloves, making an amusing gesture over a fine champagne, standing in the English Tavern under the Nouveau Cirque?"

Lautrec said thoughtfully—"But no, the color is not so simple, my friend. Now Chocolat for example,—"

"I hope, Lautrec, you will accept his color, you know the world sees his color with his name."

"Yes, yes, I know, but you forget that he is in the English Tavern."

"How do you see it there then, my good friend?"

"I see it blue."

"Chocolat, blue? But you are jesting."

"No, no, I can only see it blue."

"Very well, if you can only see it blue,—I must submit."

"And the gas—" continued Lautrec—"Not yellow as you see it, my friend. The gas in the English Tavern of the Nouveau Cirque is green, only green."[11]

Demuth must have heard many such echoes of Paris from McCarter, who may have been responsible for the strong Lautrec influence present in Demuth's paintings, his interest in illustration and his pilgrimagelike visits to Paris. Rita Wellman wrote: "Charles . . . must have received a great deal of stimulus from this artist, certainly a great deal of encouragement and appreciation."[12]

The fourth teacher with whom Demuth studied at the Academy

10 Biddle, *An American Artist's Story,* 260.
11 R. Sturgis Ingersoll, "Henry Bainbridge McCarter," in the Pennsylvania Academy of the Fine Arts catalogue, 97–98.
12 Wellman, "Pen Portraits," *Creative Art,* Vol. IX (December, 1931), 483.

was Breckenridge, whose paintings, according to Miss Wellman, "always looked like lighted matches." Yet Breckenridge probably influenced Demuth more than Chase. Miss Wellman wrote rather cruelly that if Demuth did learn anything from "Breck" it must have been "a very useful lesson not to have anything to do with lighted matches."[13] But this remark reflects the critical attitude typical of students. Though Breckenridge was not the teacher Anshutz was, he was far ahead of his day in his experimentation with abstraction.

It was with Breckenridge and Anshutz that Demuth studied during the summer of 1907 at Darby School, the Academy's camp at Fort Washington. During the summer Breckenridge became repeatedly exasperated with him. "Why do you make it like that?" the instructor would ask, looking at Demuth's drawing. "I *feel* it so," the young man would reply, whereupon Breckenridge would become angry and tell his student that *feeling* and *working* were not the same thing.[14]

Regarding the social climate which prevailed at the Academy when she was a student there with Demuth, Miss Wellman wrote:

> We were students together when we were very young. When we were very young we were very old. We were all bored with life; knew everything there was to know, and only condescended to give our time and talents to painting because it seemed to our jaded spirits the one respectable calling left.[15]

It was a time of ultrasophistication and semi-immortality in proper Philadelphia. Miss Henderson reported that at the Academy "nobody was above suspicion and the students circulated the vilest reports about themselves by way of being interesting."[16] There existed side by side a reaction against America's strict Puritan-Victorian tradition and a *fin de siècle* interest in negativity, degeneration, and degradation. Demuth, the impressionable young

[13] *Ibid.*
[14] Helen W. Henderson, Information Regarding Charles Demuth, in Weyand Scrapbook. Hereafter cited as Information.
[15] Wellman, "Pen Portraits," *Creative Art,* Vol. IX (December, 1931), 483.
[16] Henderson, Information.

man from Lancaster, was significantly influenced by the negative factors in this milieu.

In addition to the Misses Wellman and Henderson, Demuth's fellow students at the Academy included Carles, George Biddle, Clive Weed, and Charles Sheeler (who said that since he and Demuth worked in different classes they "saw little of each other while there. The same was true in the later year, a chance meeting on the street or at Walter Arensberg's"[17]). Demuth's Philadelphia friend Adolphe Borie had preceded him at the school, and Marin, with whom he was to become acquainted later in New York, had attended the Academy while Demuth was going to preparatory school in Lancaster.

The hope of the future resides not in institutions but in the occasional iconoclast or rebel whom they accidentally nurture. In the case of the Pennsylvania Academy, the weight of tradition acts as a deterrent to avant-garde spontaneity. Certainly the Academy was blind for years to its avant-garde offspring—Demuth. Yet he continued to send his paintings to the school's exhibitions long after he had achieved success in New York. He had first exhibited his work in one of the Academy's shows. It was a gesture of sentiment which prompted him to keep on sending them through the years—a sense of loyalty and affection. As late as the Academy annual of the fall of 1933, Demuth sent his work to Philadelphia, in spite of the fact that his paintings were invariably hung in an obscure corner near the ceiling.

A 1917 review, written by Miss Henderson and describing the Pennsylvania Academy's Fifteenth Annual Philadelphia Watercolor Exhibition, reads:

Childe Hassam, it is true, has a group of forty-three watercolors and pastels, occupying one long wall in the North Corridor . . . and this as the most featured thing in the show gives . . . the note of the exhibition, which is conservative to the point of insipidity. . . . For instance, there is only one watercolor by Demuth of Lancaster, and that skied, no Buehlers, no Davies, no Marins. . . .

17 Charles Sheeler to the author.

Two walls are devoted to Grafly's drawings of the nude. . . .[18]

The Pennsylvania Academy did not give Demuth his due until 1955 when, two decades following his death, it awarded him a place in its sesquicentennial exhibition among the aforementioned galaxy of its most brilliant stars—a great honor, indeed.

Demuth named his last large landscape *"After All. . . ."* (Color Plate VIII). He who always seemed to know his identity and destiny would not have been surprised at eventual recognition by the Academy. In 1929 in "Across a Greco Is Written" he had predicted: "Time [is] the final critic and only creator of legend. I feel certain time and I will agree."[19]

Demuth did not abandon Philadelphia following his final year at the Academy. Lancaster was only an hour's ride away, the train he regularly took to New York passed through Philadelphia, and he had made lasting friendships in the Quaker City—with, among others, George and Francis Biddle and Adolphe Borie. During the remainder of his life he enjoyed frequent visits to Philadelphia, where he was a member of the Borie Salon.

Adolphe Borie and his wife Edith lived in a Brown Decade house on Pine Street, beside which there was a small garden of magnolia and lilac bushes behind a gray stone wall. Inside the house a bouquet of Victorian glass flowers stood on the mantel-piece under a transparent bell, and on the walls were hung a Degas reproduction, some fine Japanese prints, and original paintings in old Venetian frames.

Perhaps there would turn up late in the afternoon George Luks or Rockwell Kent, John Carroll or Grosz, or any one of the artist friends who were passing through. . . . Here they would meet in turn Franklin Watkins, Arthur Carles, Henry McCarter, quondam teacher and beloved friend; and on other occasions came Bill Bullitt, Paul Cret, Francis Hackett, Charlie Demuth, down from Lancaster,—or any of Adolphe's and Edith's friends.

An impromptu supper might follow with much good talk. . . . Then

[18] Helen W. Henderson, "Art and Artists Pass in Review," *Philadelphia Inquirer.*
[19] Demuth, "Across a Greco," *Creative Art*, Vol. V (September 29, 1929), 629.

came an adjournment to the studio wing. . . . Among his own pictures hung an unfinished mother and child by Mary Cassatt and a figure piece by Thomas Eakins, both of whom he had intimately known.[20]

[20] George Biddle, *Adolphe Borie*, 8.

Early Visits to Paris

Proof of Demuth's 1904 visit to the French capital exists in a letter he mailed to Stieglitz from Paris on October 10, 1921. Looking back seventeen years, he wrote:

> Had I stayed when I first came over—I was only twenty, well, I might have gotten into it. Now it would take years—and work would seem so only on the surface of the scene during that time. I feel "in" America—even though its insides are empty. Maybe I can help fill them.

If the "insides" of America were empty during the early years of the twentieth century, those of Europe were not, for the year 1905 marks a high point in the intellectual history of the Western world. And much of the activity connected with this phenomenon took place in Paris. Demuth appears to have been drawn as by a magnet in 1904 to the exact geographical spot where ideas were fermenting.

In 1905, an article setting forth a theory of relativity expressed in the formula $e=mc^2$, written by Albert Einstein, appeared in an obscure scientific publication. Also in 1905 the Fauvists banded together in an expression of their sensitivity to the end of a decadent era, and a similar group of painters, calling themselves *Die Brücke*, joined forces in Dresden. In 1906 Braque and Picasso, working as a unit in the same atelier in Montmartre (actually a tenement which they facetiously dubbed Le Bateau-Lavoir, or the Floating Laundry), began to develop analytical or facet Cubism out of a study of Cézanne, a scientific interest in primitive sculpture, and the "tonic effect" of Henri Rousseau's primitivism. This new school of painting was primarily concerned with visual experimentation in the precinct of space-time concepts. In 1908 Hermann Minkowski made known his *Space and Time* theory, which he had apparently developed completely independent of Einstein's theory. And in 1909 there appeared in Italy Marinetti's first manifesto of Futurism, defining the ideas of still another school of painting fundamentally concerned with space-time concepts and the dynamics of pictorial form.

Miss Stein wrote that the first Cubist works were "some spanish landscapes" which Picasso brought back from a summer in Spain. The effective propagandist for Picasso and Gris wrote:

In these there was no african sculpture influence. There was very evidently a strong Cézanne influence, particularly the influence of the late Cézanne water colours, the cutting up the sky not in cubes but in spaces.
But the essential thing, the treatment of the houses was essentially spanish and therefore essentially Picasso. In these pictures he first emphasized the way of building in spanish villages, the line of the houses not following the landscape but cutting across and into the landscape, becoming undistinguishable in the landscape by cutting across the landscape. It was the principle of the camouflage of the guns and the ships in the war. . . .
This then was really the beginning of cubism. . . .
Gertrude Stein always says that cubism is a purely spanish conception and only spaniards can be cubists and that the only real cubism is that of Picasso and Juan Gris. Picasso created it and Juan Gris permeated it with his clarity and his exaltation.[1]

A year after Miss Stein's *Autobiography of Alice B. Toklas* appeared, Georges Braque wrote in "Testimony against Gertrude Stein": "In the early days of cubism, Picasso and I were engaged

[1] Gertrude Stein, *The Autobiography of Alice B. Toklas*, 90–91. Hereafter cited as *Alice B. Toklas*.

in what we felt was a search for the anonymous personality. We were inclined to efface our own personalities in order to find originality."[2]

According to Sigfried Giedion, "Picasso has been called the inventor of cubism, but cubism is not the invention of any individual." Rather, the end of an epoch had been gained, and sensitive intellectual forces were simultaneously approaching new ways of thinking and feeling about the nature of the universe and form in the arts. One of the painters who shared in the phenomenon expressed the situation which existed thus:

There was no invention. Still more, there could not be one. Soon it was twitching in everybody's fingers. There was a presentiment of what should come, and experiments were made. We avoided one another; a discovery was on the point of being made, and each of us distrusted his neighbors. We were standing at the end of a decadent epoch.[3]

It was no accident that Demuth got to Paris in 1904, and again in 1907. It was his nature to be where things were happening, to scent out and ally himself with what was exciting, what was new.

In a letter he wrote Dr. Williams just before departing for Paris in 1907, Demuth expressed a sense of fright at the prospect of seeing "the sights of Paris within the month." The artist's state of excited expectation bears out Hartley's description of him:

Charles seemed always, in a way, to suffer his thrills, he seemed sort of lashed with ecstasies then pacified, he seemed to sort of tremble at the approach of them, succumb to the magic of their reality, and like so many intensive natures regret their departure into the realms of memory, ...[4]

In September Demuth's passport from the State Department reached him in Lancaster, and he sailed on October 4. An impressionable young man of twenty-four, fresh from the restrictive environment of the Pennsylvania Academy and Lancaster, he

[2] Sidney Janis, *Abstract and Surrealist Art in America*, 11.
[3] Sigfried Giedion, *Space, Time and Architecture*, 431.
[4] Marsden Hartley, "Farewell, Charles," 558.

arrived in Paris about the middle of October. For a while he stayed with an old Philadelphia friend, Lawrence Fellows, at 9, rue de la Chaumière: in December he moved to 113, Notre Dam des Champs, and, after the first of the year to 35, rue Delambre. On December 12 he wrote to his Grandmother Demuth in Lancaster telling her of his plans to spend the Christmas season in Berlin with his cousin, Pauline Cooper, who was studying music there. By the end of March, a little over five months after leaving New York, the artist was on his way back to the States.

It is a fallacy to think of Demuth as having frequented Europe. He spent a few weeks in Europe in 1904, five months in Paris in 1907–1908, sixteen months in the French capital during the extended period 1912–14, and three months in the same city in 1921 —a total of only a little over two years. The years that he was there, however, were crucial ones for both European art and Demuth. The sensitive American was by nature so acutely affected by all he saw and felt that for him two years in Europe may conceivably have equaled another man's twenty years. Demuth's European visits spanned a seventeen-year period during which his art became progressively Europeanized, reflecting from 1916 on the most radical continental trends. In its turn, American art was influenced by and benefited from the Europeanization of Charles Demuth.

When he was in Paris, Demuth habitually accomplished little painting. He would make a few sketches, to be used as source material when he got back to Lancaster. Demuth's way of seeing Paris was to walk about, go to the galleries, and make friends among the artists. He knew "the wild ones" in Paris in 1907— Matisse, Braque, Derain, Dufy, Vlaminck, and Friesz, near the close of the brief Fauvist movement. The young American must have looked hard and long with his strange, piercing eyes and in his absorbed, intense way at the paintings he found in Paris at this time.

Like his idol Watteau, as described in the word portrait by Pater which Demuth illustrated, he had "been a sick man all his life. He was always a seeker after something in the world that is there in no satisfying measure, or not at all." No doubt in the milieu that was Paris in 1907, Demuth was himself a seeker after the eternal verities. He was not to discover his own way of painting for seven more years, but in 1907 he must have been probing in an intuitive and analytical way for a style that would be at once his own and universal. It is an understatement to say that "at twenty-nine he was already examining the advanced theories of modern painting and . . . well in their grip when the [1913] Armory explosion took place."[5]

Other Americans were in Paris during the first decade of the century. Alfred Maurer of Philadelphia had arrived as early as 1900, Bernard Karfiol and Walt Kuhn in 1901, Samuel Halpert in 1902, and Maurice Sterne and Walter Pach in 1904 (the year of Demuth's first visit). Marin, Carles, and Max Weber were in Paris in 1905. Hopper, the Synchromist Morgan Russell, and Abraham Walkowitz were there in 1906. James R. Hopkins, the Ohioan who became an art school administrator in his native state, maintained a studio in Paris for a ten-year period preceding World War I. In 1907, the year Demuth reached Paris for the second time, Arthur G. Dove, Edward Bruce, and Marguerite Zorach visited the French capital. Sheeler, Sheeler's friend Morton L. Schamberg, and Joseph Stella got to Paris for the first time in 1909, Preston Dickinson and William Zorach in 1910, and Hartley, Oscar Bluemner, and John Covert in 1912.

For the most part the Americans who managed to get to the city on the banks of the Loire just after the turn of the century were little affected by the radical experiments currently being made in Montmartre studios by such obscure resident painters as Matisse, Derain, Dufy, Braque, and Picasso. "Certainly Sterne went no further than Cézanne and Gauguin, Halpert no further than Picasso's Pink Period,"[6] and William Zorach no further than

[5] Jacob Getlar Smith, "The Watercolors of Charles Demuth," *American Artist*, Vol. XIX, No. 4 (May, 1955), 29.
[6] Milton W. Brown, *American Painting from the Armory Show to the Depression*, 103.

Maillol. Even the painters Marin, Dove, Hartley, and Demuth, who were eventually to comprise the progressive Stieglitz Group, seem not to have grasped Fauvist and Cubist experiments with any meaning for themselves until after 1911, the year Stieglitz staged Cézanne and Picasso shows at 291. Inspired by these exhibitions, Hartley managed to get to Paris the following year, whence he traveled to Berlin and Munich; his early abstractions dated from his 1914–16 contacts with German Expressionism in the latter city. In the fall of 1916, close upon the heels of his German experience, Hartley joined Demuth in traveling to Bermuda, where both men produced experimental Cubist paintings.

Though Demuth's 1912–19 figure pieces reflect an understanding of Cézanne's means, he did not noticeably employ Cubist theory until the historic Bermuda experiments he conducted with Hartley. There can be little doubt that the two men shared understandings about painting, but it is difficult to find parallels in their development following their commonly experienced Bermuda period—a parallel itself to the manner in which Braque and Picasso evolved following their joint participation in the invention of Cubism. Demuth's development can be said to have paralleled Picasso's, with an understandable lag in time, the lyrical, brooding content of the Spanish giant's early Blue Period being comparable to the romantic, sinister content of the American's early figure pieces, and both men turning subsequently to the classical rewards of geometric Cubism.

For Demuth the 1907 visit to Paris meant further contact with the artistic milieu of Montmartre. The artists had not yet migrated to the Left Bank but were still entrenched on the hill near Lautrec's Moulin Rouge and below Sacré Coeur, which Hartley once described as "a kind of Franco Taj Mahal, a temple of love, suspended arklike after the flood of terrible decisions of the seething emotional world upon the dry ground of the Butte."[7] It was to be a different Paris, a city under the shadow of war, to which Demuth would return five years later.

[7] Hartley, "Farewell, Charles," 558–59.

Following the completion of his last year at the Pennsylvania Academy Demuth returned to Europe, this time for his longest visit, to last from December, 1912, until the spring of 1914. The Paris he encountered when he arrived was a scene of unparalleled creativity.

In 1912 Cézanne was only six years dead. In Paris the romantic Fauvist movement had been superseded by Cubism, just as in Germany *Die Brücke* had been superseded by *Der Blaue Reiter* group, organized in Munich in 1911. Braque and Picasso had left behind both the formative years and heroic period of analytical or facet Cubism, and had arrived at the stage of collage; they were about to commence the period of Cubist synthesis. They were young men yet, both thirty-one, and very little of their work had been exhibited or created yet. Also in Paris, Mondrian was in the midst of his 1910–14 series of analytical Cubist and plus-and-minus experiments, soon to be followed (in 1917) by the founding of Neo-Plasticism in Holland. Orphism and Synchromism, the latter launched in Paris by the Americans Morgan Russell and S. Macdonald-Wright, had been born and died. In London, Vorticism was about to be established by Wyndham Lewis. In Italy, Marinetti's first *Manifesto of Futurism* (1909) had been published, as well as his *Technical Manifesto of Futurist Painting* (1910). In Russia, constructivist, nonobjective, and abstract works were being experimented with by Malevich, Rodchenko, and Tatlin. And in America, which had already seen Cézanne and Picasso works at 291, the Armory Show was imminent—signs which presaged the mid-century emergence of New York as art capital of the Western world.

At this historic moment Demuth arrived in Paris for his third visit, eager to resume life in the city he loved above all others, seek out the ateliers of friends, and walk delightedly down remembered boulevards and across familiar bridges. There was one major change in 1912 for Demuth to discover. The artists were in the process of leaving Montmartre and relocating in the Latin Quarter on the Left Bank, where they were destined to make famous certain cafés located on the Boulevard du Montparnasse by appropriating them as their headquarters.

In December, 1912, Demuth's address was 7, rue Bréa. On Christmas Eve he made the drawing *Paris: the Night before Christmas* (1912), showing a group of Parisians standing at the entrance to a crowded church. That winter he attended a life class at the Académie Moderne, going to the school in the late afternoons and evenings to sketch from the nude. According to Mrs. Malone, a Lancaster friend who maintained a studio in Paris in 1912–13 not far from Demuth's living quarters, the model at the Académie Moderne would assume difficult three-minute poses, with two-minute rest periods in between. Demuth became adept at making these rapid sketches from the nude, adding some color afterward in the manner of Rodin. The following winter, that of 1913–14, he studied at the Académie Colarossi and the Académie Julien.

Mrs. Malone wrote later that it was possible to live comfortably in Paris at this time on one dollar a day, and that Demuth "who had a room, but ate wherever he happened to be, was living on an allowance of sixty dollars a month, more than adequate if one did not become ill."[8] Demuth did become ill during the winter of 1912–13, complaining on his return to his class at the Académie Moderne that he had had difficulty with a "bad leg." Even this early in his life Demuth was the victim of chronic attacks which must have been early indications of diabetes. One wonders how he got along financially, and what he did about meals. Still, according to Miss Stein: "Painters in those days did spend a lot of money and they spent all they got hold of because in those happy days you could owe money for years for your paints and canvases and rent and restaurant and practically everything except coal and luxuries."[9]

In 1912 the Café du Dôme, Café des Lilas, and Café Lavenue, all located on the Left Bank, were the popular rendezvous of the

[8] Malone, "Charles Demuth," 8.
[9] Stein, *Alice B. Toklas*, 51.

progressive writers and painters. When he was in Paris, Demuth participated in some of the heady discussions which took place in these cafés and also in the individual artists' ateliers. Afterward, he would regale Mrs. Malone with humorous stories and descriptions of such of his friends as Miss Stein, the sculptor Joe Davidson, and the poet Pound. "He found these connections fascinating," and his reports to Lettie Malone were amusing but "full of respect for the pioneers in modern painting and writing."[10]

In a real sense Demuth's development resulted from a capacity to look sharply and listen well—most importantly, during this two-year period, which Duchamp called "the best years." Sensitive and intelligent about art, Demuth knew how to learn, and in 1912–14 in Paris the time and place were right for him to learn much.

His mind . . . was greatly broadened by travel. He discovered in himself kinship with the original thinkers, the exotics, if you will, of his day in France—Baudelaire, Huysmans, Gautier, Toulouse-Lautrec, Henry James, and later Proust. He was abundantly curious in the French sense of the word and investigated and followed up every clue that led to the revelation of the spirit of his time.[11]

It may have been this intense interest in discovering the spirit of his age which led Demuth to go frequently to 27, rue de Fleurus, where Miss Stein sat "looking like some oriental god, with the young and faithful kneeling at her feet."[12]

Gertrude Stein sat by the stove talking and listening and getting up to open the door and go up to various people talking and listening. She usually opened the door to the knock and the usual formula was, de la part de qui venez-vous, who is your introducer. The idea was that anybody could come but for form's sake and in Paris you have to have a formula, . . .[13]

In these years Miss Stein is said to have been "wholly intense," with "a deep temperamental life-quality."[14] Her atelier became a

[10] Malone, "Charles Demuth," 7–8.
[11] Helen W. Henderson, "Charles Demuth," *Philadelphia Inquirer*.
[12] Hutchins Hapgood, *A Victorian*, 533.
[13] Stein, *Alice B. Toklas*, 13.
[14] Hapgood, *A Victorian*, 131.

focus for the elite of the Parisian intellectual world, who thronged there on Saturday evenings. At first her atelier had held Japanese prints, then a mixture of pictures old and new, then only Cézannes, Renoirs, Matisses, and Picassos, for a time only Cézannes and Picassos, and finally only Sir Francis Roses. Here Demuth met many persons of note, some of them for the first time—people like Picasso, Gris, Matisse, Miss Dodge, Miss Sitwell, Hemingway, McAlmon, Delaunay, Marie Laurencin, Picabia, Duchamp, and others. Demuth felt at home here. Little Alfy "Maurer" of Philadelphia was an habitué, and Miss Stein herself had been born in Allegheny, Pennsylvania.

Demuth understood and sympathized with Miss Stein's literary effort, intimately connected as it was with modern painting. Self-consciously paralleling Impressionist theory, she was trying to express in a new literary form the total content of her stream of consciousness at a given moment in time. In addition, she went beyond this and attempted to parallel the work of Picasso, Gris, Matisse, and other twentieth-century masters by excluding from her writing all sentiment and anecdote while concentrating on the raw material of her medium—the word in the sentence, divorced from content. Intrigued by the similarities between writing and painting, she was attempting to produce literature which duplicated the burgeoning new ideas in the realm of visual art.

Demuth would have been fascinated by Miss Stein's apparent naïveté and the seeming simplicity of her writing, as well as by the effort she made to seem nonintellectual and her failure to cite authorities. He would have enjoyed the eccentricities which characterized her writing—the odd titles, pure nonsense, penchant for short, symbolic words employed emphatically, plays on rhythmic repetition, and irreverent disregard for punctuation.

It is not easy to gauge the extent of the woman writer's influence on her fellow Pennsylvanian. Her word portraits, many of them written about persons Demuth knew (McBride, Van Vechten, Duchamp, Miss Dodge, and one called *And So: To Change So: Muriel Draper Yvonne Davidson Beatrice Locher*) may conceivably have inspired his own poster portraits, full as they are of metaphor and symbolism.

In her *Autobiography of Alice B. Toklas*, Miss Stein tells how, during the winter of 1912–13 she was beginning to write plays, her first one, *It Happened a Play*, followed *by Ladies' Voices*:

> Florence Bradley, a friend of Mabel Dodge, was spending a winter in Paris. She had some stage experience and had been interested in planning a little theatre. She was vitally interested in putting these plays on the stage. Demuth was in Paris too at this time. He was then more interested in writing than in painting and particularly interested in these plays. He and Florence Bradley were always talking them over together.
>
> Gertrude Stein has never seen Demuth since. When she first heard that he was painting she was much interested. They never wrote to each other but they often sent messages by mutual friends. Demuth always sent word that some day he would do a little picture that would thoroughly please him and then he would send it to her. And sure enough after all these years, two years ago [*c.* 1930?] some one left at the rue de Fleurus during our absence a little picture with a message that this was the picture that Demuth was ready to give to Gertrude Stein. It is a remarkable little landscape in which the roofs and windows are so subtle that they are as mysterious and as alive as the roofs and windows of Hawthorne or Henry James.
>
> It was not long after this that Mabel Dodge went to America and it was the winter of the armoury show. . . .[15]

As indicated above, at this time Demuth was seriously thinking of pursuing a literary career and was also much interested in theater. In October, 1912, an article he had written entitled "Aaron Eshleman, Artist" was printed as one of the Lancaster County Historical Society Papers. And in December, 1913, the entire issue of *The Glebe*, a periodical published in New York by

---

[15] Stein, *Alice B. Toklas*, 133. The Stein Collection at Yale contains notes from Demuth to Miss Stein dated September 6, 1921, and December 26, 1922, in addition to three undated notes written at the Hôtel Lutetia (probably during the artist's 1921 stay in Paris). An undated Christmas card reads:

Wishing you and Miss Toklas a Merry Xmas, and a Happy New Year. Write me just what those Civil War pictures are called and the publisher and I'll look it up for you.

Albert and Charles Boni, was devoted to Demuth's play *The Azure Adder*. The latter appeared while Demuth was in Paris, and must have stimulated his notion of himself as an author of quality. A notice which appeared contemporaneously in a Lancaster newspaper read:

> The December issue of "The Glebe," a new monthly publication in New York, contains a playlet, "The Azure Adder," by Mr. Charles Demuth, of this city. The comedy reveals the fact that the young author is talented with the pen as well as the brush. "The Azure Adder" relates the experiences of a group of artists who temporarily discard their canvas in an endeavor to establish a magazine, to which they become the principal contributors. The application of artistic temperament, ideals and aspirations to the field of literature provides a theme that furnishes the author with productive fields of humor that he cleverly extracts. At the same time an interesting little romance is unfolded.
>
> "The Glebe" is published by Albert and Charles Boni, 96 Fifth Avenue, New York, and the price of the book is 35 cents.[16]

In addition to "Aaron Eshleman, Artist" and *The Azure Adder*, by 1913, Demuth must have completed some of his undated, unpublished manuscripts.[17] At twenty-nine he stood at a crossroads from which his career might have proceeded in either of two directions. By 1914, however, in a mood of disillusionment he wrote in "Between Four and Five," a sketch printed in Stieglitz's *Camera Work*:

> Again the forenoon had been this and that. Again the afternoon had been given to this and that—had been wasted.
>
> "Let us go in here"—and we went in again to the place which is more that than gallery—just a place in movement; just—rather, one of the few.
>
> The walls this time were emotionally hung with African carvings—

---

[16] "Play by Local Author, 'The Azure Adder,' from Pen of Charles Demuth, Appears in New York Periodical," newspaper article.

[17] These include: a poem ("In the Fields"), five plays ("Among Friends," "A Pantomime with Words," "Fantastic Lovers, a Pantomime after Paul Verlaine," "Painting, a Play," "You Must Come Over"), and two short stories (" In Black and White" and "The Voyage Was almost Over"). The last-named work was apparently written while the artist was en route to Europe in August, 1921.

there was also yellow, and orange and black. There were photographs of African carvings. There was a photograph of two hands.

That was a moment.

"Let us start a magazine—a gallery—a theatre." This is always in the air; seldom: "Let us create a moment."

"What is he trying to say?"[18]

For Demuth to "create a moment" meant to evoke the aesthetic experience by means of paint, not words. By 1929, when he was forty-six, he knew absolutely that he was a painter, not a writer. In this year he wrote his well-known essay "Across a Greco Is Written," in which he rejected the written word:

I have been urged by Mr. Lee Simonson, who if he would, could do it much better—I too have other pleasures—to write about my own paintings.

At the start: "Why?"

Haven't I, in a way, painted them?

Poems have been written by painters about their paintings, I know, and—I have heard painters, in my own time, speak excitedly about their own work. . . . Words are not to me a means. I can only paint. Many days I don't feel that this is true . . . this: "I can paint." And never that it would be true of: "I can write." . . .

If I could write and believed in having a cause—well, certainly I would write about the paintings which are being done, at the moment, in my country. . . .

The idea of having painters write about their own paintings is to me not one which is likely to produce great results—add to the medium of words. And unless this addition is accomplished; why write?[19]

On the other hand, Hartley, who wrote easily and well (if in his own peculiar style), was forever torn between writing and painting in the same way that he could never make up his mind about what was, for him, the most congenial place on the face of the earth. By comparison, Demuth's firm rejection of writing in his maturity was consistent with his loyalty to a few chosen places: Lancaster, New York, Provincetown, and Paris.

In April, 1913, Demuth attended a performance by the great

18 "Between Four and Five," *Camera Work*, No. 47 (July, 1914), 32.
19 "Across a Greco," *Creative Art*, Vol. V (September 29, 1929), 629.

71

innovator of the modern dance—Isadora Duncan. He seems not to have been influenced by her, as were so many others. The same summer at the Théâtre des Champs-Elysées, just off the boulevard of the same name, he witnessed one of the early performances in Paris of Diaghilev's Ballet Russe de Monte Carlo.

The American artist Edward Fisk, with whom Demuth was to paint during the summer of 1915 in Provincetown, was in Paris, and it may have been at this time that the two first met. At this time also, Demuth traveled to Étretat near Le Havre to paint, and journeyed to Cornwall, a county in southwest England, with a painter friend appropriately named Cornwallis. He is believed to have traveled to Berlin, probably at Hartley's urging, in the winter of 1914, at which time Arnold Rönnebeck may have modeled his sculptured head of Demuth (see Plate 5) and possibly those of Hartley and McAlmon also.[20] Rönnebeck wrote later: "For several years he [Demuth], Marsden Hartley and I would bum around in the galleries of Paris and London and suddenly meet in Berlin or Hamburg."

Demuth's friendship with McAlmon appears to have commenced during the 1912–14 visit to Paris. McAlmon, a hard-drinking American writer who gave most of his energies to the business of living, eventually contracted a disastrous marriage with Bryher Ellerman, the daughter of Sir John Ellerman, a rich manufacturer of perfumes reputed to be England's heaviest taxpayer. It was McAlmon who, using the small income he earned posing in the nude at Cooper Union while living on a scow in New York Harbor, supported at its inception the little magazine *Contact*, founded by himself and Dr. Williams. Later, as a result of having access to Sir John's fortune, McAlmon was able to publish Contact Editions, which brought out such books as Miss Stein's *The*

---

[20] Rönnebeck's sculptured head of Hartley is in the Walker Art Gallery in Minneapolis. His head of Demuth has been lost, though full-front and profile photographs of the work exist in which the artist appears to be about twenty-seven. The full-front version was published as a frontispiece in *The Dial*, September, 1925. The sculptured head of McAlmon reproduced in the *New York Times Book Review*, Sunday, January 15, 1967, appears to be a companion piece.

Making of Americans,[21] Emanuel Carnivali's *A Hurried Man,* and some of Hemingway's early efforts, parts of a noteworthy list. A fabulous figure noted for his generosity and integrity, McAlmon was interested in publishing the works of talented, neglected writers. In his *Autobiography,* Dr. Williams tells of McAlmon's close companionship with Joyce: "Bob had been useful to [a nearly blind] Joyce, whom he respected . . ., absorbed his gripes and did what he could."[22] McAlmon's own novel *The Distinguished Air,* the title of which Demuth appropriated for his last, largest, and most controversial illustration, is "now sold as red-light-district pulp in that most obscene street, Broadway."[23]

Demuth loved Paris. He found in the romantic old city what Hartley described as "unalloyed satisfaction." One wonders where at this time in Paris he saw works by such men as Lautrec, Cézanne, Matisse, Kandinsky, Nolde, Braque, Picasso, Gris, Metzinger, and Léger, all of whom influenced Demuth and some of whom are now represented in the small branch museum of the Louvre, the Musée du Jeu de Paume. In 1912–14 he could have seen paintings by these men at 27, rue de Fleurus (in the early days Miss Stein had works by Gauguin, Manguin, Vallotton, Lautrec, Maurice Denis, Daumier, Delacroix, and El Greco on the walls of her atelier; later, works by Cézanne, Renoir, Matisse, and Picasso), at Kahnweiler's shop, at the bric-a-brac shop of Berthe Weill in Montmartre (where the young Fauves, including Matisse, exhibited from 1902 on), at the gallery of Sagot on rue Laffitte, and at Vollard's.

What Demuth did when he was in the French city—other than viewing exhibitions, regularly attending a class at one of the academies, and visiting friends—came under the heading of night life. Dr. Williams wrote that when he was in Paris a decade later,

---

21 In his late, bitter years McAlmon spoke of Miss Stein as a "sumerian monument," whose "ancient, mastodonic slow idea, with slow suspicion moves agedly . . . resting to pause in the ancient slime." See Edward Dahlberg, "Beautiful Failures," *New York Times Book Review,* p. 40.

22 Williams, *Autobiography,* 190.

23 Dahlberg, "Beautiful Failures," 40.

in 1922: "The Paris of the expatriate artist was our only world—day and night—and if bread is the staff of life, whisky, as Bob [McAlmon] was fond of saying, is the staff of night life, both products of the same grain."[24] The expatriate artist's existence was probably no less enjoyable in 1912–14, and this was the period when Demuth was earning the reputation of being a *débauché* and ruining his health.[25]

In the most authoritative word portrait of Demuth that we have, the essay "Farewell, Charles, an Outline in Portraiture of Charles Demuth—Painter," Hartley gave us a detailed description of his first encounter with the other American. The two men met at the Restaurant Thomas on the Boulevard du Montparnasse in the year 1912–13, "the hour of the first meeting a certain déjeuner." A stream of colorful individuals either frequented this café or passed habitually in promenade before its doors. There were Madame Thomas herself, her daughter Yvonne, and Père Thomas. Eventually there would be the Polish artist and teacher at the Grand Chaumière, Helena Bosnańska, who always dressed in mourning for Poland, diminutive Eugene Zak walking by with his mother, and the pair from Edinburgh—Stuart Hill, a powdered and befrilled figure out of the past, and George Banks, a woman journalist who dressed mannishly and resembled Oscar Wilde.

All this très exagéré of course, but life was like that then, and it all seemed to be a part of the day's run, and brings up an amusing and funny Paris, accentuated all the more acutely by the manner of the young cubists who were over-dressing in the other extreme à la Londres, with white spats on all occasions and an air of great importance whisking about them, their style of dress quite all wrong of course for no Frenchman can wear English clothes for he can never walk like an Englishman.[26]

Dining at the Restaurant Thomas with Hartley more or less

[24] Williams, *Autobiography* . . . , 190.

[25] Van Vechten said in an interview, January 23, 1956: "Demuth drank too much and he didn't take care of his health before diabetes set in." And George Biddle wrote in the answers he gave to a Demuth questionnaire: "In his early years he was a *débauché*, drank heavily."

[26] Hartley, "Farewell, Charles," 555.

regularly was a group of expatriate artists which included Rönnebeck, the sculptor mentioned above who eventually became director of the Denver Art Museum, Alice Miriam who was studying
voice in Paris, and Simonson, the noted stage designer then studying painting in the French capital. Hartley described the meeting
with Demuth thus:

> I shall recall to Charles, perhaps more to give a setting for his own
> entrance . . . I shall recall to him the day he ambled up to our table,
> . . . there being one place left at the table at which we all sat, asking
> if he might sit with us, the request being granted without further
> thought.
> It wasn't long before Charles made us particularly aware of him
> by a quaint, incisive sort of wit with an ultra sophisticated, post-
> eighteen-ninety touch to it, for I always felt that Charles's special
> personal tone had been formed with this period, the murmur of im-
> agined deaths of superior trifles clinging to his very sensitive hands,
> and a wistful apprehension of what many a too tender soul has called
> infectious sin, alas how harmless and sentimental it all was. . . .[27]

The Maine artist continued:

> Charles, dressed always in the right degree of good taste, English
> taste of course, carrying his cane elegantly . . . coming to our table as
> I have said, we all saying yes of course, and there was immediately
> much quaint banter afloat, interspersed with veiled sous entendus, all
> of it fun, and I remember saying to Charles after the meal was over,
> I think you had better come and sit with us all the time, and so it was
> Charles became known to me over the space of the ensuing twenty-
> three years.[28]

The historic Armory Show took place in New York between
February 15 and March 15, 1913. Demuth was in Europe and
did not exhibit. Stuart Davis, a New York artist eleven years
younger than Demuth with whom the latter was to become acquainted in Provincetown during the summer of 1914, and who
once said Demuth taught him a lot about painting, exhibited in
the show. Hartley, who was six years older than Demuth and

[27] *Ibid.*, 554.
[28] *Ibid.*, 555.

75

had already been given two one-man shows at Stieglitz' 291, also exhibited. Demuth had shown his work in the Pennsylvania Academy's annual watercolor exhibitions in 1908 and 1912, and must have had works he could have shown in 1913, but in addition to being in Europe he was in the process of finding himself as an artist. Less than a year after the Armory Show, in the fall of 1914 when he was thirty-one, Demuth had his first one-man show, an exhibition of watercolors at New York's Daniel Gallery.

The 1912–14 sojourn abroad occurred at a crucial time in Demuth's development. He was able to make a lightning-quick selection of what he as an individual wanted, of what was right for him, out of the abundant intellectual climate he found in Paris. He returned with sure knowledge of the means to dynamic form employed by the masters throughout the centuries. In other words, in the critical years of the emergence of twentieth-century painting out of a dead academicism and the superficiality of *art nouveau*, Paris provided Demuth with contact with other artists of stature, both past and present, an experience which resulted in his gaining an intellectual understanding of pictorial form. Hartley stated it this way: "He knew the laws of picture making, and that is something that not all painters know."[29]

Demuth sailed from Europe in the spring of 1914 shortly before the outbreak of war. He was met in New York by Augusta Demuth, his Aunt Kate Buckius, and Locher. When he stepped off the boat, he was thirty-one, an impeccable cosmopolitan, and a potential artist of rare promise ripe for the distinguished career which lay ahead. The next five years were to be his most prolific, when he was to produce his great illustrations and other figurative works depicting circus people, dancers, and acrobats, bathers on the beach, sailors just arrived in port, and scenes in jazz-age night clubs and saloons.

Demuth had had a good time in Paris, and a happy existence lay immediately ahead. Until 1920, in spite of occasional attacks of illness involving his "bad leg," life was, on the surface, a con-

[29] *Ibid.*, 561.

tinuous round of successful painting and sophisticated social events. Yet Demuth's life was ever a mixture of delight and tragedy.

So it was with the rest of the world in 1914. As though people sensed the imminence of disaster, an intangible spirit of recklessness filled the air.

5

Early Productive Years (1914-23)

The early Provincetown group consisted mostly of writers. They arrived during the summer of 1911, three years before the New York artists. And, as is always curiously the case even when given such slight precedence in time, they considered themselves the elite. The 1911 group included such authors as Mary Heaton Vorse, George Cram Cook and Susan Glaspell, Wilbur Daniel Steele and his wife Margaret, and Hutchins Hapgood and his wife Neith.

In those days the picturesque little fishing village displayed an unspoiled charm with its Cape Cod houses, colonial mansions (a few with widow's walks), tall monument commemorating the arrival of the Pilgrims, and handsome church graced with a Wren-influenced steeple. Then as today there were authentic fishhouses, shanties, and wharves down on the shore of the bay. And then as today Portuguese fishermen left with their nets at dawn for the day's work, returning, boats loaded, with the tide.

In 1914, the summer peace of Provincetown came to an end when, in search of psychological release from the threat of war, the habitués of New York's Greenwich Village descended. Like a swarm of bees, the Villagers had found their permanent summer home. That particular summer, 1914, was to be marked not only by the initial appearance of the Villagers. It was to reach a certain climax, a typical Greenwich Village–Provincetown Happening, as an outcome of the reaction of the artists to the reality of war. According to Hapgood, who was there: "Even before the climax, which took place the week the Great War broke out, that summer marked a strange union of strangely unlike elements, and yet a real union."[1]

In his book of personal recollections, *A Victorian in the Modern World*, Hapgood noted that the Villagers appeared to arrive upon the heels of Hippolyte Havel and Polly Holliday, Louis Holliday and Christine Ell. He described the invaders as "revolutionists of various kinds . . . the Anarchists, the I.W.W.'s, the extreme left wing of the Socialists, the females militantly revolutionary about sex-freedom, and the Cubists and Post-Impressionists in art."[2] The newcomers belonged to certain bohemian groups which, sustained by their associations with the Parisian Latin Quarter, had been active in the Village for several years.

Stuart Davis, then twenty, roomed at the same place Demuth did. Miss Henderson of Philadelphia, Miss Street and Elaine Freeman of New York, and Helene Iungerich were there; also, an I.W.W. poet whose name was Joe O'Carroll, an I.W.W. named Fred Boyd who had just been released from jail where he had been placed for preaching sabotage, Max Eastman, who had recently become editor of the *Masses*, a Cubist illustrator named Stuart, and Bayard Boyeson. Eastman was there with his first wife Ida Rauh, from whom he had not yet separated.

Years later Miss Henderson recalled:

It was a fruitful and interesting summer to both of us and Charles made friends of all the people of note who had adopted Province-town as a sort of Europeanized resort. What Provincetown thought of all this is something else. . . . Suddenly it was invaded with the most extraordinary people, bringing the atmosphere of Greenwich Village with them. Lodgings were very cheap, we found rooms with the natives. There were two art schools in full force—under Hawthorne and Webster.

---

[1] Hapgood, *A Victorian*, 380.
[2] *Ibid.*, 379.

Demuth, of course, worked independently.[3]

Demuth painted the boats in the bay, getting what may have been his first detailed acquaintance with the masts and rigging of small sailboats. He also painted the dunes situated several miles down the road from the village near the beach.

An article apparently written by Miss Henderson entitled "Cape Cod Town Is an Artistic Haven" which appeared on August 15, 1914 (?), in an unidentified newspaper, read:

> Demuth, of Lancaster, has been here since June and may remain the winter, as he finds the place rich in resources. He paints chiefly the wonderful desert-like dunes which lie behind the town and which one must cross to reach the ocean side of the cape. . . .
>
> It has been left, apparently, for Demuth to discover the immense lure of the sand dunes, which are protected from the vulgar gaze by heavy sand roads and a mosquito belt almost impassable except to the most courageous. . . .
>
> Demuth has made the most of his opportunity and has a series of remarkable impressions of the dunes in both oil and watercolor, treating them as dunes have not been treated before. . . .
>
> Stuart Davis, a youngster of promise whose work has appeared in the illustrated weeklies, is working here in his studio at portraiture. He and Demuth have had a small exhibition in the Greenwich Village Inn, the headquarters of the nuts' congress and the rendezvous of the literary contingent of Provincetown.[4]

Polly, Louis' sister, ran a restaurant in Provincetown that summer with the help of Havel, that "anarchist philosopher, journalist, and bohemian" from Bohemia. He and Polly "loved one another, and they had started a *ménage* together"[5] in the Village where Polly ran her Manhattan restaurant. First called Polly's and then the Greenwich Village Inn, the New York restaurant was a small basement café on the west side of Washington Square. It may have been the first café in the Village. In her book *Part of a Long Story*, Agnes Boulton O'Neill wrote that Miss Holliday's mother had been an actress, and that in her restaurant Polly always "domi-

[3] Helen W. Henderson, "Charles Demuth," paper.
[4] "Cape Cod Is an Artistic Haven," in unknown Provincetown newspaper.
[5] Hapgood, *A Victorian*, 317.

nated the scene—tall, dark-eyed, and calm, with an interesting and receptive mind, she gave her place the air of a club . . ."

Mrs. O'Neill continued:

It seems to me that the Holliday family were in some way connected with the O'Neill family in the sense of being old friends. Adele Holliday had been a protégé [sic] of Otis Skinner—who was probably a friend of the elder O'Neill. She had been on the stage for awhile, then given it up to marry and to give birth to two children, Polly and her brother Louis. Polly, at some time when money was scarce, had started a restaurant. Her brother Louis had been a friend of Gene's for years.[6]

Christine, the restaurateur who later married Louis Ell, decided that Demuth was a finished individual because he possessed a subtle variety of charm and an unprejudiced mind; Demuth's youth appealed also to Christine. But it was Polly who fell in love with Demuth. Stuart Davis said: "Polly could be crazy about a lot of people, and she got crazy about Demuth"[7] in the summer of 1914 in Provincetown. Polly also "got crazy" about the I. W. W. poet O'Carroll, the I. W. W. revolutionary Boyd, and the young Cubist illustrator Stuart. As a result, Havel burst frequently into tirades against not only Demuth, O'Carroll, Boyd, and Stuart, but the entire universe.

On his part, Demuth became interested in Helene Iungerich, a beautiful young woman with a noble, mysterious countenance enhanced by heavy-lidded, deep set eyes. He would go to call on her at the place where she was rooming with Miss Freeman. During the summer he helped Helene stage a show, Living Japanese Prints, which consisted of real-life facsimilies. Miss Henderson, who saw the performance, reported that at one moment when Miss Iungerich was to appear onstage "after the most incredible delay the curtain was drawn aside, [and] nothing was to be seen but Helene's foot sticking out at one side of the flies."[8]

It was the summer of 1914 that Demuth formed his enduring

[6] Agnes Boulton, *Part of a Long Story*, 84. Hereafter cited as *Long Story*.
[7] Interview with Stuart Davis.
[8] Henderson, Information.

friendship with Miss Street, who later described how elegantly Demuth dressed in Provincetown, and how attractively his olive skin tanned, leaving only "little white untanned smile lines" at the corners of his eyes. According to Miss Street, Demuth spent his evenings in Provincetown walking down Commercial Street with his friends, stopping at the drugstores along the way, and was much more interested in riding the local bus up and down the single main street of the village (which strings itself out along the curve of the bay) than in going out on the harbor in a boat. Demuth would climb into the side of the bus, which was equipped with board seats, sit down at the front alongside the driver, and go "hell-bent from one end of the town to the other,"[9] waving to his friends as he went by.

According to Miss Street, people called the artist "Deem"[10] in Provincetown. But Davis said a group of young men who roomed at the same place where he and Demuth stayed began calling him "Chuck" just to tease him. "He was too elegant to be called 'Chuck,' "[11] Davis stated.

It was a period when there was a great deal of drinking. Mr. Cook brought the first cask of red wine to Provincetown, from Brooklyn, christening this and subsequent importations Sappho, Aeschylus, Sophocles, and Euripides. With the advent of the bohemians from the Village, wine flowed more freely. It was Provincetown, where in season a heady vacation spirit always prevails, and Prohibition and the Eighteenth Amendment were six years away. Stuart maintained "a little studio on the beach where they all danced and drank and went in swimming at night, with Cubist costumes and without them."[12] It was the custom to go boating on the harbor at night.

Demuth is reported to have drunk heavily that summer, along with the others. Davis took him home a few times. Davis, who

[9] Interview with Miss Street.
[10] The name "Demuth" is correctly pronounced as though it were spelled Dee'-muth, with the accent on the first syllable.
[11] Interview with Davis.
[12] Hapgood, A Victorian, 380.

said that Demuth "wasn't trivial, nor was he stupid—he was extremely sensitive, and interested in his own sensations," also stated: "Demuth was a playboy in his own terms. . . . In those days only people of distinction were the go-to-hellers. Not everybody, like it is to-day."[13]

Demuth himself once commented in a letter he wrote to Stieglitz in July, 1927:

Still, a few of us have lived, although it almost killed me, will in the end, I suppose—and are able through this living to see, before a thing is a safe Old Master, its living qualities.

Through the misleading surface aspects of their way of life, artists tend to camouflage their basic seriousness of purpose. Undoubtedly this fundamental seriousness of the artistic nature contributed to the violent reaction of Provincetown artists in 1914 to the announcement that war had been declared in Europe. People gathered in the local stationery store where newspapers were sold, straining to keep in touch with the latest news from Europe. Hapgood wrote afterward: "The War went to our heads, the whisky helping merely to set free the emotions resulting from the war." He recalled the psychological impact thus: "[The artists] felt the war as social upheaval rather than as war. . . . It was personal and impersonal, a turmoil from within as well as from without. Where was our [Socialist] propaganda now? What part had our ideas held with reality? Where were we? What were we?"[14]

Boyd proposed a conference of Provincetown's leading personalities for the purpose of putting a stop to the war. A conference was duly held, attended by Boyd, Boyeson, O'Carroll, Hapgood, Havel, Eastman, Miss Vorse (social arbiter of Provincetown), and Mrs. Cook (George Cram Cook's mother). Following the meeting O'Carroll recited some of his poetry, which "narrated the woes of the workers and heralded the dawn of freedom," after

[13] Interview with Davis.
[14] Hapgood, *A Victorian*, 385.

83

which he was put to bed. Later, "naked and ecstatic,"[15] he was rescued by friends while running toward the water in an apparent effort to end it all. That same night Polly, the sensuous, designing charmer who had attracted the simultaneous attentions of Demuth, Boyd, O'Carroll, Stuart, and Havel, became so confused she attempted to drown herself at the identical spot where O'Carroll had just been rescued, but she was discouraged by the coldness of the water.

Two days later Boyd left Provincetown by invitation after organizing one of many riotous parties resulting from the announcement of war, and Havel departed of his own volition. After that Polly breathed a sigh of relief and "gave herself over to the subtle charm of Demuth,"[16] who seems to have remained aloof from all the excitement.

The impact of World War I on Provincetown artists paralleled reactions at all levels of society. People sensed that an end had come to the particular world which they had known—that carefree, ordered, principled world of the Absolute where each idea was firmly labeled, wine flowed freely, and the sun shone bright.

The initial reaction of the revolutionary element in America was a visionary, hopeful expectation that war might bring the fruition of the Socialist dream. But in spite of the Russian Revolution, even the Socialists emerged from the war with shaken beliefs. Nearly everyone in America and Europe became disillusioned and despairing, gripped by a deep sense of personal loss which degenerated, on the plane of society as a whole, into moral permissiveness. Theirs was "the lost generation," theirs the Wasteland. Hapgood expressed the situation accurately when he wrote: "We poured out our disappointment and our skepticism upon ourselves, and our virtue suffered. We were less admirable human beings; responsibility had little meaning, relatively, to our imaginations."[17]

15 *Ibid.*, 386.
16 *Ibid.*, 390.
17 *Ibid.*, 391.

Demuth stands out against this emotional cataclysm as one relatively untouched. He seems not to have been affected by the pall of hopelessness which fell over the Western world in the wake of war, and not to have felt appreciably the Depression years of the early thirties, through which he also lived. True, he painted soldiers in New York cafés and sailors just arrived in port, but in his paintings the soldiers and sailors appear to be jolly playmates gotten up in military and nautical costume.

The reasons for Demuth's imperviousness to world disaster are complex and multiple. In 1914, he had just returned from an extended stay in Paris and visits to Berlin, Hamburg, and other cities on the continent; as a result he must have been acutely aware of war developments, so that the official announcement of war came as no surprise. His personal life had always been so beset with problems of the most drastic order that world catastrophe seemed only more of the same, if on a wider, more impersonal scale. He knew, of course, that he was physically unfit for service—that, as usual, due to his infirmities he would be forced to play the vicarious role of an onlooker outside of normal experience.

But there is more than this to Demuth's controlled, insulated aloofness to war, world disillusionment, and widespread financial depression. One is reminded of Leonardo's imperviousness to the motives behind Cesare Borgia's wars, in which the Florentine was intimately involved, and of his accompanying a group of condemned persons to the execution block so that he might sketch their fear-ridden faces. Perhaps as a matter of self-preservation sensitive men necessarily develop a philosophy which permits nonparticipation—that is, emotional noninvolvement—in the political events of their day.

Hartley wrote afterward regarding the summer of 1915 in Provincetown: "The summer was really huge in import, and huge in various satisfaction."[18] It was in a way an important epoch in American art history when, largely as a matter of personal rehabil-

[18] Hartley, "Farewell, Charles," 557.

itation in connection with the effects of war, the Provincetown Players Group was spontaneously organized and performed for the first time in Miss Vorse's fishhouse on the bay.

Hartley was a guest that summer in the house of John Reed (the gifted Socialist who had just returned from consummating his famous interviews with Pancho Villa in Mexico and who was destined to be buried in the Kremlin with full military honors). Havel was functioning as cook in the Reed *ménage*. Across from Reed's house O'Neill was living in a fishhouse along with Terry Carlin, that "insatiable searcher after deeper knowledge, accumulator of incredible experiences, from flop-house luxury on the Thames Embankment . . . Terry always alive to whatever it was."[19] Ann Harding, who was to win fame as an actress, Louise Bryant, the journalist who was to marry first Reed and then diplomat Bullitt, and Carl Sprinchorn were in Provincetown that summer, in addition to a host of others.

Demuth was there with Fisk, an American painter he had met in Paris. According to Daniel, Fisk was "a very handsome fellow with regular features. He married [Agnes O'Neill's sister] eventually and went West. Taught for awhile in Tennessee."[20] The two young men painted assiduously during the summer and in November and December, 1917, Daniel gave them a two-man show, called Watercolors by Charles Demuth and Oils by Edward Fisk, at his New York Gallery. At the close of the 1915 season in Provincetown, Demuth exhibited in various end-of-the-summer shows; and just before Miss Street left for New York, she purchased one of his watercolors, *Flower Piece* (1915).

Hartley has told how during this summer there were "long night sessions" when the day's work was done, during which "playtime was likewise a matter of big business." And out of the amalgam of hard work and hard play there emerged a strong intellectual affinity between members of a remarkable group of gifted persons, among whom were Miss Vorse, Miss Harding,

[19] *Ibid.*, 556–57.
[20] Interview with Daniel.

Miss Glaspell and her husband George Cram Cook, Hapgood and his wife Neith, O'Neill, Reed, Hartley, and Demuth. "Suddenly it was decided that there was to be and must be a little theatre,"[21] to be located at Miss Vorse's dock, which had a fishhouse on it.

Hartley recorded that in all the activity and camaraderie surrounding the founding of the Provincetown Players Group, which was to continue at the Macdougal Street theater in the Village, Demuth was "a special figure."

And he would enjoy having himself set out against all that background.

Charles liked being in on these parties, those tiger-like stalkings after amusement down the courses of the night, he liked being swept into atmospheres and getting his own funny kick out of them, and they were big ideas and issues for Charles, bringing some of the best of his work out of him, and I am sure he gave them far-reaching importance by virtue of the fact that his imagination was essentially of the spiral variety.[22]

It must have been this summer that Demuth appeared in one of Miss Vorse's plays. His Lancaster friend Elsie Everts, the little Polish girl who attended the Pennsylvania Academy when he did, recalled that the title of the play in which he appeared was *A Girl on the Wharf*. And it must have been this summer also, when he was on intimate terms with the Provincetown Players, that Demuth painted the crucifix on a bedroom door in the Provincetown home of Miss Glaspell. Elsie said that the painted cross occupied the raised moldings between four sunken panels. The recessed panels and cross were painted with gilt or else laid in golf leaf, and the body of the dead Christ was painted in flesh tones. Elsewhere on the door appeared areas of scarlet and purple. A tenant who subsequently rented the house for the summer refused to occupy until the crucifix had been removed. This was done, but the gold panels and some of the other painted areas remained until Miss Glaspell's death in 1947.

[21] Hartley, "Farewell, Charles," 557.
[22] *Ibid.*, 557–58.

During the summer of 1915, Demuth was still painting in his early amorphous, formative style. A watercolor landscape from this period, *The Bay* (c. 1914–15), shows a view of Provincetown seen from the water. The work is technically free, with broad washes and delicate brushwork, but lacks the sure grasp of form which the artist exhibited later. Another watercolor landscape from this period, *Dunes* (1915), is a loosely executed, painterly work in which the profiles of dark blue dunes undulate upward into a turbulent blue sunset sky. Demuth also painted some beach scenes that summer, and some flower still lifes.

Demuth and Hartley spent the summer of 1916, also, in Provincetown on the Cape.[23] The following fall Demuth went to Bermuda, remaining at St. George on St. George's Island until the following spring. Since Hartley is known to have been in Bermuda at the same time,[24] in all probability the two friends went there together. Because of his lameness and chronic attacks of what he termed a "bad leg," Demuth, who was thirty-three, was unfit for military service, and Hartley, who was thirty-nine, was too old. Both men apparently felt the need in 1916 for an island apart, a place to get away from the pressures of war.

Both artists were in their prime at this time, ripe for making rapid gains in thinking about twentieth-century painting in America, though they no doubt felt enmeshed in the historic conflict between intellectual European aesthetic values and the curious American penchant for realism. That Hartley was never to explore the avenues of Cubism as searchingly as Demuth is understandable. Hartley was too fundamentally a romantic: he felt too strongly the pull of a poetic nature.

During the months that he was in Bermuda, Demuth produced

[23] Reprinted from Emily Farnham, "Charles Demuth's Bermuda Landscapes," *Art Journal*, Vol. XXV, No. 2 (Winter, 1965–66), 130–37.

[24] See Elizabeth McCausland, *Marsden Hartley*, 28, for a reproduction of Hartley's painting *A Bermuda Window in a Semitropic Character, 1916*. Miss McCausland states: "It is difficult to find documentation to fit *A Bermuda Window* into the sequence of his [Hartley's] evolution."

a brilliant series of architectural landscapes (see Plates 16 and 17), some of them apparently unfinished, in which he experimented with Cubist theory in regard to subject matter content and form. These landscapes—exquisite, perfectionist works of great delicacy, yet solidly structured—bear the mark of mastery and ought probably to be considered a landmark not only in the artist's career, but also in the history of American art. Severe, restrained, and incisive, like the superb Italian landscapes Corot painted when he was thirty, they eclipse the artist's better-known, more popular later works.

The following descriptions indicate the general character of these landscapes, which tend to be of a piece:

Bermuda #4 (1917).
Ruled planes define a square tower in lower right. Curved lines symbolize hills and trees above and to the left of tower. Darkest darks (red, green, violet) are also located above and to the left of tower, pulling composition into upper left. *Very pastel.*

Bermuda: Houses (1917).
A yellow pile of buildings which have primitive forms (cubical, some with sloping walls). Blue sky and blue mountain (merely indicated) in background. Green foliage suggested. A single black triangular roof in upper left, used as staccato weight and directional arrow. Three fourths of format left unpainted.

Landscape (c. 1917).
The roofs and gables of ridgepole structures are discernible, but this painting is very close to pure abstraction. Stress has been laid solely on form created by manipulation of the straight line and plane divorced from realistic subject matter.[25]

The most important influence on Demuth from 1916 forward was unquestionably that of Cézanne, the body of whose work lay at the root of Cubism. Demuth had considerable opportunity to study Cézanne works—at 291 in Stieglitz' 1911 show of works by Cézanne and Picasso, in the Barnes Collection at nearby Merion

[25] These descriptions have been excerpted from the author's catalogue of Demuth works, on file in the Main Library of Ohio State University, Columbus, Ohio.

(where Demuth was always welcome as a friend of Dr. Barnes), in Paris at Miss Stein's atelier, and elsewhere in Paris and New York. There is every reason to believe that Demuth carefully studied those of the great Frenchman's works which he was privileged to see.

The fact that the American's watercolors resemble the Frenchman's, as it became the fashion to record, results from the fact that both men habitually painted delicately and with muted colors, subtly and with understatement, the problem of form being their constant, ruling passion. Cézanne and Demuth were both masters of a sensitive approach to painting, and, though their most serious works were accomplished in oil, both artists were possibly more at home in the watercolor medium. The watercolors of both men usually contain a considerable amount of left paper, and frequently present an unfinished appearance. Both artists employed unpainted white spots in the ground as organic, plastically operating neutral foils for activity present elsewhere in a painting. Watercolor suited the common character traits of the two men, both of whom were retiring by nature, modest, gentle, ultrasensitive, and introverted.

Demuth made no attempt to employ Cézanne's *petite sensation*, his system of grading color from cool darks to warm lights. He seems to have understood, as did Braque and Picasso, that Cézanne's greatness lay not in his method of modeling objects but in his capacity for creating a dynamic variety of space wedded to the flatness of the plane. The American substituted a dazzling chiaroscuro technique combined with various kinds of texture— his individual "tree-forms" texture and textures which were pooled, mottled, speckled, grained, and hatched. What Demuth learned most conspicuously from Cézanne lay in the precinct of abstract means for structuring a painting—such means as the upward expanding conformation (regarded here as a pictorial principle used in all painting which subscribes to the romantic variety of open form), the split wall, general tectonic composition by means of planes, and the turning of total form about an axis.

90

As in the paintings of Cézanne, in the Bermuda works there occur few true verticals or horizontals. Paint is applied sparingly and kept rigidly under control, in part by means of the dexterous blotted textures which Demuth began to use at this time. The textures vary in nature, being refined or coarse according to the artist's need, and they are usually employed for purposes of value gradation (both for typically Cubist value transition within a given plane and for the gaining of a vignetted effect). Patterned effects and facets are obtained in these works by manipulation of the edge of the blotter.

All of the Bermuda landscapes are extremely pale in color, even for Demuth (who could employ powerful color when he was so inclined). They are so light, the values so close, that in some works the pattern of the whole is nearly indistinguishable. When in later years he became more confident in his handling of straight lines and planes, his color came back to life, as it were (as in the large oil *My Egypt*, completed in 1927), and strong value contrasts reappeared.

An examination of the Bermuda works and subsequent Demuth landscapes[26] reveals that, among the many devices employed by the Cubists, he experimented with the following: over-all unity and the reduction of deep space, the facet technique (with which he was particularly enthralled), distortion and dislocation of parts, shifting, pluralism or duality, the arbitrary use of shadows which occasionally became substance, planes at once transparent and opaque, interlocking light and dark planes with interchangeable positive-negative qualities, overlapping planes, interpenetrating planes, geometrically exact lines (straight and curved), coincidental edges, the projection of lines of force, the refraction of lines, and fusions or *passages*. As Winthrop O. Judkins has suggested, such devices result in "a deliberate oscillation of appearances, a

[26] Demuth's landscapes break down into four groups:
1. The early amorphous landscapes (1911–15).
2. The Bermuda Cubist-influenced landscapes (1916–17).
3. The transitional landscapes (1918–21).
4. The late architectural-industrial landscapes (1927–33).

studied multiplicity of readings . . . an iridescence of form"[27]—all qualities which would have appealed to Demuth's love of vitality and ambiguity. Demuth did not use *collage*, simultaneity (the twisting of objects *en face*), or elevations—all part of Cubist vocabulary—nor does he appear to have been interested in the automatic action of materials and tools.

Demuth does not appear to have been influenced by the Futurists, some of whose means were appropriated from the Cubists and expanded by the Italian school. An exception may be his extensive use of the ray technique (a device also employed by Feininger, Joseph Stella, Marin, Lozowick, and O'Keeffe), in connection with which he may have been interested in the breaking up of light in the Futurist manner.

Obviously something critical happened to Demuth's approach to painting while he was in Bermuda. The taut Bermuda landscapes are drastically different from the illustrations and figure pieces of the same period, works crammed with interest in anecdote, humanism, and wit, and executed in what was habitually a loosely scribbled calligraphic line combined with amorphous washes. What happened was that while he was in Bermuda, Demuth possessed the brilliance to analyze and effectively employ advanced painting ideology. In a great surge of creativity which became somehow possible for him while he was there, he was able to advance rapidly toward mastery of the art of twentieth-century painting.

At Bermuda, Demuth attempted one of the most difficult things in the realm of painting, and succeeded in it; namely, to retain a high degree of recognizability and communication in a given work and at the same time maintain a primary concern with the great pictorial dichotomy of two-dimensionality allied to dynamic form. In Bermuda for the first time art became a "quest, through forms, of . . . an inner pattern, or schema, which subsequently takes (or does not take) the form of actual objects, but of which, in any

<hr/>

[27] Winthrop Otis Judkins, "Towards a Reinterpretation of Cubism," *Art Bulletin*, (December, 1948), 275

case, these objects are merely the expression, no more than that."[28] In his maturity Demuth had acquired sure conviction about the death of chronicle, and shucked off literary content and the figure. He had gained confidence that only studied simplification can lead to great art, and learned to limit his means, in the right direction. He had felt and responded to the newly discovered world art, in which there exists a visual language independent of the subject portrayed, and had arrived at a point where he could think about pure painting as a creative act instead of as representation.

For a period of approximately three years following his Bermuda experience Demuth was pulled simultaneously in two directions: toward his old concern with naturalistic line, anecdote, humanism, and a Renaissance variety of three-dimensionality, in which he had been influenced by El Greco, Lautrec, Watteau, Blake, Kandinsky, and Rodin; and toward his new-found interest in the use of classical exactitude, the plane, antihumanism, and two-dimensionality integrated with form, in which he was influenced by Cézanne, Picasso, Braque, Gris, Metzinger, and Léger. During the years 1916–20 Demuth moved steadily away from a romantic variety of line (of which he was a master) toward a classical variety of emphasis on the plane, away from illusory space toward nonillusory abstract space, from fluidity toward immobility, and from a humanistic (if negatively humanistic) art toward abstraction and nonhumanism. By 1920, Demuth's course was firmly set in the new direction; henceforth, until the end of his life in 1935, he was to paint in terms of twentieth-century nonillusory expression. Some of his illustrations and figure pieces had been masterpieces, but he was to achieve his goal, which was to create significant paintings in the idiom of the Great Style, in the majestic, sometimes monumental, architectural-industrial landscapes of the last years of his life.

Demuth reached two summits of accomplishment, either of which is sufficient to establish him on the level of the masters: the psychology-imbued illustrations of 1915–19, taken as a group, and

[28] André Malraux, *Museum without Walls*, 79.

the superbly structured Cubist-influenced landscapes of 1916–21. Unfortunately but intriguingly, in both groups of paintings the power is latent, subtle, and obscure—on the one hand because of understatement, on the other as the result of a sophisticated knowledge of form.

Sherman E. Lee underscored the above judgment when, in "A Critical Survey of American Water-Color Painting," he wrote: "[The 1916–18 landscapes,] with the narrative and circus pictures . . . are of great importance in modern art and . . . should be considered equally with the work of such men as Braque, Gris, Ozenfant, Feininger, Klee, and Picasso."[29]

That one man, within the short period of two years (1915–17), could have produced both the hot, intense, psychology-ridden Zola illustrations and the cool, austere Bermuda landscapes is indicative of Demuth's complexity as an artist. The answer lies not altogether in what Daniel Catton Rich termed the artist's inability "to fuse both sides of a complicated personality," though many of the riddles in Demuth's nature are certainly traceable to his homosexuality. Surely part of the answer lies in the artist's versatility, his capacity for rapid development and change, his passion for new ideas in art, and his penchant for what can only be called a scholarly variety of experimentation.

Oddly—though it is a sign of creativity and versatility—the fact that Demuth's art is many-faceted has caused him to be only partially appreciated on all fronts. Few, if any, persons have been able to react with equal enthusiasm to all five of his subject-matter categories. To one who has seen only his illustrations, he appears to be a major illustrator; to one who is conscious primarily of his watercolor still lifes, his work seems fragile, light, a bit precious and overdelicate; to one who is oriented toward his tempera and oil landscapes he appears to be a pioneer in hard-edge abstraction; and to one who is aware of his *hommages* or poster portraits he appears to be either a decorative painter or precursor of Pop. Pos-

---

[29] Sherman E. Lee, "A Critical Survey of American Water-Color Painting," 297–98. Hereafter cited as "A Critical Survey."

94

sibly Demuth would emerge sooner as an artist of major significance if we knew only his landscapes, just as we know only Marin's.

The fact that Demuth's works lean toward lightness, in both subject matter and technique, also militates against a ready appreciation of his art, as he himself predicted when he wrote: "Lightness is seldom understood. . . . Things tedious, over long, or, over large and slightly Freudian, at the moment, have a much better chance of being acclaimed great."[30]

But one must not assume because of this that his works are not profound. "Behind his delicacies lies the strength of Cézanne and Toulouse-Lautrec."[31] And beneath the subtle nuances of a Demuth landscape, figure piece, or flower painting frequently resides a complex, subterranean contribution of sensuous, erotic undertones much like those one encounters in Henry James and Proust.

Still another reason for the slow realization of Demuth's stature may be found in the fact that much of his best work has lain hidden away for years in cloistered private and semiprivate collections. The illustrations of literary works by Zola, Wedekind, Henry James, Poe, Pater, and Balzac were acquired by private collectors soon after they were produced. For instance, at least six of the nine illustrations for Franz Wedekind's *Pandora's Box* and *Erdgeist* were purchased by Dr. Albert C. Barnes and Miss Violette de Mazia of Merion, Pennsylvania. Dr. Barnes, who possessed unerring taste, acquired forty Demuth works, including seven of the Bermuda landscapes—every one a superb painting, and each suffering the fate of disappearance into the resplendent depths of the exclusive Barnes Foundation museum.

As a result of the 1913 Armory Show, the American art world was radically changed—almost overnight. And, as is always the case with change, the process was painful. It was the first time modern art had been experienced by a Philistine Ameri-

[30] Demuth, "Peggy Bacon."
[31] Lee, "A Critical Survey," 278.

95

can public or by most American artists. Lloyd Goodrich wrote later: "As one who saw the show in my pre-art-student days, I can testify to its impact—the revelation of a new world of art, alive with a vitality beyond anything I had ever seen."[32]

Approximately eleven hundred works were exhibited, including an impressive survey of French painting from Impressionism, Post-Impressionism, and Fauvism through Cubism. It was the foreign section that most disturbed the public: works by the Fauvists Matisse, Camoin, Manguin, and Rouault, the Expressionists Munch and Kandinsky, and the Cubists Braque, Picasso, Gleizes, Picabia, Duchamp, and Jacques Villon. The American exhibits, intended by the Eight of Philadelphia who organized the show to be limited to those in revolt against academic idealism, ended up being "a great hodgepodge, ranging from stray academicians to modernists."[33] Americans exhibiting included Henri, Sloan, and Davies (all members of the Eight who, along with Walt Kuhn, formed the show), and ranged all the way from such academicians as Kenneth Hayes Miller to the avant-garde men Hartley, Marin, and Stuart Davis.

Concerning the American section, Lloyd Goodrich wrote:

Among the modernists there were some important absences, for one reason or another: Weber, Sterne, Dove, Macdonald-Wright, Man Ray, Demuth, Preston Dickinson, and others. . . . To some intelligent sympathizers the effect was not impressive; Frederick James Gregg wrote that "the vast mass of the American works exhibited [they occupied three-fourths of the space] represented simply arrested development."[34]

Though Demuth did not exhibit in the Armory Show nor see it since he was in Europe at the time, he was one of those who actively participated in the international movement which caught fire in Paris immediately before World War I. He felt as keenly as any the influences of Post-Impressionism, Fauvism, Cubism, and

[32] Quoted from Lloyd Goodrich, "The Decade of the Armory Show," *Art in America,* Vol. LI, No. 1 (February, 1963), 61.
[33] *Ibid.*
[34] *Ibid.*

primitivism (African, Polynesian, Melanesian, and Pre-Columbian art). According to George Biddle, Demuth was one of a loosely knit group of artists who, following the Armory Show, rebelled against the Eight and all "sentimentality, realism, the anecdotal, the academic outlook and John Singer Sargent."[35] Their quarrel with the Eight was that their revolution had concerned only subject matter. Biddle wrote: "The American modernists of 1913 and the following years were swinging away from the American 'human interest' note of . . . Luks, Henri, Glackens, Sloan and Bellows. And we did not willingly exhibit with these other rebels of an earlier decade."[36]

The members of this new group, who were united by youth, idealism, and a commonly shared experimental attitude toward form, included the sculptors Diederich, Nadelman, and Zorach, and the painters Carles, Dasburg, Demuth, Hartley, Man Ray, Marin, Maurer, Pascin, Walkowitz, Weber, Biddle himself, and others.

In the fall of 1915 Demuth rented an apartment at 45 Washington Square South, on the third floor at the front of the building. He converted this apartment into a studio and kept it until sometime in the spring of 1916. He was probably living at this address when Walter Arensberg and Van Vechten went down to the harbor to greet Duchamp on the occasion of his arrival from France.

As mentioned above, Demuth had been given his first one-man show at the Daniel Gallery in the fall of 1914. A year later, during the season that he occupied his Washington Square apartment, Daniel staged Demuth's second one-man show. And it was while he was living in New York in 1915–16 that Demuth began his series of watercolor paintings of New York night clubs and bars— such works as *At Marshall's* (1915), *The Drinkers* (1915), and *The Nut, Pre-Volstead Days* (1916). Demuth produced his great series of twelve illustrations for Zola's *Nana* in 1915–16, probably in New York, and in 1916 he painted his single illustration for

35 Biddle, *An American Artist's Story*, 258–59.
36 *Ibid.*, 259.

Zola's *L'Assommoir*. At this time Demuth executed the first of his Turkish bath series at the Lafayette Baths in the hotel of the same name, and produced other figurative works in great variety such as the street scene entitled *The Shine* (1916). It was a prolific period, the fact that he was maintaining a studio on Washington Square apparently contributing significantly to the quantity and variety of the artist's production.

Demuth spent the following winter (1916–17) in Bermuda. He was never to live in New York for any great length of time thereafter; instead, making brief but frequent weekly sojourns to the city, where he would stay at either the Brevoort or the Lafayette Hotel in the Village. After his return from Bermuda, Demuth returned to figure painting,[37] employing night-club, vaudeville, and circus subjects. According to Locher, all of the vaudeville pieces were accomplished in Lancaster, where "Charles used to go every week to vaudeville at the Colonial Theatre [on the city square]." It was in 1917 that Demuth began his series of sailor pieces and painted his two views of bachelor quarters, *Eight O'Clock–Morning* (1917) and *Eight O'Clock–Evening* (1917).

In 1918 he produced more figure paintings of acrobats, vaudeville performers, and sailors, and painted another Turkish bath picture (see Plate 18). In the same year he made his five illustrations for Henry James's *The Turn of the Screw*, his nine illustrations for Wedekind's *Erdgeist* and *Pandora's Box*, and his single illustration for Poe's "The Masque of the Red Death."

In 1919 Demuth did three illustrations for Henry James's *The Beast in the Jungle* and the night-club scene *At "The Golden Swan" Sometimes Called "Hell Hole,"* which contains portraits of himself and Marcel Duchamp seated at a table. One of the mysteries of the art world lies in the fact that he ceased almost altogether to produce figurative works about the year 1920.

[37] Demuth's figurative works fall into four categories, as follows:
1. The nonillustrative figure pieces (c. 1914–19).
2. The illustrative figure pieces (1915–19).
3. The pornographic watercolors of sailors on the beach (c. 1930).
4. The 1934 sketchbook.

The above résumé of figurative works accomplished by the artist during World War I years and immediately thereafter constitutes, in a sense, a summary of Demuth's life during the same period. He was enjoying the existence of a *bon vivant*, that of a habitué of certain cafés and saloons in the Village, night clubs in downtown Manhattan and Harlem, and avant-garde galleries. Simultaneously, he was devouring those nineteenth-century literary works which affected him so profoundly that he felt compelled to create moving illustrations for them.

The years immediately following the Armory Show witnessed an unprecedented creative flowering in New York. Gleizes, Picabia, and an already famous Duchamp arrived in the New World in 1915, Picabia for the second time. Duchamp immediately became part of the Arensberg Salon, so named because the artists and writers belonging to the group met frequently in the New York apartment of W. C. Arensberg on West Sixty-seventh Street. In his book *The World of Marcel Duchamp* Calvin Tomkins describes this salon thus:

New York at this time was the center of an extremely active avant-garde group that included the American painters Walter Pach, Charles Demuth, Marsden Hartley and Joseph Stella; the Walter C. Arensbergs, wealthy collectors of the most advanced art; Katherine S. Dreier, a strong-willed heiress who had also started collecting modern art after her conversion to it at the Armory Show; and a growing number of Europeans cast up by the War—Albert Gleizes, Jean Crotti, Marius de Zayas, Edgard Varèse, and later on Picabia, who had arranged to have himself sent on a military mission to buy molasses in Cuba (a mission that he forgot all about when he reached New York). At the center of this lively circle was Alfred Stieglitz, the great pioneer photographer, whose gallery at 291 Fifth Avenue had become a center for the development and display of the most advanced tendencies in the arts a good five years before the Armory Show gave them wider currency. Stieglitz's magazine, *291*, published in 1915, carried reproductions of Cubist and other advanced works, and Stieglitz himself constantly encouraged his artist friends to break decisively with the old representational traditions in art—traditions that had been permanently undermined by the invention of photography.

Duchamp and Picabia became the brightest stars of this glittering circle.[38]

The walls of the Arensberg apartment were hung with works by Matisse, Brancusi, Braque, Gris, and, eventually, one of the versions of Duchamp's *Nu Descendant un Escalier*. Demuth had absorbed much about Cubism during his protracted 1912–14 sojourn in Paris. Membership in the Arensberg Salon prolonged his association with Cubist ideology, increasing the substantial total influence upon him of the French Cézanne-oriented school.

The little magazines burst forth like buds on a tree. Among them *The Dial, The Bookman, Seven Arts,* and *Creative Art* championed the young, experimental artists. *The Dial* had been preceded by *Others,* and Dr. Williams' and McAlmon's *Contact* was soon to follow. In his *Autobiography* Williams described the fecund atmosphere of New York at this time:

> *The Dial* had set up shop, and as usual the intellectuals began to intrude upon the terrain opened by the lunatic fringe. . . .
> It's hard to summarize those days. The *Little Review* was putting up a fight for Joyce's *Ulysses;* Gertrude Stein was having everyone by the ears. Then one night at Lola Ridge's, Hartley, whose pictures, along with those of Demuth and Charles Sheeler, I always went to see, brought a young man with him named Robert McAlmon.
> Marianne [Moore] was there and read her "Those Various Scalpels"; Marsden read his "On the Hills of Caledonia"; I read something, I don't remember what, and something clicked for me. Before long McAlmon, who was drifting after having done a bit in one of the Canadian regiments, had set up plans with me for the magazine *Contact.* Djuna's [Djuna Barnes's] comment was that "the one thing about it you could be sure of was that there wouldn't be any contact!"[39]

In 1916 while Demuth was occupying his apartment-studio on Washington Square, he telephoned his old friend Carlos asking him to come over from Rutherford to make a professional call.

[38] Calvin Tomkins and the Editors of Time-Life Books, *The World of Marcel Duchamp,* 37.

At this time Dr. Williams, who was the same age as Demuth, was thirty-three and not only practicing medicine full time but also writing both on the job and off—an amazing feat made possible by extraordinary energy. It was only a twenty-minute drive across the Hudson to New York, and the doctor managed to get to the Village frequently. This time when he arrived he found Demuth's back looking "as though a young tiger had clawed it from top to bottom." Dr. Williams reminisced in his *Autobiography*:

> They were deep, long digs, recently scabbed over. Charley was worried about infection.
> "What in God's name happened to you?" I asked him.
> "Do you think it is dangerous?" said he.
> "No. But how did you get such digs?"
> "A friend."
> "Charming gal," said I thoughtlessly.[40]

Demuth's most famous poster portrait (Plate 30–a) is the one he did of Williams, who said that the artist was never satisfied with this particular work. In his *Autobiography* the doctor related the circumstances which led to his writing "The Great Figure," the poem which in turn inspired the poster portrait:

> Once on a hot July day coming back exhausted from the Post Graduate Clinic, I dropped in as I sometimes did at Marsden's studio on Fifteenth Street for a talk, a little drink maybe and to see what he was doing. As I approached his number I heard a great clatter of bells and the roar of a fire engine passing the end of the street down Ninth Avenue. I turned just in time to see a golden figure 5 on a red background flash by. The impression was so sudden and forceful that I took a piece of paper out of my pocket and wrote a short poem about it.[41]

Williams' poem, "The Great Figure," reads:

> *Among the rain*
> *and lights*
> *I saw the figure 5*

39 Williams, *Autobiography*, 171–72.
40 *Ibid.*, 151.
41 *Ibid.*, 172.

in gold
on a red
firetruck
moving
with weight and urgency
tense
unheeded
to gong clangs
siren howls
and wheels rumbling
through the dark city.[42]

I Saw the Figure 5 in Gold (1928) gained considerable importance during the early sixties as a result of being used as a source by Pop artists. A red, gold, and blue-gray abstraction depicting a fire engine rushing through the theater district of New York, its dominating feature is a large motif consisting of three diminishing figures five, the innermost figure laid in gold leaf. As a portrait the work is most apt, since in personality and character Dr. Williams was much like a red, clanging fire engine—bold, honest, brutal, and, as his autobiography reveals, egotistical to the point of depreciating nearly all others. Yet he was a genuine intellectual possessed of great vitality and deep feeling for beauty, along with the kind of brilliance which is frequently the result of mixed genetic heritage.

That Demuth was capable of simultaneous friendship with Williams and Duchamp is an indication of the complexity of his nature, since in contrast to the hard-working doctor's aggressive character that of the French artist was retiring, gentle, and sweet —traits curiously governed by a towering mentality and lack of ambition.

Though the Village boasted cafés and saloons at the time Duchamp arrived, there was no night club in Greenwich Village in 1915. Duchamp recalled that the artists attended a masquerade

[42] William Carlos Williams, *Sour Grapes*, 78.

ball at Webster Hall, and that "Demuth took me to Harlem for the first time, to Barron Wilkins' café there."[43] Originally on West Thirty-fifth Street, Barron Wilkins' Little Savoy moved to Harlem about the year 1920. The Marshall, another Negro club which Demuth frequented, was on West Fifty-third Street under the Sixth Avenue El. Demuth is said to have spent a great deal of time in these clubs, accompanied variously by Duchamp, Hartley, or Fisk.

According to Duchamp, Demuth was "very interested in Negro music, ragtime, [and] jazz at that time."[44] It was the period which witnessed the emergence of jazz, and Demuth created valuable first-hand visual records, the only ones in art, of this cultural phenomenon and its milieu. A description of Demuth's night-club painting *Negro Jazz Band* (1916), taken from the author's catalogue of Demuth works reads: "Florence Dunbar in an Irene Castle dress is seen dancing 'The Seven Veils' while singing 'Fatima Brown.' Behind her appear three black musicians and various instruments—a piano (the sheet music on the piano rack reads: BILL BAILEY), drums, etc. The front edge of a stage is depicted at the base of the composition." In addition to *Negro Jazz Band*, Demuth also painted *At Marshall's* (1915), *Negro Girl Dancer* (1916), and *At Marshall's* (1917) as by-products of his visits to black clubs.

The Negro night clubs are effectively described by James Weldon Johnson, who lived with his wife, Grace, at the Marshall Hotel, in his book *Black Manhattan*. He listed eight clubs which both functioned as gathering places for professional black vaudeville performers and entertained unsegregated clienteles: Barron Wilkins' Little Savoy (mentioned above), the Anderson Club, the Douglass Club, Ike Hines's, Johnny Johnson's, Joe Stewart's Criterion, the Waldorf, and the Marshall.[45] But it was particularly the last-named club, situated in the basement of the hotel of the

43 Interview with Duchamp.
44 From the answers by Duchamp to a Demuth questionnaire.
45 James Weldon Johnson, *Black Manhattan*, 74–75.

same name and presided over by hotel owner Jimmie Marshall, which acquired fame as the rendezvous of such upper-echelon black professionals as Ford Dabney, Will Marion Cook, Ernest Hogan, Williams, and Walker, and their hangers-on.[46]

According to Johnson, one of the earliest jazz bands ever formed, the Memphis Students, appeared at the Marshall during the first decade of the century.[47] The group which Demuth depicted in his 1916 watercolor *Negro Jazz Band*, described above, was probably not much different.

Fascinated by the exotic contrasts and carnival aspects of this lively milieu, which offered tawdry as well as aesthetic satisfactions, some of New York's most sophisticated white musicians, actors, and artists frequented the Marshall. Among these, during the second decade of the century, were Demuth, Hartley, Duchamp, and Fisk.

Demuth's fellow Pennsylvanian McBride entertained misgivings concerning these sorties into colored clubs. In an article called "An Underground Search for Higher Moralities," which appeared November 25, 1917, he gently chided the younger men from his post as art critic on the *New York Evening Sun*:

His [Demuth's] studies of downstairs restaurants and upstairs vaudevillists are tinged with wit. I don't know why it is, but the moment you go downstairs into a restaurant in New York you begin to see life. Or so I judge from Mr. Demuth's drawings. How revolting, for instance, must not have been "Baron Wilks's" [*sic*] establishment? It has been closed by the police some time since. Races of various colors intermingled, danced and drank there. Yet I hold it was entirely right of Mr. Demuth to have studied it, so evidently in the interests of higher morality. What excuses young Mr. Duchamp and young Mr. Fisk can offer for descending into such resorts I cannot imagine. They may say they went along to protect Mr. Demuth in the performance of his duty, but in that case surely it was unnecessary for Mr. Fisk to place his arm quite so caressingly about the colored lady with whom he is taking wine in the picture. . . . Perhaps Mr. Fisk

[46] *Ibid.*, 119. The fact that jazz emerged first in New Orleans and Chicago has been well chronicled elsewhere.
[47] *Ibid.*, 120.

will say that his arm composes better in that position, but I reject that explanation also as inadequate.

In 1917 the second issue of *The Blind Man*, edited by Duchamp, appeared with contributions by Arensberg, G. Buffet, Demuth, Louis Eilshemius, Satie, Stieglitz, and others. The frontispiece of this issue was a Stieglitz photograph of the ready-made which Duchamp fashioned out of a urinal and submitted to an exhibition of the Society of Independent Artists, where it was rejected. Entitled *Fountain*, this ready-made was signed "Richard Mutt, 1917," and Demuth's contribution to *The Blind Man* was dedicated to the artist:

FOR RICHARD MUTT

One must say everything—then no one will know.
To know nothing is to say a great deal.
So many say that they say nothing—but these never
    really send.
For some there is no stopping.
    Most stop or get a style.

When they stop they make a convention.
That is their end.
For the going every thing has an idea.
The going run right along.
The going just keep going.

In the light of time, this poem appears to be an indictment of not only the ready-mades as being nonpainting and nonsculpture, but also of Duchamp's eventual forsaking of the art of painting, which Demuth appears to have anticipated. Although he greatly admired the Frenchman and enjoyed his companionship, Demuth was not a Duchamp disciple.

In 1920, Société Anonyme, Inc. was founded by Duchamp, Katherine S. Dreier, and Duchamp's disciple Man Ray. Demuth showed in the new society's initial exhibition.

Demuth had many haunts in New York besides the Negro clubs. One of these was the Brevoort Hotel, which had been taken over about the time of the outbreak of World War I by Raymond Orteig, the man who later contributed twenty-five thousand dollars as a reward (won by Charles A. Lindbergh) for the first nonstop transatlantic flight between New York and Paris. Under Orteig's management the Brevoort became a glittering, sophisticated place invested with the glamor of Paris where patrons spoke French to one another.

Several of Demuth's watercolors in his night-club and café series (*Bartender at Brevoort* [c. 1912] and *Waiters at the Brevoort* [c. 1915], among others) were inspired by the Brevoort Café, at this time the rendezvous of the artists. The Café, which offered delicious French cuisine to compensate for somewhat dingy rooms in the hotel proper, was done in a florid Victorian décor with elegant crystal chandeliers, marble-topped tables, red leather benches, and mirrored walls. Hapgood caught the flavor of the place when he wrote: "I went into the Brevoort. I entered the bar and saw Jo Davidson and Maurice Sterne, Mabel's [Mabel Dodge's] new husband, sitting there. When Jo saw me, he said, 'Hello, Hutch!' and then, turning to the bartender, he said, 'Les Dieux ont soif! Donnez à boire!' "[48]

It was a creative, intellectual, and often inebriated group which, during the war years, flowed regularly down to the Brevoort Café from Mabel Dodge's salon at 23 Fifth Avenue and the Arensbergs' apartment on West Sixty-seventh Street. Those who frequented the Brevoort included "artists, poets, journalists, sociologists, suffragists, anarchists, feminists; everybody who was, in even a small degree, differentiated from the inexpressive mass, and in all stages of genial intoxication."[49] Among these were the painters Marin and Dove, the poets Harry Kemp and Orrick Johns, the sculptor Davidson, the writers Dreiser and O'Neill, the leftist Havel, and the loafer Carlin. At dawn when the Brevoort would

[48] Hapgood, *A Victorian*, 362.
[49] *Ibid.*, 358.

finally close its doors, people would drift over to either of two saloons—the one run by Luke O'Connor at the corner of Eighth Street and Sixth Avenue called the Working Girls' Home, or the one at the corner of Fourth and Sixth Avenues officially named The Golden Swan but known more familiarly as Hell-hole. The latter was frequented by a band of hoodlums called the Hudson Dusters, and "also by a certain rather sinister girl with whose name Charles Demuth, the painter, was oddly infatuated. . . ."[50] Hapgood wrote: "In the back-room of Hell-hole, Terry Carlin and Gene O'Neill, it is said, were often drunk together. . . ."[51]

Demuth roomed with O'Neill one summer, probably in 1916, at the Francis Apartments in Provincetown. As O'Neill's close friend, he must have known Carlin, the beautiful loafer so like the psychedelic hippies of the sixties, about whom both Hapgood and Hartley wrote with awe and admiration. Once when he was questioned regarding the extent of O'Neill's drinking during the summer he lived with him, Demuth replied: "By four o'clock in the afternoon O'Neill was high." In later years when the great playwright was living with his second wife, Agnes, and their two children, Shane and Oona, at the Life-Saving Station in Provincetown, Demuth was always going over the dunes to see O'Neill.

One morning while Hapgood was breakfasting in the Brevoort Café, Demuth entered looking "like a crazy man. He literally seemed a being in hell." Hapgood wrote: "I never saw such a look of complete horror on any human being's face. He walked right by me without noticing my existence, or anything but the terrible image in his mind."[52]

Louis Holliday had returned the preceding night from a trip west where, in accordance with a premarital pact made with a Village girl named Louise, he had worked outdoors in an effort to conquer his alcoholism. On reaching New York, he had telephoned Louise, who arranged to meet him at Hell-hole. But while

[50] Boulton, *Long Story*, 15.
[51] Hapgood, *A Victorian*, 360–61.
[52] *Ibid.*, 426–27.

Louis' friends gathered to celebrate his return, Louise arrived and informed Louis she now planned to marry someone else.

The friends who had assembled to welcome Louis included Demuth, O'Neill, Carlin, and a girl named Dorothy. When Hell-hole closed, the group proceeded to Romany Marie's. Hapgood noted that it was unfortunate Carlin was along, since he alone knew where to get heroin, the drug Louis allegedly wanted. Louis apparently took too much heroin and died that night. Agnes O'Neill, who saw Louis' body at Romany Marie's shortly after the young man died, quoted Dorothy as saying: "He [O'Neill] left. It was obvious that Louis was dying. Everyone left except Demuth."[53]

In addition to the Brevoort Café, Demuth frequented Polly Holliday's Greenwich Village Inn, located in a basement on the west side of Washington Square. It will be recalled that the apartment he maintained during the winter of 1915–16 was on the south side of this same square, and that during the summer of 1914 in Provincetown, Polly had been "in love" with Demuth, among others.

Polly shared an apartment in the Village with Havel, the Bohemian leftist who worked for a period as cook for Hutchins Hapgood's family at Dobbs Ferry. Havel was surprisingly jealous, and as a result he frequently created scenes in Polly's restaurant: one wonders whether the Bohemian might not have been responsible for the deep scratches on Demuth's back which were inflicted while he was living in New York.

Another restaurant Demuth frequented was Christine's, located above the Provincetown Theater on Macdougal Alley. After a play the people who frequented the Brevoort, the Working Girls' Home, and Hell-hole would go upstairs to Christine's.

[There would be] Harry Kemp and Mary Pyne; Alice Macdougal; Bobby Jones [Robert Edmond Jones, the stage designer]; Gene O'Neill; George Cram Cook; Eleanor Fitzgerald; Edna Kenton; occasionally Justus Sheffield, who was one of the most accomplished of the actors . . . ; Edna [St. Vincent] and Norma Millay, the latter the

[53] Boulton, *Long Story*, 89.

wife of Charley Ellis; Polly and Louis Holliday; Hippolyte Havel and Terry Carlin; Djuna Barnes; Ida Rauh and Susan Glaspell; and Wilbur [Daniel] Steele, Alice Palmer, and a host of others. . . .

Many wild scenes took place at Christine's after the shows . . . these meetings . . . were bohemian in the best sense. Once, I remember taking my old friend Abraham Cahan down to Christine's. . . . He said to me, "This is really a Russian atmosphere, this is the atmosphere of Dostoevsky, there is a tumultuous inner life here, externally expressed."[54]

Demuth was a frequent guest in two elegant New York homes —Miss Street's and that of the four Stettheimer sisters. The latter home, on Seventy-eighth Street, boasted a fountain indoors near the entrance. The sisters were Ettie, who held a Doctor of Philosophy degree from the University of Göttingen, Florine, who wrote poetry and painted charming, decorative works, Stella, who became the first Mrs. Walter Wanger, and Carrie, who kept house for the family. Mrs. Stettheimer, who was white-haired, invariably wore a black velvet ribbon around her neck and a gown with a train. The Stettheimers had come to America from Germany at the start of World War I, and all of the sisters, in the manner of educated Europeans, spoke German, French, and Italian fluently. Demuth was invited to the festive Stettheimer parties, actually the outward aspect of a salon which helped to shape the artistic direction of the period. At these events there regularly appeared many noted persons, "most of them in the *avant garde*, such as Gaston Lachaise, Charles Demuth, Pavel Tchelitchew," Henry McBride, Marcel Duchamp, Carl Van Vechten, Edward Steichen, Edna Kenton, Fania Marinoff, Avery Hopwood, Elie Nadelman, Dr. Arnold Genthe, Jo Davidson, Francis Picabia, Albert Gleizes, Leo Stein, Elizabeth Duncan, Albert Sterner, and others.

Between 1915 and 1918, Demuth went periodically to the New York Aquarium in Battery Park, where he painted a series of colorful, amorphous fish pieces. These are unpretentious, unique little works unparalleled in the world of art, which the artist seems to have created for the sake of pure enjoyment. In these paintings

54 Hapgood, *A Victorian*, 421–22.

(see Plates 15–a and 15–b) the fish remind one of flowers; just as Demuth's flowers remind one of people, and his figures, of fish.

It must have been in the spring of 1914, soon after Demuth returned from his extended visit to Paris, that Hartley introduced him to Daniel. Hartley was interested in helping his friend find a sponsor, and it couldn't be Stieglitz for the reason that, as Daniel said: "Alfred Stieglitz didn't want to carry someone who would be in competition with Marin."[55] The dealer took a liking to the young man with the cane and the cast in his eye, and offered to give Demuth a show during the approaching fall season. It was the beginning of a long association, for between 1914 and 1923 Daniel was to sponsor eight Demuth shows in his gallery.

Daniel was a slight man of approximately the same build as Demuth, and of Germanic extraction. He differed from Demuth in that he lacked subtlety, being a downright, direct sort of person wanting in finesse of nearly every kind, including business acumen. For a time Daniel had been the proprietor of a bar which he inherited, and had stumbled upon the picture-dealing business after accepting from Ernest Lawson a large number of oil paintings in payment for drinks. After he had acquired a considerable cache of Lawsons (certainly a potential fortune), in addition to a number of works presented to him by other talented, penniless, and thirsty artists, Daniel decided to become a dealer. He rented suitable rooms at 2 West Forty-seventh Street, had them fashionably decorated, hired a clever assistant (Alanson Hartpence),[56] and began to deal in paintings.

Daniel and Stieglitz ran the only galleries in New York during the early years of the century which exhibited radical modern works. The Daniel Gallery opened in 1913, eight years after Stieg-

---

[55] Interview with Daniel.

[56] Hartpence's sister, Mrs. Frank Barnes Burns, once peddled in New York a group of twelve torn watercolors which Hartpence had rescued from the wastebasket where Demuth, tearing them first into four neat pieces, had thrown them in anger after Daniel had either rejected them or offered what the artist considered to be too low a price. They were purchased by Edith Gregor Halpert of the Downtown Gallery.

PLATE 17 *Old Houses*. 1917. Watercolor, 9½ x 13½ in. The Los Angeles County Museum of Art: The Mr. and Mrs. William Preston Harrison Collection.

PLATE 18　*Turkish Bath Scene with Self-Portrait at Center.* 1918. Watercolor, $10^{15}/_{16}$ x $8^{9}/_{16}$ in. (mat opening). Collection of Mr. Richard H. Hopf, Lancaster, Pennsylvania.

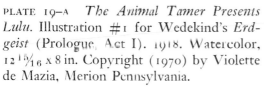

PLATE 19–A *The Animal Tamer Presents Lulu.* Illustration #1 for Wedekind's *Erdgeist* (Prologue, Act I). 1918. Watercolor, 12 15/16 x 8 in. Copyright (1970) by Violette de Mazia, Merion Pennsylvania.

19–B Roy Lichtenstein, *Flatten —Sand Fleas!* 1962. Synthetic polymer paint and oil on canvas, 34⅛ x 44⅛ in. Collection of the Museum of Modern Art, New York: Philip Johnson Fund.

PLATE 20   *"No, No O God! . . ."* Illustration #2 for Wedekind's *Erdgeist* (Act III). c. 1918. Watercolor, $7\frac{7}{8}$ x $12\frac{15}{16}$ in. (mat opening). Copyright (1970) by the Barnes Foundation, Merion, Pennsylvania.

PLATE 21   *Interior with Group of People Around Red-headed Woman.*
Illustration #4 for Wedekind's *Erdgeist* (Act IV). c. 1918. Watercolor,
c. 7 x 9½ in. (sight). Copyright (1970) by the Barnes Foundation, Merion,
Pennsylvania.

PLATE 22   *The Ladies Will Pardon My Mouth's Being Full.* Illustration #2 for Wedekind's *Die Büchse der Pandora* (Act II). 1918. Watercolor, 7⅞ x 12¹⁵⁄₁₆ in. (mat opening). Copyright (1970) by the Barnes Foundation, Merion, Pennsylvania.

PLATE 23 *In Vaudeville: Dancer with Chorus.* 1918. Watercolor, 12¾ x 8 in. The Philadelphia Museum of Art: A. E. Gallatin Collection.

PLATE 24 *In Vaudeville:* Columbia. 1919. Watercolor, 11 $^{15}/_{16}$ x 8 $^{1}/_{16}$ in. The Columbus Gallery of Fine Arts, Columbus, Ohio: The Ferdinand Howald Collection.

litz' Photo-Secession Gallery at 291 Fifth Avenue; and Daniel kept his gallery going until about 1929, the year the market crashed and the Depression began. When Stieglitz' 291 closed in 1917, Daniel carried both Demuth and Marin. At various times he carried the works of Lawson, Hartley, Demuth, Marin, Sheeler, Spencer, Preston Dickinson, Raphael Soyer, and Kuniyoshi. Daniel said: "Dealing went on in a wilderness. . . . People were afraid to buy the work of advanced artists."[57]

An excellent description of the Daniel Gallery was given by Helen Henderson in the December 1, 1918, version of her column: "Art and Artists Pass in Review" in the *Philadelphia Inquirer*:

Recent watercolors by Charles Demuth occupy the rarified atmosphere of the Daniel Gallery, New York. . . . Stepping from the lift, which passes in its brief ascent Elsie de Wolff's domain, and leaving the sharp bark of the actress decorator's red-haired spaniel in the nether regions, the advance through glass portals, as into a conservatory is well followed up by the aspect of the clean, crisp Daniel Gallery. . . .

Demuth's first one-man show, Watercolors by Charles Demuth, was held at the Daniel Gallery during October and November, 1914. From the beginning the artist's works sold well and were well received by the critics. The *New York Herald* notice which appeared October 26, 1914, under the general heading "Art of Painter, Etcher and Sculptor Fills the Galleries," read:

At the Daniel Gallery, No. 2 West 47th St., Mr. Charles Demuth, a young New York artist, is having his first presentation to the public. His work has the strictly modern "color music" note without any of the grotesqueness which some of the moderns have given it. . . . His work represents the very best fruition of the new movement.

Nearly all of the twenty-five pictures were inspired by what the artist saw in the neighborhood of Provincetown, Mass. One of the best works is "The Bay," having a brilliant yet soft pattern of surf, beach and sky. The one entitled "Conestoga" shows how eloquent a mere suggestion of landscape can be when informed by a color purpose.

[57] Interview with Daniel.

McBride, covering the same fledgling exhibition in his October 30, 1914, column in the *Sun*, wrote:

Charles Demuth, whose watercolors are on view at the Daniel Gallery . . . loves a certain little bay, with green shores and blue water and rainbow skies. He has painted it over and over again, and if any old cynic tries to maintain that the real skies there are not like Browning's "Star that Dartles the Red and the Blue," the pictures will confound him. They are stamped with the authenticity of affection. They are rich in color delight.

Included in this first exhibition may have been a series of illustrations of emotions, such as grief, pathos, and joy. These works, which no longer exist, seem to have been nonobjective paintings produced under the influence of Kandinsky, excerpts from whose 1910 book *Concerning the Spiritual in Art* were reprinted in Stieglitz' organ *Camera Work* as early as 1912.

Demuth's second show, Watercolors by Charles Demuth, was on view at the Daniel Gallery from October 30 to November 9, 1915. The catalogue was somewhat unusual.

Regarding the cryptic nature of this catalogue McBride wrote in the *Sun*: "Charles Demuth's catalogue for his first exhibition was laconic. That for his present show of watercolors in the Daniel Gallery is more so. The first nineteen are simply called 'flowers,' the next ten 'dunes.' Brevity is not only the soul of catalogues, Mr. Demuth thinks, but also of watercolors."

The third exhibition of Demuth's works at the Daniel Gallery was called Watercolors and Drawings by Charles Demuth, and was on view during the month of December, 1916. A catalogue in the Demuth folder at the New York Public Library appears to have been printed in connection with this show.

In spite of McBride's witty criticism, Demuth's catalogue was still terse.

It will be recalled that Demuth and Fisk painted assiduously in Provincetown during the summer of 1915, and that the former spent the winter of 1916–17 in Bermuda, where he experimented

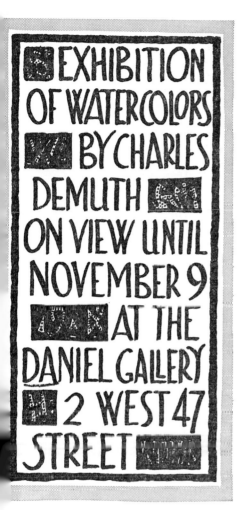

CATALOGUE

FLOWERS

1 2 3 4 5 6 7 8 9 10
11 12 13 14 15 16 17 18 19

DUNES

20 21 22 23 24. 25 26 27 28 29

DRAWINGS

Catalogue for Demuth's second one-man show at the Daniel Gallery, on view from October 30-November 9, 1915.

with the application of the theories of Cézanne and Cubism to landscape subject matter. During November and December, 1917, Daniel gave both men an exhibition at his gallery called Water-

WATER COLORS & DRAWINGS
BY CHARLES DEMUTH
CLOSING DECEMBER 12

THE DANIEL GALLERY
2 WEST 47 STREET

CATALOGUE

"FLOWERS"
1-2-3-4-5

"LANDSCAPES"
6-7-8-9-10

"TREE FORMS"
11-12-13-14-15-16-17-18

"THE BEACH"
19-20-21-22-23-24-25-26

"THE AQUARIUM"
27-28-29

VAUDEVILLE DRAWINGS

Catalogue for Demuth's third one-man show at the Daniel Gallery, on view until December 12, 1916.

colors by Charles Demuth and Oils by Edward Fisk. The accompanying cut shows the catalogue of the Demuth section of this show, his fourth at the Daniel Gallery.

On November 30, 1917, the *New York Globe and Commercial Advertiser* printed an uncomplimentary review regarding the Demuth works in this two-man show, as follows:

Exhibitions of water colors by Charles Demuth and oils by Edward Fisk are at the Daniel Gallery. Mr. Fisk portrays with considerable vigor and directness Provincetown dunes, sand marshes, and groups of still life. . . . Mr. Demuth shows among other things "Interpretive Landscapes," executed at St. Georges, Bermuda. This we learn from the catalogue, not from the water colors. He exhibits a quite

WATER COLORS
BY
CHARLES DEMUTH

PAINTINGS
BY
EDWARD FISK

CLOSING DECEMBER 4th

DANIEL GALLERY
2 WEST 47th STREET

CATALOGUE

CHARLES DEMUTH

INTERPRETATIVE LANDSCAPES
ST. GEORGES, BERMUDA

DRAWINGS

Catalogue for a two-man show of works by Demuth and Fisk, on view at the Daniel Gallery[58] from sometime in November until December 4, 1917.

tangible arrangement of calla lilies which has charm. All are more or less sensitive in color.

In a more appreciative vein Willard Huntington Wright, in an article which appeared in the January, 1918, issue of *International Studio*, wrote:

At the Daniel Gallery are to be seen the oils of Fisk and the water-colours of Demuth. Demuth's pictures constitute, for me, the most important modern show of the month. The painter had made great strides since last he showed his work, especially in his landscapes, which are charming as Picasso's early oils of the same type. In De-

[58] All of the catalogues quoted here in connection with the Daniel Gallery are from the Demuth folder in the New York Public Library.

115

muth's figure pieces and scenes of circus and music-hall folk is much that is Picasso, and a great deal that is Toulouse-Lautrec. . . .

The unfortunate thing about Demuth's work is that it reveals in the artist a contentment with his tricks and mannerisms, and a lack of striving for more solid and masculine attributes. Occasionally, however, there are real balances of volume, as, for instance, in the picture of the ballet girl on horseback. And Demuth has a real feeling for complete color scales.

At bottom, of course, he is a draughtsman who reinforces his drawings with colour, and not an aquarellist at all, as is Marin. But, it is to be hoped this painter, in the near future, will devote his entire time to organizing his sensations, not into interesting illustrations, but into aesthetically moving pictures. Already he is beginning to grapple with the deeper problems of aesthetics.

This review is a highly intelligent, informed appraisal of Demuth's work as it stood in 1917 at the moment of his turning from an expressionistic variety of figure painting toward a classical variety of Cubist-influenced abstraction. Demuth must have regarded it as such. By 1919 Demuth had produced his great illustrations but was dissatisfied. (Actually, all of his life Demuth was dissatisfied with his paintings, a state of mind stemming from his passion for perfection. He once wrote Stieglitz that it was because he did not like his work that he kept painting.) Wright's suggestion that the artist concern himself henceforth not with illustration, but with "aesthetically moving pictures," is exactly what occurred. Demuth's direction from about 1919 on was more ambitious, involving the production of large, classical works in both tempera and oil.

The *Nana* illustrations, produced during the years 1915–16, were covertly shown by Daniel to a chosen few. McBride made mention of this in the *Sun* in his 1917 review of the Demuth-Fisk show: "There are some watercolors of Mr. Demuth that have not been hung upon the walls. The subjects were suggested by a reading of Zola's 'Nana.' They are kept hidden in a portfolio, and are only shown to museum directors and proved lovers of modern art upon presentation of visiting cards. They are quite advanced in style—. . . ."

116

The *Nana* watercolors were clandestinely kept under cover, a fate which was to continue to be that of these particular illustrations until the publication in 1950 of Andrew Carnduff Ritchie's monograph on Demuth, in which all twelve of the *Nana* works were reproduced, including both versions of *Scene after Georges Stabs Himself with the Scissors.* Twelve years after he had first mentioned the *Nana* paintings, in an article entitled "Watercolours by Charles Demuth" which appeared in the September 29, 1929, issue of *Creative Art*, McBride wrote:

When the flower pictures had already made Demuth known and it had become fashionable to own one, Mr. Daniel, who was then Mr. Demuth's merchant, showed us all, surreptitiously, some figure drawings. They were not precisely shocking, but one or two of the drawings illustrated points in Zola's *Nana*, and just before the war we were sufficiently Victorian to shudder at the thought of exposing pictures of reprehensible *Nana* on the walls. . . . Times, of course, have greatly changed since then and now *Nana*, poor dear, can go anywhere she wants to, but by the time our collectors had realized that "Nanas" had become perfectly all right, and rather better company than most, the entire lot of Mr. Demuth's figure drawings had been swept into some especially well-hidden collection—and it was announced that the artist was not to do any more figures!

The collection into which the *Nana* illustrations disappeared was, of course, that of Dr. Albert C. Barnes of Merion.

Demuth's fifth show at the Daniel Gallery, *Recent Drawings in Watercolor by Charles Demuth*, was held from sometime in November until December 14, 1918. The catalogue for this exhibition was only slightly amplified beyond the earlier ones.

An undated newspaper notice relating to this show, apparently written by Helen Henderson of the *Philadelphia Inquirer*, was preserved in Richard Weyand's Scrapbook No. III. It reads:

An exhibition displaying the works of Charles Demuth, of Lancaster, is now being held in the Daniel Gallery in New York City. The collection is noted for its variety, including landscapes, figure work, and floral effects. Mr. Daniel told us that Demuth's work is being appreciated and picked up by connoisseurs, that he seems

RECENT

DRAWINGS IN WATER COLOR

BY

CHARLES DEMUTH

CLOSING DECEMBER 14th

DANIEL GALLERY
2 WEST 47th STREET

CATALOGUE

DRAWINGS

FLOWERS
1–8

DRAWINGS

NEW ENGLAND HOUSES
9–21

ILLUSTRATIONS

"THE TURN OF THE SCREW"
BY
HENRY JAMES
22–25

Catalogue for Demuth's fifth show at the Daniel Gallery, on view from sometime in November until December 14, 1918.

to have a distinctive quality in his work and that it is being sought by national collectors.

Demuth's five illustrations for Henry James's *The Turn of the Screw* were all painted in 1918. Four of the five, very possibly the same four listed above, were soon acquired by Mr. and Mrs. Frank Calvin Osborn of Manchester, Vermont. After her husband's death, Mrs. Osborn gave the four illustrations she and her husband owned to the Philadelphia Museum of Art, the logical repository for Demuth works.

In connection with his sixth show at the Daniel Gallery, which was on view during the month of December, 1920 (Daniel frequently gave him the month of December, the best month for making sales), Demuth attempted a more extravagant use of

ARRANGEMENTS OF THE

AMERICAN LANDSCAPE FORMS

BY

CHARLES DEMUTH

DURING DECEMBER

THE DANIEL GALLERY
2 WEST FORTY-SEVENTH STREET

CATALOGUE

1. PENNSYLVANIA
2. AFTER SIR CHRISTOPHER WREN
3. NEW ENGLAND
4. WAITING
5. PENNSYLVANIA
6. THE MERRY-GO-ROUND
7. FOR W. CARLOS W.
8. NEW ENGLAND
9. THE END OF THE PARADE
10. NEW ENGLAND
11. CHIMNIES, VENTILATORS OR WHATEVER
12. NEW ENGLAND

Catalogue for Demuth's sixth show at the Daniel Gallery, on view during December, 1920. (See footnotes 59 and 60.)

words. The exhibition was called Arrangements of the American Landscape Forms, and, for the first time, individual works were named instead of being merely numbered.

The title *New England* appears in this 1920 catalogue four times; the title *Pennsylvania*, twice. Obviously Demuth was at a loss for words when it came to naming his pictures and habitually gave one name to several different works. He would just as soon have called all of his flower pieces *Flowers*, all of the landscapes he did in Gloucester and Provincetown *New England*, and those

[59] The tempera called *Waiting* owned by the Art Institute of Chicago is signed and dated in the lower left: *C. Demuth 1930 Lan Pa.*—but the date may be read erroneously. No 1920 work by this name is listed in either Weyand's or the author's catalogue of Demuth works.
[60] *Machinery* (or *For W. Carlos W.*). 1920.

119

he accomplished in his home town, *Lancaster* or *In the Province*. This seems incredible in view of the artist's acute capacity to distinguish between different varieties of flowers in his paintings. Apparently Demuth possessed a visually oriented mind but little feeling for words—a fact which has led to much confusion in the cataloguing of his works.[61]

The catalogue for the exhibition Recent Paintings by Charles Demuth, presented at the Daniel Gallery from December 1(?), 1922, to January 2, 1923, read:

CATALOGUE

1. WELCOME TO OUR CITY	6. FRUIT
2. NOSPMAS M. EGAP NOSPMAS M.	7. VEGETABLES
	8. SPRING
3. AUCASSIN AND NICOLLETE [sic]	9. MODERN CONVENIENCES (il)
4. FROM THE GARDEN OF THE CHÂTEAU	10. INCENSE OF A NEW CHURCH
5. OUR MARY IN "AS YOU LIKE IT"	11. PAQUEBOT "PARIS"
	12. RUE DU SINGE QUI PÊCHE

WATER COLORS

This show included some of the most ambitious and effective works Demuth had accomplished to date, but afterward an unsympathetic, hostile notice appeared in an unidentified New York paper, as follows:

The Daniel Gallery presents a number of new pieces by Mr. Charles Demuth. This gentleman has a humorous turn of mind. He paints a pair of chimneys and calls it "Aucassin and Nicolete [sic]." To a picture of some large-leaved green growth he affixes the title "Our Mary in 'As You Like It.' " A minutely exact reproduction of a num-

[61] Two of Demuth's best-known paintings had for some time the title *After Sir Christopher Wren*, the matter being finally clarified when the Worcester Museum listed its painting as *After Sir Christopher Wren* (also called *New England*), and the Columbus Gallery of Fine Arts adopted the title *The Tower* (also called *After Sir Christopher Wren*).

ber of samples of materials for new shirts is labeled "Spring." Just what Mr. Demuth is driving at we cannot imagine, nor does it much matter, for his rigidly careful drawings of dull objects, though redeemed by an occasional flash of agreeable color, do not seem to us to have any artistic interest whatever.

The artist's eighth and last show at the Daniel Gallery, Watercolors by Charles Demuth, took place during November and December, 1923. No catalogue or notices relating to this final exhibition at the Daniel Gallery seem to have survived.

History has revealed that Daniel displayed as much courage as Stieglitz in championing young, unknown pioneer artists. For instance, he gave Hartley a hundred dollars a month for a year, so that he could go west to paint. But Stieglitz, the brilliant entrepreneur of 291, affected people in such a way that they believed in him in a fanatical manner, whereas Daniel was more adept at alienating others than at winning their esteem. Sympathetic to the cause of the young moderns and instrumental in the building of the reputations of several, Daniel failed to propagandize himself, so that in the end his unselfishness brought about anonymity in conjunction with financial ruin.

Unfortunately, Demuth's well-preserved letters to Stieglitz condemn Daniel and consistently refer to him and his gallery in a derogatory manner. Demuth had much to gain by winning Stieglitz' favor. Apparently he was not averse to joining the latter in a mutual spirit of negativity toward Daniel.

Nevertheless, it was Daniel who, between 1914 and 1923, forged Demuth's reputation (as Duchamp said, he was never launched, like some painters), so that by the time he became part of the Stieglitz stable, Demuth was already well known. In March, 1925, he appeared in the exhibition Seven Americans as an official part of the Stieglitz Group, which included Marin, O'Keeffe, Dove, Hartley, Demuth, Stieglitz himself, and the photographer Paul Strand. It was the beginning of a fortunate professional association which was to last until Demuth's death ten years later.

6

Last Visit to Paris — Serious Illness

In the first volume of *The Psychology of Art* André Malraux wrote:

The powers of darkness of the Christian past, the Freudian devil, and the devil of Bikini—all wear the same aspect. And the more ground these new demons gain in Europe, the more her art tends to hark back to the mood of earlier cultures plagued by their appropriate devils. . . . The devil lurks behind all arts of immobility. . . . And almost always Satan paints in two dimensions.[1]

Although Demuth died before World War II began, he experienced World War I vicariously. One of the most sensitive of individuals, he was extremely aware of the nature of his disturbed times, which witnessed not only war but also moral decay and financial depression. In addition, he possessed personal demons in profusion. He knew well "the Freudian devil" referred to by Malraux, and those of social disapproval, lameness, and tuberculosis. About the year 1920 the outline of another demon, the artist's most fearsome and destructive, became clear—that of the demon diabetes. And in exact fulfillment of Malraux's psychological pattern, he who bore the multiple cross of being homosexual, halt, consumptive, and diabetic, and whose brief life spanned a period of world conflict, disillusionment, and despair, came eventually to express himself in an art marked by two-dimensionality and

[1] Malraux, *Museum without Walls*, 128.

122

immobility; an art not of sweet, perfumed flowers, but of *fleurs du mal*.

As has been mentioned above, Demuth was subject to recurrent attacks of an unidentified chronic illness. As early as the winter of 1912–13 when he was twenty-nine and studying in Paris, occasional attacks of this illness occurred following which he would return to the Académie Moderne speaking of his "bad leg." He appears to have suffered simultaneously from his hip infirmity and the chronic illness which was eventually to be diagnosed as diabetes.

Demuth went occasionally to Rutherford to stay with Dr. Williams and his wife Flossie, for visits of several days' duration. Once, in the years before he knew he had diabetes (that is, before 1921), the artist went to Rutherford plagued with a carbuncle which Dr. Williams lanced. Williams said later: "In diabetes a carbuncle is often a pretty dangerous thing. This time the carbuncle healed all right."[2]

It is not known just when Demuth's chronic illness became finally diagnosed as diabetes. Mrs. Malone wrote: "It was not until 1919 that the doctor discovered it in Charles."[3] However, the artist seems not to have known he was suffering from diabetes during the summer of 1920, which he spent in Provincetown. Prohibition had gone into effect on January 16, 1920, and the little resort on the Cape was a changed place. Miss Street, who had rented a house for the summer, made beer privately in her kitchen and "everybody came and took it, even Gene O'Neill." One day Demuth said to Miss Street: "I don't know what it is, Susie, but I have a craving for canned pineapple, for canned sweets."[4] During this summer while he was on the Cape he suffered the most severe diabetic attacks he had yet experienced, becoming completely incapacitated.

From this time forward, Demuth lived in the shadow of death.

2 Interview with Dr. Williams.
3 Malone, "Charles Demuth," 8.
4 Interview with Miss Street.

Yet, though incapacitated at times, he proceeded as usual. No stranger to disability and always courageous, he continued to paint in Lancaster and make his regular visits to Philadelphia and New York in search of congenial companionship and intellectual stimulation. Duchamp said: "How long does it take to get to New York from Lancaster? Three hours? . . . Demuth used to come to New York at least once a week. Think of the time consumed en route."[5]

The regularity of Demuth's weekly visits to New York must have changed to a more erratic pattern after 1920, but he did not cease going. And he continued to paint in the secluded family garden and small upstairs studio, producing both still lifes and landscapes in transparent watercolor and tempera; working, in the case of landscapes, from pencil notes sketched previously on the spot. In spite of the condition of his health, he sent some paintings to New York and managed to get in to see his December, 1920, show at the Daniel Gallery. Daniel said that at this time Demuth "looked terrible."

In a review of the artist's 1920 show, "News and Reviews: Charles Demuth Displays His Beautiful Landscapes at Daniel's," which appeared in the *Sun* on December 5, 1920, McBride reported perceptively regarding the psychological-philosophical changes which were taking place in Demuth concurrently with the progress of disease:

He grows more earnest and eloquent with the times; . . . but he also grows more ascetic. His studies of aspects of New England and Pennsylvania would be quite terrible—if they were not so beautiful. Whether he has studied Nietzsche or not I do not know, but he certainly sees plenty of applied Nietzscheanism in this beloved but hard country of ours. Mr. Demuth must have gone through the period of terror into which most sensitive artists plunge upon returning to this country from the *dolce far niente* of the Paris school days. . . .

In the little gallery to the left as you enter . . . hangs a series of little water colors . . . of Zola's "Nana."

The change from the warm, perfumed atmosphere of the "Nana"

[5] Interview with Duchamp.

124

drawings to the chill of the "Coatesville Steel Mills" . . . [is remarkable].

Demuth had, indeed, gone through a period of terror. He had emerged from his joyous, wild years onto a stage which presented only one scene, really. It was a setting of grim, unrelenting reality crowded with his various personal demons, and illumined by a light which was gradually growing dimmer—not a congenial scene for any man, and particularly disheartening for one who "was often overcome by the highly defined appearance of things." Yet it was the stage on which Demuth would be forced to play for a decade and a half longer.

At thirty-eight, emaciated, depressed, and made more serious by severe illness, Demuth decided in 1921 to visit Paris once more. As he wrote to Stieglitz from London soon after landing, he wanted "to do something to stop the 'wheels' [from] going around backwards." On June 28, 1921, he received his passport from the State Department marked for travel in England and France, and on July 27 was issued British and French visas in Philadelphia.

Two days before his boat docked Demuth wrote a reassuring letter to Augusta Demuth, who appears to have been understandably concerned about the state of her son's health, mailing it in Southampton on August 12, 1921, the day he went through customs. In this letter Demuth said:

Miss Sand whom I knew in Étretat the summer that I was there is on the ship, also Mr. Mercer, Mrs. Eshleman's brother.

We will land on Friday. The boat made a very slow run.

I've felt pretty well—the last few days not so well. The food on the ship is getting low. No doubt I'll be all right when I land.

Bob sent me a book. I don't know how it got aboard. . . .

Stayed quite warm all the way over. . . . To-night it is quite cool. It's too bad you didn't come along. I think that my biscuits will hold out.

I'll write you from London after a day or so. . . .

We've had several dances, and will have one to-night. . . .

The mention of biscuits in this letter suggests that diabetes had already been diagnosed, perhaps immediately following the violent attacks the artist had experienced in Provincetown during the summer of 1920, as a result of which Demuth had departed for Europe with a supply of saltless bread.

In the same letter, Demuth mentioned "several dances" on board ship. In all likelihood it was the last of these gala events he described in his autobiographical piece, "The Voyage Was Almost Over." In this story, wherein he revealed a deep sense of loneliness and a surprising, pathetic yearning for marriage, the artist wrote that on the last evening aboard ship "dinner had been gay":

The table boys distributed crackers which opened with tiny explosives and contained paper hats wrapped in sentimental verse. Dinner was over. Everyone, wearing their hats, rose and moved toward the stairway which led to the upper decks. . . .

When group after group reached the first landing and the light struck . . . their everyday clothes together with the paper hats, the picture was droll and sad; sad as comedies are sad.

Demuth went on to define the after-dinner atmosphere on deck; the parties of twos, threes, and fours enjoying the sea, the distant land, and the moonlight. At last there remained on deck only "one man who still lingered alone. However, if one looked (this he had done) into the shadows cast by stacks and funnels" one could discern "vague outlines. Outlines of forms which stood or sat but always in pairs."

The lone man walking the deck, rapidly at times and at others slowly, with head bent, saw the sea, the moon and the couples in the shadows. He gazed in turn at the golden moon, out upon the sea, and stole fleeting glances at the lovers in the purple black shadows of the ship. He saw these things; better and more fully than anyone on board, perhaps.

126

And all of these things, with the exception of the lovers, appeared beautiful to him in the sense that they evoked in him poetic similes: "How like the ocean is to that and how like the golden moon in her turquoise sky is to this."

⟶ And the lovers on the deck, what were they like? He wondered. Vague lines of forgotten looks half-awakened in his memory as he glanced into the shadows which held a pair. But, somehow, he could not say of these, they are like this or that, as he could of the sea or night or of the moon.

He had felt all this before. Felt it in gay and noisy cafés, in crowded parks, at night when the music of a band was wafted to him by the hot summer breeze or on the streets crowded for a holiday or fete.

But to-night, above all preceding ones, he realized it more fully than ever before, and as he walked a great anger against some unknown Thing filled him completely.

"Why, why was everything wonderfully made, perfectly made, and I given the power, among many, to appreciate this wonder and perfection? And yet denied the one thing which would perfect me, truly? If only a little white hand would beckon from without one of those mysterious shadows—then—well, then, to hell with these borrowed ideas. Then the sea would be no silly purple fish or blue flower but only a mighty living thing which somewhere beats against mightier existing coasts. . . ."

And hate against some unknown Thing filled his soul.[6]

When the artist had been twenty-one, he had spent the summer painting in New Hope, Pennsylvania, along with Weed, a fellow student who became a successful cartoonist on a Philadelphia newspaper. During this summer Demuth had courted and proposed to a divorcée, Emmasita Register (Mrs. Charles) Corson. According to Miss Henderson:

[6] Demuth, "Voyage."

127

[Emmasita] was a very beautiful girl and interesting. She lived, when a student at the academy, with her uncle, Leyton Register, at Haverford. He was her father's brother, a wealthy man and very kind to Emmasita, building her a studio and paying Thomas Anshutz to come out to give her private criticism. Mr. A. considered her very talented. . . . Against her uncle's wish she married Charlie Corson, who had been football coach for the University of Pennsylvania and was extremely handsome. . . . But he was flagrantly unfaithful and left her and that summer of which we speak Charles and Weed used to go there [to Emmasita's home on the tow-path] at all hours and eat meals on the lawn under the trees with candles and were the scandal of New Hope, of course. It was too much like Paris.

Charles told me a tale of the finale of this romance in his inimitable style. It was all by hints and innuendo but I gathered that he had proposed, and Emmasita . . . had refused him. . . .[7]

Two years later in December, 1907, Demuth traveled from Paris to Berlin to spend the Christmas holidays with his cousin, Pauline Cooper. Not long after this he sent Pauline a photograph of a young woman seated on the edge of a fountain, possibly in Paris, with the following message written in longhand on the reverse:

⎯⎯⎯ Marco Sullivan as she is. Incidentally, this will serve to announce the fact that we are engaged.[8]

Sometime during the 1920's, when Demuth was in his forties, he was approached by the brother-in-law of one of his women friends, who had been delegated to sound him out regarding the possibility of marriage. His reply, as he escorted the man to the door: "Nobody's going to lay their hands on my soul." Surely there were other proposals, and other rejections comparable to those which Van Gogh experienced.

On his return to the States following his 1921 European visit, the artist made sketches on board ship which he used later as source material for his well known oil *Paquebot Paris* (1921 or

7 Helen W. Henderson, Information.
8 Weyand Scrapbooks.

1922). No human figures appear in these sketches, no "vague outlines" in the "shadows cast by stacks and funnels," as though with
the descent of serious illness the man who had been a superlative
figure artist arrived simultaneously at a denial of society. Certainly it was at about this time that Demuth's art became nonfig-
urative, and his story "The Voyage Was Almost Over" supports
a theory that this transformation was psychological.

Soon after he arrived in Southhampton, Demuth wrote a letter
to Stieglitz on stationery which carried the letterhead of the Hotel
Rembrandt, London, S.W. 7. This letter, which is dated August
13, 1921, reads in part:

> You will, no doubt, be surprised to get this from me from
> this place. . . .
>
> I wanted so to feel it once more—so, here I am, and will go to
> Paris next week.
>
> I wish that you were here to look at an exhibition of Blake's,
> now on at the Tate, with me. They [Blake's works] have been
> loaned. . . . They hang next [to] the great Turners—it is wonder-
> ful. Marin could be there—how simple it seems. . . .
>
> It is more difficult in America to work—perhaps that will add a
> quality. My God, where are they? And how little fun they are
> having. . . .
>
> Best regards to O'Kief [sic].

The artist remained in London only three days, leaving immediately for France, where he arrived August 15. On September 6,
he wrote the following note to Miss Stein:

> PARIS, Sept. 6, 1921
> Will you be home tomorrow evening—Wed.? Marcel
> and I would like to come to see you. If it is all right don't answer,
> and we will come.

Late in September the artist became a patient in the American

Hospital, Neuilly-sur-Seine, where he remained for about a week. A few days later, on October 10, he sold two watercolor landscapes. The receipt of the sale read:

> Received on deposit from M. C. Demuth 2 watercolors called "Views of the City," of a value of 500 fr. each. Paris Oct. 10, 1921.
> (Signed) LEONCE ROSENBERG, pr. L'Effort Moderne.[9]

Demuth was so pleased about this transaction that on the same day he sold the paintings, writing with black ink on pink paper, he composed another letter to Stieglitz. This letter reads:

All the French painters, the great ones, and the men interested in the two magazines "L'Amour de l'Art" and "L'Esprit Nouveau" are very anxious to have the best of the Americans in with them. It is a thrill, really, to hear what they think of us, knowing us so slightly (mostly through the "Dial"—strange, isn't it? but it is thought very well of in France & England). I am told either of the Rosenbergs will have our things; and, they have very impressive galleries. All the moderns are shown with great spirit, and there is no showing of the Old Masters as an excuse for their being—the spirit of often showing the younger men only to sell a Lawson is lacking entirely! . . .

Pound has done a lot, but he really doesn't know about painting. It is all very amazing, to me, to find this enthusiasm here . . .; and, the great French men telling us that we are very good. It seems rather grand. It is like Baudelaire and Poe. I wish that you could be here to get the thrill of it, after the work and love you have given the painters French & American. It seems almost as though the dream were "coming true," that after all, Art is not only in pictures, books, etc. but also the nearest we can get to—you can call it what you like—I'll write, Sympathetic Order!

Paris is as you see rather wonderful. It seems to shine. One feels, perhaps it is the last grand flair—I don't know—it seems almost too grand. . . .

[9] *Ibid.*

Sometimes it seems almost impossible to come back, we are so out of it. Then one sees Marcel or Gleizes and they will say: "Oh! Paris. New York is the place—there are the modern ideas—Europe is finished." ...

Hartley is going to Berlin, in a week or two. After Xmas he expects to go to Rome with Rönnebeck who is to have a class there. He may help. Germany is having an "inning" in Italy at the moment.

Saw Gertrude Stein—she is fat & handsome and rides in the smallest "Ford" Henry ever turned out, also the most ugly. She is rather grand. But unlike the French, thinks that we are very dull. I do think that she should have a few months in the home land. I took some friends of mine to see her, and she liked them—and then asked me on the quiet if they really hadn't been over here a long time. ... I suppose in 17 years things have changed.

So you see where we are—or maybe where we are not. I wish you were here.

Best regards for OKieff [*sic*], and too, for you.

During this visit Demuth stayed at the Hôtel Lutetia, which boasted hot and cold running water, on the Boulevard Raspail. He was in the French capital by plan at the same time as his old friends Beatrice and Robert Locher and Miss Street, who were staying in an apartment at 82 rue de Sèvres. Demuth went frequently to his friends' apartment, but took his meals at the Lutetia because he could procure the special dietary foods he needed there.

Hartley was often with the other Americans that fall. He had been assisted to go abroad in 1921 by the combined efforts of Stieglitz and Mitchell Kennerly, who had staged an auction of his paintings from which the artist had netted approximately five thousand dollars. On this then magnificent sum Hartley managed to remain in Europe until the spring of 1928—a period of nearly seven years. At the commencement of this sustained visit he remained in Paris in order to be near his American friends for a while before departing for his beloved Germany.

On October 15, 1921, Demuth wrote another letter to Augusta Demuth, this time from Paris. It read:

～～ Your latest letters—the two with the four-leafed clovers—have been received. I hope with you that they bring me luck.

Bob, who got back from the South to-day, says that I'm looking, he thinks, as when I was well. I'm not quite that fat, as yet, but do feel and look pretty well. . . .

Sue has taken a nice apartment—. . . .

I think that you can count on my coming home about the 30th of November, that is, leaving here about that time.

One of the galleries in Paris has taken my things—a quite good place. . . .

In lots of ways, I would like to stay, but I think I've been lucky to get three or four months the way things are at present.

A lot of people are going to Germany. Arnold Rönnebeck writes that I should come up with Hartley, but I don't think that I will this time. I would love to go, but it's rather a long trip, and I get tired carrying bread and stuff around Europe. No, I suppose I won't go, or try to go to Italy. I [had] thought that I would, maybe.

I'm glad that the flowers did so well. . . . The gardens [here] look fine and gay—although it never seems to rain. Other times I've been here it was raining all the time; now it never rains.

If you send me Mrs. McKnight's address, I will send her a card. . . .

Paris is livening up for the winter—the picture exhibitions are starting and the theatres are opening with new plays. I went to the opera last week—it was quite grand, but ours is really better.

According to this letter, it was because of his poor health that Demuth never got to Italy. One can only surmise how much his life and art might have been influenced by such a contact.

Demuth also failed to see Proust during this visit to Paris. As mentioned above, his mind and temperament were so similar to those of Proust that he responded with reluctant but deep sympathy to *À la Recherche du Temps Perdu*, dreamed of illustrating this great work, and held onto the dream for many years. The French writer, who died in 1922 shortly after Demuth attempted to talk with him, may have been ill at the time the American, himself critically ill with diabetes, tried to see him.

Demuth had always been close to his mother, but now that he was living on the brink of death, she became more important than ever in his life. The strong bond between them followed the classic psychological pattern, as Duchamp pointed out when he said: "The relation between Demuth and his mother was what you call a Freudian relationship. . . . He kept going back to her in Lancaster. He was very devoted to his mother."[10]

On October 17, just two days after he had written the October 15 letter quoted from above, Demuth wrote to his mother again, saying:

Your letter with the photos just came, and as I was writing to Barnes about a picture that he wishes me to buy for him, I thought that I would write you just a short letter, too.

I think the pictures quite good of you and Ida and the moonflower, and was glad to hear that the Kaufmanns were with you. . . .

I write to Barnes quite often. . . .

If I need any money, I'll let you know. . . . The way things look my money would hold out until about March. Of course, if I come back at the end of November, I'll still have some. I haven't gotten passage [yet], but will in a week or so if I decide to come back [early].

I've put all of the four-leafed clovers in my shoes.

When Demuth and Hartley had been in Paris in 1912–14, the French artists were in the process of transferring their studios from Montmartre on the hill to the Latin Quarter on the Left

[10] Interview with Duchamp.

Bank. Now it was that famous 1921 period when the artists who
frequented the Café du Dôme quarreled with Père Jambon and
moved across the Boulevard du Montparnasse to the Rotonde.

Hartley, who like Demuth seems to have possessed a flair for
being in Paris at historic moments, wrote afterward in his epitaph
"Farewell, Charles":

> The picture turns now to a moment in an upper room of the Hôtel
> Lutetia on Raspail, finding Charles looking out of a given and what
> has always seemed to me that remarkable dormer window which
> afforded one of the most amazing views of Paris to be had anywhere
> on the Left Bank, and this room and window therefore, always sought
> by him.
> It was a visual operatic Paris that one beheld, and I can never fathom
> just how this angle was obtained, but you had to a striking degree,
> all that Paris had to offer, or most all.[11]

Out of this window could be seen simultaneously St. Sulpice,
the majestic outline of Notre Dame de Paris, the somber domed
Panthéon, and rising above all else Sacré Coeur, transformed into
a pagan "temple of love" by the "peculiar dovelike tonality" of
the Parisian atmosphere.

> Charles is at the right of this amazing dormer window, I at the left,
> and the disheartening news has been revealed, he saying to me, and
> I recall it so well—O well, I've seen it all—I've done it all, and the
> throat thickened with the sense of sudden revealment—Charles learns
> that he is really ill, and that he must go home.
> Summer was on the way to being over. . . .[12]

Judging from what Hartley wrote, it may have been at this
time that Demuth first learned that his serious illness was diabetes;
or, perhaps, that he suffered from a fatal variety of the disease.
The fact that he went to Paris at all in 1921 indicates nonrealiza-
tion of the seriousness or extent of his sickness. Apparently he
knew now, for the first time, that he must die soon. Hartley wrote:

He booked passage home to begin the scientific experiments with

[11] Hartley, "Farewell, Charles," 558.
[12] Ibid., 559.

the now so famous insulin treatments, being one of the first patients, and as he was the inheritor of its virtues, for it let him live fifteen years longer than he assumed he could, he was also inheritor of its dangerous variations, for he never knew when he would be overtaken with those violent and terrifying collapses.[13]

In his October 17 letter to his mother Demuth had indicated that he might return to the States about "the end of November." In a subsequent letter to her, written November 7, the artist revealed plans to leave still sooner:

My lovely birthday present came a day or two ago. It was a little early, as this is Monday the 7th as I write, and tomorrow will be my birthday. . . . I gave Bob what you wanted him to have, [and] I gave it to him at once, as they are rather hard up on account of some money still owed him from the theatre job of the past summer.

The bread and cakes I get here are very good, not as good maybe as those in London, but all right. The other things, vegetables, I'm afraid have something in them sometimes which does not agree with me. . . .

I've decided to come home on the *Paris*, sailing next Saturday— that will be the 12th of November, and will land on the 19th, I hope. I will cable you today, and I hope that you get this letter a few days before the 19th, but I'm afraid that there are few boats sailing before the Paris, so this [letter] may cross with me

Altogether it has been a nice trip. . . .

If you want to meet me, all right. The boat lands on a Saturday if it is on time. We can stay in New York over Sunday. If you don't want to come, and I don't find you on the dock, I'll call you up at once from New York.

Bob is doing some work for Poiret. It may lead to a good job....

In a week or two, now, I can tell you all about my trip.

I will not bother about the bag for Christopher. . . . I've gotten something for Ida, and the muffler for Christopher.

13 *Ibid.*

The trunks and things like that are almost as expensive as they are at home, and no better.

Hoping you get this before the boat lands, and to see you soon. Don't worry, I'm really all right, or almost—. . . .

Demuth returned as planned on the *Paris*, sailing from Le Havre on November 12. Two days after he arrived in Lancaster, he received a letter from Stieglitz, and on November 28, 1921, writing again in black ink on pink stationery, he replied:

You made a good guess—the letter found me at home—two days at home. Your letter made me glad to be home, and I will see you soon in New York.

It was all very wonderful, but I must work, here. Had I stayed in France when I went to it for the first time, by now I would be into it. It would take years and, after all, there are many able Frenchmen. And New York is something which Europe is not— and I feel of that something, awful as most of it is. Marcel and all the others, those who count, say that all the "modern" [progress] is [now up] to us, and of course they are right. . . .

The Autumn Salon was dead—about five years dead. Braque seemed to be growing in quality—they [his paintings] are quite lovely. And Marcel, dear Marcel, is doing, and doing, and doing. He has a new wife, a real wife—that is, she is getting him away from all his old friends. There is a great deal to tell you of Europe —Marcel seems to be the only one really working.

At the moment I feel that I wish to grow fast, even, to Lancaster. I am so tired—maybe it is my health, but I suspect it is more from hearing so often: "I must go to Berlin, or Rome, or Vienna, or Florence, or the East, or the South Seas—I know there must be something there for *me*." I so often wished at hearing them that some would, or all would go to hell.

What work I do will be done here; terrible as it is to work in this "our land of the free."

We will talk it out together, soon. I could write a book about it, of course, but all that is left of my energy, I suspect, had better go into painting!

Together we will add to the American scene. . . .

Love to you and O'Kieffe [*sic*].

Soon after he had been released from the American Hospital, Neuilly-sur-Seine, and three days after he had sold his watercolor landscapes to L'Effort Moderne in Paris, Demuth had written Dr. Williams a letter dated October 13, 1921, in which he said that he was sending his friend a "little book, on Matisse" and that "Paris is more wonderful than ever, but I must hurry back to Lancaster and work—I'm too old to stay." He had not written a word to his physician friend about his physical condition. Evidently Dr. Williams heard about the seriousness of Demuth's illness anyway, as he visited the artist in Lancaster soon after his return. In his *Autobiography* Williams wrote:

> Upon his return to this country Demuth was in bad shape. That, I think, was when I first saw his mother. She was a horse of a woman, a strange mother for such a wisp of a man: . . . .
> His mother had taken him home to Lancaster, Pa., to care for him.[14]

Demuth had need of his tall, deep-voiced mother now; she whom he sometimes called "Augusta the Iron-Clad." As Miss Street said: "After 1920 and the onset of diabetes, Demuth needed his mother. His food had to be weighed."[15] The man who was dying from diabetes turned to Augusta Demuth now as to a tower of strength for assistance in sustaining his life.

Fortunately, a sanitarium designed expressly for the dietary treatment of diabetes was established in 1922 at Morristown, New Jersey, in the old Otto Kahn house. And Augusta Demuth possessed the intelligence and means to take her son to Morristown, where he became one of the Physiatric Institute's first patients. Simultaneously, for the first time in medical history the use of

14 Williams, *Autobiography*, 151–52.
15 Interview with Miss Street.

insulin in the treatment of diabetes, discovered by a Canadian physician, came into general use.

In 1922 doctors were experimenting with the treatment of diabetes. The particular form of the disease from which Demuth appears to have suffered, *diabetes mellitus*, is characterized by emaciation accompanied by excessive hunger and thirst, and is commonly fatal. In 1922 doctors realized that diet was an important factor in treating the disease, but what they did lay principally in the area of taking food away from the patient.

Dr. James Winn Sherrill in consultation with the other doctors at Morristown reduced Demuth's intake to a caloric minimum —a sure method for removing disturbing dietary factors. Dr. Williams, practicing nearby in Rutherford and much interested in the case, wrote afterward:

The result was frightening. Charley faded to mere bones, but he was able to live. They occasionally permitted him to be taken home to us for a short visit but I had to return him the same evening. He brought with him a pair of scales and weighed his food carefully. I never saw a thinner active person (this, as I say, was before the discovery of insulin), who could stand on his feet and move about.[16]

Eventually the doctors at the Physiatric Institute began treating Demuth with insulin. The Morristown institution was the first in the United States to use the new drug, and Demuth is reputed to have been the second individual to be treated with insulin at Morristown. The result was immediate. The artist began at once to gain in weight and general well-being.

While Demuth was a resident at Morristown, Miss Street was one of several friends who went to see him there. Busy as Dr. Williams was with his own practice, he drove down from Rutherford occasionally, and on one such trip took Marianne Moore along; at least, she visited Demuth there, and "he was grateful to her for it."

On June 9, 1922, toward the close of his initial term of residency in the sanitarium, Demuth wrote in a brief letter to Williams:

16 Williams, *Autobiography*, 152.

Box 308
MORRISTOWN, N. J.

CHER CARLOS:

We had such a nice ride over.

Don't worry—it is all, all right. What you want is only what we all want only in this part of the scene, there isn't really very much, if any, of "That."

Do take the month abroad. It is almost enough, really quite [enough].

Am sending you the poems of Emily Dickinson—what a treat —there was a girl, the biggest New Englander of them all.

By coincidence, the Alexander Lieberman of Demuth's generation was a patient at Morristown at the same time Demuth was. In a letter to Weyand composed years later, on October 5, 1940, Lieberman wrote:

I met Mr. Demuth for the first time in the Spring of 1922. Both of us were patients at the Physiatric Institute. . . . Mine was a corner room with a large round balcony overlooking a magnificent valley with a rather profuse growth of spring flowers. Mr. Demuth and I picked these blooms and he asked permission to use my balcony which had a northern exposure and it was there that he actually painted . . . three watercolors.

By late July, 1922, Demuth was back in Lancaster. Stieglitz had written asking him to compose something with regard to the question: Can a photograph have the significance of art? On July 30 Demuth wrote a brief reply, enclosing with the letter the photograph which depicts himself, so emaciated he resembles a cadaver, standing in a garden. An excerpt from this letter was printed in the fourth (December, 1922) issue of Stieglitz' publication *Manuscripts*. It read:

Just a line, in the heat and, in other things as trying. . . .

I'm working a bit. My old age has started—at least, middle period! "It's great fun."

139

Am enclosing, I think, a very good report of myself (and garden) in July, 1922—hope you like it. Sorry couldn't do something for "M. S. S." about camera. Couldn't. Very little left after I do my daily (sometimes, now, weekly) painting.

Two and a half months later, apparently in triumphant announcement of his miraculous return to both Lancaster and the world of the living, as well as in apology for having been remiss in his correspondence, Demuth sent a telegram to William Carlos Williams which read:

FY LANCASTER PENN 812A OCT 16 1922

DR W C WILLIAMS

9 RIDGE ROAD RUTHERFORD N J

FORGIVE LONG SILENCE LOVE

DEMUTH

Nine weeks after sending this telegram to Rutherford, Demuth mailed his engraved calling card to Stieglitz and his wife, Georgia O'Keeffe, with the following Christmas message written on it:

Wishing you & O'Kief [*sic*] merry holidays, and a great coming year—'23—it contains one of "our" numbers!

Whereas the July 30 answer to Stieglitz' question about the significance of a photograph had obviously been composed during a period of depression and exhaustion, the tone of the last two messages is one of optimism, even jubilation. Demuth was slowly regaining weight and, by the time these communications were sent, had apparently begun to feel well.

In a letter he wrote Stieglitz on January 19, 1923, Demuth mentioned having sent the New York dealer some watercolors, among which the "one of the egg-plant and the two of the cyclamen" were recent paintings. In the same letter the artist said he

was "trying to write something about Washington Allston" for
Arts, and painting some.

Ten days later, on January 29, 1923, Demuth wrote another
letter to the same correspondent, as follows:

◄━━━ Will you be terribly upset if I say that you & O'K may
have them and must not go to Hell; not yet, as I'm still hanging
onto this world, and, don't want you to be in a sphere where I
am not.

I do want you to have the water-colours . . . as Daniel has sold
one or two, well, below the "thousands." . . . Between us, I'd
rather you'd have them than Warren G. Harding or the Museum
at 5th & 81st!

I will try to come on for O'K's first day—the 29th—it's my
mother's birthday.

Perhaps you can do my hands then. . . . It, if you wish to do
them, would . . . be well to do them soon, for in the language of
the moment: Every day they grow thinner & thinner.

I'm glad you want the egg-plant. I kept it here; it turned into a
heart—maybe mine. Anyway, I hope no one will discover "Art"
or "Painting" engraved on it.

Good luck for the show, & love. Will see you when in town,
at Anderson, or will call you if I don't find you there, as soon as I
get in, so we can arrange about photo of hands.

Writing to Stieglitz again two months later, in a letter dated
March 12, 1923, Demuth said:

◄━━━ Could we take those drawings [or] water-colours which
you bought to Off's sometime before Thurs. I'll be in town Thurs.
and Fri. I'll clean them up at Off's and select some moulding for
the frames, something white and very simple. In the general excitement that day we forgot about the frames.

Am going to Morristown Fri. Will see you at the Marin show.
Have two more water-colours which if you do not mind I

will leave at Off's. You can look at them and if you would like to have them for a while I would be glad. 2 W. 47[th St.] is so awful these days. . . .

P.S. I have written and talked to Barnes, I hope to some end— but, God knows—about the Marins. I think that he will be in [to see you]. Don't . . . have Montross fuss over him. I think this might help a possible sale. I hope that he takes those sea things. They are the only really great marines since Courbet, I think. Homer's after all, were illustrations—of course, really good illustrations, but still only that. Martin and Marin will be some day a great vogue—Martin, almost (at this late day, for him), almost as unknown as Marin.

Demuth traveled to New York for a few days in February, and again toward the middle of March. While he was there, he visited the Daniel Gallery where, on January 2, his seventh New York exhibition had recently closed, and where his eighth New York (and last Daniel) show would open in November. According to Daniel, at this time "he was almost fat. That's what insulin had done for him. He was courageous—never a murmur about his condition. He would roll up his sleeve at the gallery, nonchalantly take a shot of insulin, and be off."[17]

In mid-March Demuth returned to Morristown to commence his second period of confinement there. The artist's second stay, which occurred almost exactly one year following his first, lasted from approximately March 15 through May 2, 1923.

Writing to Stieglitz from Morristown on April 16, 1923, in green ink on pink paper, Demuth expressed enthusiasm regarding the Marin show he had recently seen in New York, and spoke of reports which had reached him concerning the photographic portraits Stieglitz had made of Duchamp and himself, apparently during his mid-March visit. In this letter Demuth said:

I got your catalogue, [the one] of your show, several

17 Interview with Daniel.

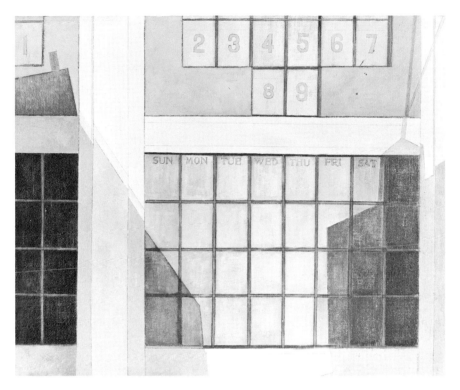

PLATE 25–A *Business.* 1921 (or 1929). Oil on canvas, 20 x 24¼ in. The Art Institute of Chicago: Alfred Stieglitz Collection.

25–B Andy Warhol, *Seven Decades of Janis.* 1967. Synthetic polymer paint silk-screened on eight joined canvases, each 8⅛ x 8⅛ in.; over-all, 16¼ x 32¼ in. The Museum of Modern Art, New York: Sidney and Harriet Janis Collection.

PLATE 26 *Incense of a New Church*. 1921. Oil on canvas, 26¼ x 20 in.
(back of stretcher bars). The Columbus Gallery of Fine Arts, Columbus,
Ohio: The Ferdinand Howald Collection.

PLATE 27 *Poster Portrait: Georgia O'Keeffe.* 1924. Oil on panel, 20½ x 16½ in. Courtesy of the Yale University Art Gallery: Gift of Georgia O'Keeffe for the Alfred Stieglitz Archive, Collection of American Literature, Yale University Library.

PLATE 28 *African Daisies.* 1925. Watercolor, 17¾ x 11½ in. The Wichita Art Museum, Wichita, Kansas: The Roland P. Murdock Collection.

PLATE 29 *Eggplant and Tomatoes.* 1926. Watercolor, 14⅛ x 20 in. The Museum of Modern Art, New York: The Philip L. Goodwin Collection.

PLATE 30–A *Poster Portrait: I Saw the Figure 5 in Gold* (*Hommage to William Carlos Williams*). 1928. Oil on composition board, 36 x 29¾ in. The Metropolitan Museum of Art, New York: The Alfred Stieglitz Collection, 1949.

30–B Jasper Johns, *The Large Black Five*. 1960. Encaustic, newsprint, burlap, and paper bags on canvas, 72¼ x 54⅜ in. Collection of Mr. and Mrs. Robert C. Scull, New York.

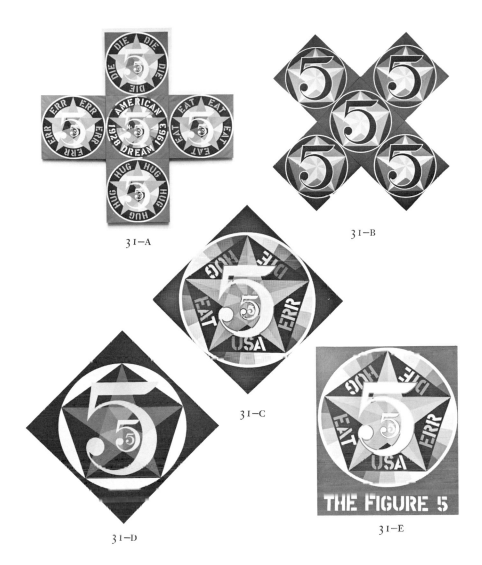

31-A

31-B

31-C

31-D

31-E

PLATE 31 *Five Studies by Robert Indiana*

A *The Demuth American Dream N. 5*, 1963, oil on canvas, 144 x 144 in., in 5 panels, each 48 x 48 in., assembled; Collection of the Art Gallery of Ontario, Canada, gift from the Women's Committee Fund, 1964. B *X-5*, 1963, oil on canvas, 102 in. square, 5 panels, each 36 in. square; Collection of the Whitney Museum of American Art, New York. C *The Demuth Five*, 1963, oil on canvas, 68 x 68 in., diamond; Collection of Mr. and Mrs. Robert C. Scull, New York. D *The Small Demuth Five*, 1963, oil on canvas, 51 x 51 in.; Collection of Mr. John A. Kloss, New York. E *The Figure 5*, 1963, oil on canvas, 60 x 50 in.; Collection of the Artist, New York.

PLATE 32–A *Poster Portrait: Love, Love, Love (Hommage to Gertrude Stein).* c. 1928. Oil, 19½ x 23½ in. Collection of Mrs. Edith Gregor Halpert of the Downtown Gallery, New York.

32–B Robert Indiana, *Love.* 1962(?). Serigraph, plate size 34 x 34 in. Collection of the Artist, New York, and Owners of Prints.

days ago, but could not make [it to] town. Missing your show and O'Kieff's [*sic*]—too bad. But I saw Marin's! It was, as "we" all know it was.

Mother said (out of the blue): "This—these are the only pictures which I have seen since the Ryder show." It was such a strange remark from her—of course, you don't know her. She is not easily impressed; and, I did not think, very responsive to "Art," so-called.

From varied sources comes great enthusiasm [concerning] what you did of me and, too, Marcel. Could you send me some of the old proofs or, any scraps, of mine so that I might see [what you have done]. I don't know when I will get to town.

The serum seems to be—well, it seems like a sort of trick. I feel [that] I will waken. It is not possible. If it be true what it is doing, then . . . there must be a few who "know."

In a letter he wrote Stieglitz five days later, Demuth appeared jubilant because of having just sold a watercolor to the Metropolitan Museum, apparently through the Daniel Gallery. This letter, which is dated April 21, 1923, reflects a curious mixture of elation and dismay, the latter emotion because of the fact that the other artists Stieglitz officially sponsored had not yet been similarly honored. Demuth wrote:

However, I want to tell you, myself (having wired Mother & phoned Bobby), that the Met did buy one of my old watercolours. As you know, and I confess, it means nothing to us unless it leads to more. Why mine should be there and others missing —well, the gods alone can tell. . . . Of course, I don't want to seem to pose as not being pleased . . . for I am, but also a bit embarrassed. . . .

Dear Stieglitz, I would love to see you—but, I must grow fat. Already I've gained ten pounds—so, you see, it may not be so long until I do see you.

Love—yes, I send you both that. It is all we really have, after all.

A letter written to Stieglitz at Morristown eleven days later, on May 2, 1923, consists mainly of an expression of appreciation for the great portrait the photographer had made of him. Evidently Stieglitz had sent Demuth proofs of both the portrait (which shows the artist standing with coat and scarf on in a gallery) and the photograph he had made of Demuth's hands—as a sketch of two overlapping hands appears on page two of the letter. This letter, which reveals Demuth's inordinate vanity, reads in part:

I think the head is one of the most beautiful things that I have ever known in the world of art. . . . I send it this morning to my mother.

The hands, too, Stieglitz—how do you do it? The texture in this one is, simply is! I hope that I see you soon. Thank you—it seems so little to write just that. But, as I say, I hope that I see you soon.

Thank O'Kief [*sic*] for the placing of the water-colour. The returns came in very handily. All waters-of-life are expensive, be they waters for the emotions, or for the flesh.

Yes, I grow fat 12 or 13 pounds. It is beyond belief the power and subtility of the serum. . . .

I heard of Martin's sales. God—what wonderful things the old man got. I really envy him. It was fine for Marin, I hope he got prices worthwhile.

Give my kindest regards to O'Kieff [*sic*]. I hope she is painting.

In a letter to the same correspondent, written in Lancaster four months later on September 4, Demuth again reassured Stieglitz concerning the state of his health:

I was thinking about you for the whole day Sunday, two weeks ago. And then your letter [on] Monday morning. Even started to write you that Sunday—funny.

There is so little to write. Of course, you know the meagre

background we all have to work before, and with this fact and the fact that I am completely cut off from any contact with ones interested in the "thing," makes writing hard. I don't know what will come of it—if I were a genius it might be all right. Complete isolation—and it is that here.

On the other hand, I grow fat, and fatter—which is something! And I garden & cut grass and stay on the move, as is expected, it seems.

There will be some water-colours for you to see in the autumn. Already there are ten or twelve which you could see—and how I would like you to see them—but you will.

Though Demuth had, literally, been returned to the land of the living by means of the new miracle drug insulin, "his hands, as photographed . . . by Stieglitz were those of one virtually dead." In addition to being forced into a strict regimen involving adequate rest and exercise, correct diet and insulin injections, for the remainder of his life Demuth had to cope with the constant threat of the sudden, terrifying collapses which occurred whenever his body chemistry contained too little or too much insulin, too little or too much starch. When he had been younger, Demuth had been fond of saying: "Appearances must be kept up." Now the fluctuating chemical balance within his body had to be maintained with as much personal dignity as possible. It was done with a stiff upper lip and no complaining, McBride said. "Charles never mentioned diabetes to me."[18]

Once when he was mounting the steps to one of the Longchamps restaurants in New York along with Miss O'Keeffe, Stieglitz, and McBride, Demuth suffered one of his swift attacks. The two other men managed to get him into the restaurant, where McBride found him a chair. Somebody gave Demuth some sugar, and "in a few minutes he was all right."

This same scene was repeated over and over in different settings and under varying circumstances. For instance, sometime

[18] Interview with Henry McBride.

in the year 1929 the artist was calling on Miss Street at her New York apartment when he had a diabetic attack. He lay down on a couch and said: "Please give me a little sugar." After Miss Street had fed him some sugar or saccharin ("I don't remember which," she said),[19] Demuth recovered.

In the summer of the same year, 1929, Demuth accompanied Edith Gregor Halpert to Atlantic City to attend the first municipal art show ever presented in America. Mrs. Halpert, owner of New York's Downtown Gallery and wife of the American painter Samuel Halpert, managed the show. While they were there, the two friends attended a dinner party given by the sponsors of the exhibition. Mrs. Halpert recalled that "just before dinner Demuth had one of his attacks. We gave him some orange juice, and in a few minutes he was all right—just as elegant as ever."[20]

The artist's attacks, which apparently resulted from the wrong amount of insulin present in the injections which he gave himself, were violent. According to Van Vechten: "[Demuth] would try to climb the walls, and generally didn't know what he was doing. When he had these spells the way he got over them was to take sugar, or some substitute for sugar. But he wouldn't eat the sugar voluntarily. People had to force sugar into his mouth."[21]

19 Interview with Miss Street.
20 Interview with Edith Gregor (Mrs. Samuel) Halpert.
21 Interview with Van Vechten.

146

7

Late Productive Years (1919-34)

After his release from the Morristown sanitarium in 1923, Demuth continued to paint as much as he was able in his neat white-washed studio and in his mother's garden. Immediately following his return from Paris in 1921 he had written Stieglitz from Lancaster saying: "All that is left of my energy, I suspect, had better go into painting." Two years later, on September 4, 1923, he reported in a letter to the same correspondent that during the preceding summer he had "only painted in water-colour; the strain is greater, but I don't have to return and fuss if it goes bad as one always does in oil or tempera." He found watercolor easier in spite of its demanding nature, because a painting done in this medium is either a success or failure and cannot be successfully worked over.

From 1919 through 1921, Demuth used both oil and tempera, occasionally combining the latter experimentally with pencil, crayon, and transparent watercolor, and employing slightly larger formats than he had used before. From 1922 to 1930, because of loss of energy, he painted mostly in transparent watercolor on small papers (the *hommages* and *My Egypt* [1927] are exceptions). From 1930 on for a period of three years he again produced large oils and temperas in a series of landscapes which were the largest and possibly the most successful paintings of his career. It should be noted that the strong 1919–21 period immediately preceded the time that Demuth nearly succumbed to diabetes, and that the important 1930–33 period immediately preceded the artist's death, which occurred in 1935.

Demuth had begun his Cubist-influenced transparent watercolor landscapes in Bermuda in 1916–17. In 1919, he began his Cubist-influenced tempera landscapes, some of which were done on composition board. These include, among others: *Back-drop of East Lynne* (1919), *Box of Tricks* (1919), *In the Key of Blue* (c. 1919), *Mackerel 35 Cents a Pound* (or *Gloucester*) (1919), *Sails* (or *Sailboats*) (c. 1919), and *A Sky After El Greco* (1919). The two temperas in the Ferdinand Howald Collection in the Columbus Gallery of Fine Arts, *Cottage Window* (c. 1919) and *The Primrose* (c. 1919), were crudely painted on thick yellow cardboard and appear to be transitional, as though they may have been the artist's first temperas.

It will be recalled that during the summer of 1920 in Provincetown Demuth experienced such severe diabetic attacks that he became temporarily incapacitated. Yet this same year he painted his watercolor masterpiece *Stairs, Provincetown* (1920) and his important tempera landscape *End of the Parade—Coatesville, Pa.* (or *Milltown*) (1920). He also produced several relatively large tempera landscapes during the year 1920, among them: *After Sir Christopher Wren* (or *New England*) (1920), *In the Province #1* (or *Roofs*) (1920), *Lancaster* (1920), *Machinery* (1920), and *The Tower* (or *After Sir Christopher Wren*) (1920). Of the last five paintings named, four are approximately twenty by twenty-four inches in size, larger than any of Demuth's previous works. *In the Province #1* is twenty-eight by twenty-four inches, larger still. It was not until the 1950's and 1960's that American artists became mesmerized by scale.

The following year, during which he spent a week in the American Hospital near Paris, Demuth painted the large oils *Aucassin and Nicolletta* (1921), *Incense of a New Church* (1921), *Modern Conveniences* (1921), *Paquebot Paris* (c. 1921); the tempera *Rue du Singe Qui Pêche* (1921); and one of his most accomplished transparent watercolor flower pieces, *August Lilies* (1921).

Demuth spent part of the year 1922 as a patient at the Physiatric Institute in Morristown, and at this time was so thin he could hardly stand. All that his diminished strength permitted him to produce amounted to a few watercolor still lifes. These included *Eggplant and Peppers* (1922) (the first of the eggplant series, most of which were painted in the years 1925–27), *Fruit No. 1* (1922), *Fruit No. 2* (1922), *Still Life No. 2* (1922), *Tuberoses* (1922), and *Yellow Calla Lily Leaves* (1922).

In 1923 Demuth accomplished some more flower pieces, such as *Amaryllis* (or *Flower Study*) (c. 1923), *Flower Study No. 1* (1923), and *White Lilacs* (1923) and painted some still lifes using peaches as subject matter. These were all transparent watercolors on small papers, indication of the artist's poor physical condition. It will be recalled that Demuth spent some time at Morristown this year also.

In 1924, the artist painted more watercolor still lifes, a figure piece entitled *Mme. Delaunois* (1924) (the only figurative work he had done since 1919) and his first two *hommages*—the *Arthur G. Dove Poster Portrait* (c. 1924) and the *Georgia O'Keeffe Poster Portrait* (1924) (Plate 27). All of his *hommages* were painted in oil.

From the year 1922 forward Demuth was content to paint mostly small transparent watercolor still lifes,[1] which exacted a

---

[1] Demuth's still lifes fall readily into nine classifications, according to technique or structural nature. In approximate chronological order these categories are:
1. The early, amorphous, wet paintings of c. 1915.
2. The compositions playing light-colored objects against a dark ground (c. 1915).
3. The vignetted oval compositions (c. 1920–21).
4. The diagonal compositions in which the principal motifs were left unpainted (c. 1922).
5. The upward-expanding V or hourglass conformations placed against unpainted grounds (c. 1923–28).
6. The diamond-shaped compositions placed against unpainted grounds (c. 1925–28).
7. The extravagant still lifes with fruit or vegetables, flowers in a vase, and a basket or dish placed against white cloth (c. 1925–26).

relatively small toll from his slight reservoir of strength. Exceptions are to be found in the *hommages* (which seem in retrospect to have been farewell tokens of affection), *My Egypt* (1927), which is considered to be his most monumental painting, and the important series of architectural-industrial landscapes produced late in the artist's life, between 1930 and 1933. The last named works, which include such relatively large oil and tempera paintings as *Buildings, Lancaster* (1930) (Color Plate VII), *Waiting* (1930), ". . . *and the Home of the Brave*" (1931), *Buildings Abstraction—Lancaster, 1931*, *Chimney and Water Tower* (1931), and "*After All...*" (1933) (Color Plate VIII), represent a curious resurgence of Demuth's energies immediately preceding his death.

Demuth's genius, then, was at its peak in the period 1916–21 (years which include both the 1916–17 Bermuda experiment and the 1919–21 productivity paralleling the onslaught of diabetes) and 1930–33, immediately antedating his death. His art bears silent, irrefutable witness to the fact that the flow of his talent displayed a direct relation to the ebb and flow of his strength, but an indirect relation to the approach of death. Diabetes appears to have drained the artist of his creative founts and strength for painting, except when it assumed its most destructive role and threatened imminent death. At such times it seems to have caused the artist to produce prolifically at a high mental and emotional pitch. This phenomenon can be satisfactorily explained on medical and psychological levels: it has been so explained by Dr. Williams.[2]

The doors of 291, Stieglitz' Photo-Secession (or Little) Gallery, located at 291 Fifth Avenue, were closed in 1917 because of the war. In 1925 he opened the Intimate Gallery in Room 303 of the Anderson Galleries, located on Park Avenue at Fifty-ninth Street.

---

8. The figure-eight compositions (c. 1925–28).
9. The close-ups of a few objects placed against unpainted grounds (c. 1927–29).
2 See Williams quotation herein, p. 14.

He maintained this gallery from 1925 to 1929, moving to An American Place on the seventeenth floor at 509 Madison Avenue in the year 1929.

Not long after the doors of the Intimate Gallery opened, Stieglitz wrote an undated letter to Demuth in which he said:

THE INTIMATE GALLERY
ROOM 303, ANDERSON GALLERIES
489 PARK AVENUE, NEW YORK CITY

DEAR DEMUTH

I've been thinking an awful lot about the whole situation. That is, the situation of the, what I call, A–1 men. And amongst the A–1 men of course is the woman, O'Keeffe. I feel more and more that the so-called dealers have no idea of handling the situation. That is, the situation of these few people I have in mind. I think it an outrage that so little has been achieved for you, considering what has been written about you and what you are really doing.

If I were only young enough I'd really finally hang out my shingle, not to make money, but just to show these wise men called art dealers what rotten business men they are.
. . .

For remember my fight for O'Keeffe and Marin is my fight for you as well. You may not understand but somehow or other I'm sure you must feel what I've said to be absolutely true.
. . .

Visitors still are sparse in the Room. But those who come count and that is what I am after. The mob is welcome to go elsewhere. . . . With love as always,

Your old
———

Kalonyme and Seligmann who are in the Room here send their best regards.

As mentioned above, Demuth exhibited with the Stieglitz Group for the first time in the show Seven Americans, presented in the Intimate Gallery at the Anderson Galleries from March 9 through March 28, 1925. Altogether, Demuth was given three

LIST OF PAINTINGS

PROVINCETOWN—1918

LONGHI ON BROADWAY—1927

"I SAW THE FIGURE 5 IN GOLD"
—WILLIAM CARLOS WILLIAMS—1927

DESIGN FOR A BROADWAY POSTER
(UNFINISHED)—1929

CABBAGE & RHUBARB—1929

THE CHARLES W. KRAUSHAAR GALLERY
IS AGENT FOR MR. DEMUTH'S
WATERCOLORS

CHARLES DEMUTH

FIVE PAINTINGS

The Intimate Gallery: Room 303

APRIL 29—MAY 18
1929

THE ANDERSON GALLERIES BUILDING
489 PARK AVENUE, NEW YORK

Catalogue for Demuth's 1929 show at The Intimate Gallery.

one-man shows at Stieglitz's galleries and exhibited in four Stieglitz Group shows. His 1926 one-man show at the Intimate Gallery was called Recent Paintings by Charles Demuth and lasted from April 5 through May 2. From April 29 through May 18, 1929, he was given an exhibition at the same gallery entitled Charles Demuth—Five Paintings. And in April, 1931, he had a show at An American Place called Paintings by Charles Demuth.

As well as exhibiting in the 1925 show Seven Americans, Demuth was included in three other Stieglitz Group shows: an exhibition of the work of O'Keeffe, Demuth, Marin, Hartley, and Dove shown at An American Place in April and May, 1930; Impromptu Exhibition of Selected Paintings by the same Stieglitz Group of Five presented at An American Place during May, 1931; and Impromptu Exhibition of Selected Paintings by the Group of Five shown at the same gallery from May 20 through June 14, 1932.

In the comprehensive Stieglitz memorial exhibition held at the Philadelphia Museum of Art in 1944, called History of an American—Alfred Stieglitz: "291" and After, a number of Demuth's works were shown as representative of Demuth's participation in the Stieglitz Group of Five, as the accompanying cut indicates.

Although Demuth exhibited at the Stieglitz galleries from 1925 on as part of the Stieglitz Group, and although for years he was a close friend of the pioneer photographer and his wife, "Stieglitz never acted as his [Demuth's] guarantor."[3] The great entrepreneur's principal enthusiasms were always Marin (whose work he exhibited as early as 1909), O'Keeffe (whom he married), and, curiously, Dove.

At this distance in time the role of Stieglitz in the history of American art appears to have been principally that of proselytist for the twentieth-century style. Sensitive and paternal, he was eminently suited to play the part of shepherd to the newborn lamb, and intelligent enough to know exactly what he was doing.

[3] Henry Clifford and Carl Zigrosser, "History of an American—Alfred Stieglitz: '291' and After," catalogue, 36.

CHARLES DEMUTH

American painter, born at Lancaster, Pa., in 1883, and died in 1937. Studied at the Pennsylvania Academy of Fine Arts. Although Demuth frequented "291" (see Stieglitz's portrait of him standing in front of a Picasso drawing) and was a close friend of Stieglitz and O'Keeffe, Stieglitz never acted as his guarantor. He did, however, have numerous exhibitions of his work beginning in 1925.

283. BERMUDA No. 1—TREE AND HOUSE, 1917   signed watercolor

284. BERMUDA No. 2—THE SCHOONER, 1917   signed watercolor

285. BERMUDA No. 3—THE TOWER, 1917   signed watercolor

286. VENTILATORS, 1920   signed pencil and gouache

287. BUSINESS, 1921   oil painting

288. AFTER ALL, 1921?   oil painting

289. EGGPLANT AND PEPPERS, 1922   signed watercolor

290. GEORGIA O'KEEFFE—POSTER PORTRAIT, 1924   oil painting

This and the three succeeding pictures were a series of combination posters and symbolic portraits of his artist friends.

291. DOVE—POSTER PORTRAIT, 1924   oil painting

292. DUNCAN—POSTER PORTRAIT, 1925   gouache painting

293. MARIN—POSTER PORTRAIT, 1925   oil painting

294. FLOWERS, 1925   signed watercolor

295. CARROTS AND APPLES, 1928   signed watercolor

296. CALLA LILIES AND SHELL, 1926–1929?   oil painting

297. "I SAW THE FIGURE 5 IN GOLD," 1928   oil painting

A symbolic portrait of the poet, William Carlos Williams.

298. LONGHI ON BROADWAY, 1928   oil painting

299. DAFFODILS, 1928   signed watercolor

300. RED CABBAGES, RHUBARB, AND ORANGE, 1929   signed watercolor

36

Demuth section in catalogue for the exhibition History of an American—Alfred Stieglitz: "291" and After, the Philadelphia Museum of Art, 1944. (See Plates 25–a, 27, 28, 31–a, and Color Plates IV, V–a, VI, and VIII.)

He knew the caliber of the lambs in his barn, whom he called the "A–1 men." He possessed a true evangelical passion for the new art form, along with a genius for spreading the Word among the Philistines. What Stieglitz did was "stir into flame," by means of the exhibitions in his galleries and printed material in his publications *Camera Work* and *Manuscripts*, the minds and emotions of an entire generation of Americans. He also made ceaseless and effective use of the spoken word, and out of all his talk, passion for living, and genuine feeling for people emerged a sort of magnetic flux which inspired and vitalized everyone it touched.

Hapgood wrote that "most of the men around Stieglitz didn't understand him," that the photographer was not essentially an artist but a man driven by a restless desire to live and make live. Probably this is as sound an estimate of the "directing Spirit" of 291, the Intimate Gallery, and An American Place as will ever be made.

The Demuth-Stieglitz letters in the Collection of American Literature at Yale, which cover a period of twenty years, stand as evidence of the psychological alchemy Stieglitz wrought. People trusted him, were prodded by him into thinking deeply on a high plane about art, and an accompanying spiritual growth comparable to the springing of green grass out of black earth occurred. This parallels the art of teaching, and as much as he was anything Stieglitz was a teacher, a professor who used his gallery as a classroom.

In the letter he wrote Stieglitz on November 28, 1921, two days after he had returned to Lancaster from his last trip to Europe, Demuth said:

~~~~~ Together we will add to the American scene, more than has been added since the '60's and '70's—maybe more than they [the artists of that time] added. I feel that all together we are more or less fine.

As his contribution to the book *America and Alfred Stieglitz*, published in 1934, Demuth wrote "Lighthouses and Fog," a brief essay which displays exceptional insight into Stieglitz' life-function. It reads:

> For no reason, perhaps a very good reason, after all—as I start to write this—I have been thinking, when really not thinking, of lighthouses and fog.
>
> Lighthouses and fog—a lighthouse and many fogs. There really are not many lighthouses, and fogs seem to be always rolling in from most distinguished shores and seas.
>
> Lighthouses are fixed. Sometimes they seem to have moved but—they really haven't. Lights in lighthouses sometimes move but they do not move as lights in a political street parade move. Lights in lighthouses sometimes wink, and I've seen them myself twinkle.
>
> "But you said you were writing about Stieglitz—"
>
> "Well, I am writing about Stieglitz—here, this is what I have been doing—writing about Stieglitz!"[4]

In a way Stieglitz was a fanatic, a man of inordinate zeal launched irrevocably upon an "endless quest." And one of the subjects dear to Stieglitz' heart was the American cause. The letters which Demuth, a sixth-generation American, wrote to him are studded with references to America. For instance, in a letter to Stieglitz dated August 6, 1928, Demuth wrote:

Thanks for sending me *Creative Art*—the Hartley number. . . . Has he [Hartley] gone back? Europe was to us all nearer & dearer, but—well, you know. What could any of us add to Europe? Perhaps I like to suffer; at times, I think that I do. It may never flower, this our state, but if it does I should like to feel from some star, or whatever, that my living added a bit. For in [comparison to] this flower, if it [America] does [flower], I can imagine Rome in its glory looking very mild.

And in a letter dated October 12, 1930, mailed to Stieglitz at his Lake George summer place and written on Hotel Brevoort stationery, Demuth said:

[4] Demuth, "Lighthouses and Fog."

Didn't work at all—but have been again painting before I came to town; for the past couple of weeks. Was going to bring what I've finished, one oil . . . but didn't; just as well now that I find you still in the country. You will see it next time I come over. I think you will like it. It's quite American, I think . . . .

During the twenties a self-conscious quest for an American form of art was being carried on throughout the land, and out of this quest came, first of all, the shallow regionalist movement of the thirties. Two Ohio cities, Cleveland and Cincinnati, promoted annual shows which stressed an American theme; and in December, 1929, a show entitled Paintings by 19 Living Americans opened at the new Museum of Modern Art in New York.

Demuth's humorous comment concerning the last-named exhibition, in which he was included, was made at the close of a letter he wrote Stieglitz on October 16, 1929:

> Hotel Brevoort
> Fifth Avenue at
> Eighth Street

DEAR STIEGLITZ:

Again, New York. Again, this & that. Nothing really, but Helen Morgan.

Those drawings, the ones I sent you for Mrs. Nauman to look at, didn't you say that you would send them to Kraushaar? . . . Some one in Boston must have a drawing, it seems, of that vintage—. . . .

I hear that the Bliss-Crowninshield-Luxembourg after its opening show of French is to have a show of 15 living Americans! I don't think there are that many, myself—but that's another matter, again.

Love for you & Georgia.

Stieglitz took pride in his disinterest in financial gain—according to O'Keeffe, "he made no money from anything [he] sold." This is traditionally the concept which separates the commercial from the fine arts, and Stieglitz was fundamentally a fine arts person—a great photographer who incidentally ran a gallery. This apparent contradiction in his functions resulted in an avant-garde gallery coupled with high prices. Stieglitz discussed this predicament in a letter he wrote Demuth on January 28, 1930:

MY DEAR DEMUTH:

Several people have been after your "Green Pears," but balked at $2500.00 saying that at Kraushaar's, etc., etc. Always the same old story. They concede the particular picture to be finer than any one "there," but—yes, ye gods—*but*! I seem always to be in the position of money-gouger—most amusing when in all the years of gouging I have yet to receive a penny from the gouging! And none of the artists I have gouged for have become rich like the French artists so lovingly supported by art loving America! Why aren't you & Marin & O'Keeffe & Dove Frenchmen?—& I at least a Man Ray in Paris? I can't be a Steichen or a Sheeler in America. Am too old to join the game.

But it's great to have the clean Place & not be overrun by the mob. Occasionally an at least semi-intelligent person shows up & that's a lot. I'm neither encouraged or discouraged; nor does it take any courage merely to be. One can laugh at one's own imbecilities, and gape at the shrewdness of those waxing fast & furious in the game! And what a game it has become.

Dear France! Priceless France—where would America be without its art dealers—& its hosts of great artists. . . . It's all very wonderful.

& Goodyear, Pres. of the Modern Museum has bought a Kenneth Hayes Miller for the Modern Museum! . . . Mrs. Rockefeller presented the Karfiol to the Museum. Amen.

I hope Miller is proud—& Karfiol prouder. Poor Walt Kuhn, what an injustice to his genius. But Matisse is coming from France for the next Carnegie. Then all will be perfect.

I hope you are at work. Some one recently came in & asked me what ailed you when you were in town recently. I wondered. The person said: Why, he didn't have a kind word to say about any of his friends. I laughed & merely said: Well!

So here's "Well!" & good luck. We're all in one Boat guaranteed Non-Sinkable.

The notice entitled "Alfred Stieglitz Dies Here at 82" which

THE
INTIMATE
GALLERY
ROOM 303
ANDERSON GALLERIES BUILDING
489 PARK AVENUE AT FIFTY-NINTH STREET, NEW YORK

announces its Fourth Exhibition — April 5 to May 2 —

RECENT PAINTINGS BY CHARLES DEMUTH

The Intimate Gallery is an American Room. It is now used more particularly for the intimate study of Seven Americans: John Marin, Georgia O'Keeffe, Arthur G. Dove, Marsden Hartley, Paul Strand, Alfred Stieglitz, and Number Seven.

It is in the Intimate Gallery only that the complete evolution and the more important examples of these American workers can be seen and studied.

Intimacy and Concentration, we believe, in this instance will lead to a broader appreciation.

The Intimate Gallery is a Direct Point of Contact between Public and Artist. It is the Artists' Room. It is a Room with but One Standard. Alfred Stieglitz has volunteered his services and is its directing Spirit.

Every picture is clearly marked with its price. No effort will be made to sell anything to any one. Rent is the only overhead charge.

The Intimate Gallery is not a Business nor is it a "Social" Function. The Intimate Gallery competes with no one nor with anything.

The Gallery will be open daily, Sundays excepted, from 10 A.M. till 6 P.M.

Exhibition I —JOHN MARIN, December 7, 1925-January 11, 1926.
Exhibition II —ARTHUR G. DOVE, January 11-February 7.
Exhibition III—GEORGIA O'KEEFFE, February 11-April 3.
Exhibition IV—CHARLES DEMUTH, April 5-May 2.
Marsden Hartley Exhibition to be announced.

All but Time-killers are welcome

Recent Paintings by Charles Demuth, statement emanating from Stieglitz' Intimate Gallery.

appeared in the *New York Times* July 14, 1946, stated that the photographer "never took money for a photograph," that once when he needed money and in contrast to his practice reluctantly sold a photographic portrait for fifteen hundred dollars, he expressed his regret in the words: "I hated to take the money. It was against all that I had stood for and fought for. What is a masterpiece worth? A million dollars, if one has the money. But ... as public property, it has no selling price."

Nothing lays bare Stieglitz' fanatical devotion to the cause of art so clearly as the announcement made in connection with the Intimate Gallery's Fourth Exhibition, presented at the Anderson Galleries from April 5 through May 2, 1926 (see accompanying cut).[5]

This announcement lends credence to Daniel's charge that Stieglitz was "the biggest egotist that ever lived."[6] It reads like the manifesto of a narrow cult under the leadership of a high priest or prophet. And this is what Stieglitz was, as well as what the new art desperately needed in America during the first decades of the century—a "directing Spirit."

The same self-conscious prose so characteristic of the twenties appears again in another publication, which emanated from An American Place and was related in intent to Demuth's distinguished architectural-industrial landscape *My Egypt* (1927).

Naturally sympathetic toward other artists, especially those whom he knew personally, Demuth joined enthusiastically in the philosophy and activity of the Stieglitz Group. He had been drawn to the group by his long-standing admiration for Marin and his friendships with Hartley, Stieglitz, and O'Keeffe. It was with the last-named artist that his relationship ran deepest.

Van Vechten said that Georgia "adored" Demuth with a devotion which stemmed from the fact that "she and Demuth were very much alike. Georgia is an introvert. She is a wonderful per-

---

[5] Weyand Scrapbooks No. II, 149 (back of page), and No. III, 271.
[6] Interview with Daniel.
[7] Weyand Scrapbook No. 1, 55.

gift is giving. this we learn. hard to learn. recompense we

dont understand. hence talk, effort, search, research.

in the Whitney museum is a painting by Charles Demuth

called "MY EGYPT". it represents gift - giving. it is small,

obscure, delicate—a study of factory buildings—dextrous,

acute, perhaps the finest sense of a modern age that has been

expressed. this painting has a history. its history may some

day be known. a slow process, this knowing, knowing history.

hard to know. the painting may then be seen, be received.

hard to see, to receive.

the American Indians express what they know by means

of dance. within their dance occurs a gesture, simple gesture

—body in balance, slight almost imperceptible step forward,

shoulders dropped, elbows flexed, wrists and hands in con-

stant rhythmic motion—palms out—palms in. it makes one

wonder if giving and receiving—giving and seeing—are not

the same thing.

"IT MUST BE SAID"

NUMBER FOUR

AN AMERICAN PLACE

509 MADISON AVENUE

NEW YORK CITY

NOVEMBER 1935

"It Must Be Said," statement about *My Egypt* which originated at Stieglitz' American Place.[7]

son, but very hard to get to know, just as he was."[8] O'Keeffe told Dorothy Seiberling: "Demuth and I always talked about doing a big picture together, all flowers. I was going to do the tall things up high, he was going to do the little things below."[9] A great admirer of the other artist's painting, she purchased the watercolor *Carrots and Apples* (1926) when it was on consignment at An American Place, and was influenced by Demuth in the precisionist, craftsmanlike nature of her work, which outdoes him in simplicity and consistent monumentality. Demuth's admiration for and trust in O'Keeffe became evident after his death when it was learned he had willed her his unsold oil paintings[10]—a gesture which may also have meant he believed she would know how to get his work to the public. This faith was magnificently fulfilled in the gifts of Demuth works (those owned by O'Keeffe and Stieglitz) made to the Metropolitan Museum, the Art Institute of Chicago, Fisk University, Yale University, and other institutions.

Demuth wrote introductory paragraphs for the catalogues of

[8] Interview with Van Vechten.

[9] Dorothy Seiberling, "Horizons of a Pioneer," *Life*, Vol. LXIX, No. 9 (March 1, 1968), 52.

[10] A notice entitled "Mother and Two Artists Share Demuth Estate" which appeared in an unknown New York newspaper January 30, 1936, read:

The estate of Charles Henry Buckius Demuth, American artist, of Lancaster, who died there October 23, 1935, was appraised here this morning for transfer tax purposes at $22,527 gross and $21,207 net.

Mr. Demuth, whose paintings hang in the Metropolitan Museum of Art, the Whitney Museum and the Brooklyn Museum of Arts and Sciences, left his watercolors [an error] to Georgia O'Keeffe, an artist, of the Hotel Shelton, this city. His other paintings were left to Robert E. Locher, of 331 East 17th Street, New York. The value of Mr. Locher's legacy was placed at $6,025.

The residue passes to Mr. Demuth's mother, Mrs. Augusta W. Demuth, Lancaster.

After Locher's death in 1956, the unsold watercolors were inherited by his associate, Weyand. On Weyand's death which occurred approximately five months after Locher's, the watercolors went to Weyand's four brothers and sisters, who had never known Demuth. On October 16, 1957, and February 5, 1958, the watercolors along with a few oils and drawings were auctioned off at the Parke-Bernet Galleries in New York. According to Elsie Everts, whose source of information remains obscure but whose figures agree substantially with those found elsewhere, the 1957 auction of Demuth works brought $44,475, the 1958 auction, $37,660.

three O'Keeffe exhibitions. For the catalogue of a 1927 O'Keeffe show at the Intimate Gallery he wrote:

Flowers and flames. And color. Color as color, not as volume, or light—only as color. The last mad throb of red just as it turns green, the ultimate shriek of orange calling upon all the blues of heaven for relief or for support; these Georgia O'Keeffe is able to use. In her canvases each color almost regains the fun it must have felt within itself, on forming the first rainbow.[11]

A sentence from his essay "Across a Greco Is Written" was used as the introduction for O'Keeffe's February 4–March 17, 1929, show at the Intimate Gallery: "Across the final surface—the touchable bloom, if it were a peach—of any fine painting is written for those who dare to read that which the painter knew, that which he hoped to find out, or, that which he—whatever!"[12]

And for the (apparently unprinted) catalogue of a Georgia O'Keeffe exhibition presented at An American Place early in 1931, Demuth prepared the following paragraph, commenting in the accompanying note he sent the Stieglitzes that he was "rather pleased with this fragment":

With these go a movement of flames. Flame of the spirit? Flame of the flesh?—perhaps the flame, only, of creation, however, it consumes—that is success in a flame. Sometimes it burns vermillion, sometimes it burns emraud with violet edgings, but, it always burns and moves. Moves at times like great flames fanned by great winds from the sea, at other times like things burn indoors, as candles behind the elevated Host. At times like the electric arch; then the movement and the colour seem not to be movement and colour anymore—the movement being that slight rest before any consummation which is supreme movement, or balance, and the colour being some colour beyond those we see.[13]

[11] Demuth, Introduction to "Georgia O'Keeffe Paintings," catalogue.
[12] Demuth, Introduction to catalogue for Georgia O'Keeffe exhibition, 1929.
[13] Demuth, Introduction to (apparently unprinted) catalogue for Georgia O'Keeffe exhibition, 1931.

GEORGIA O'KEEFFE
PAINTINGS, 1926

The Intimate Gallery: Room 303

JANUARY 11—FEBRUARY 27
1927

FLOWERS AND FLAMES. AND COLOUR. COL-
OUR AS COLOUR, NOT AS VOLUME, OR LIGHT,—
ONLY AS COLOUR. THE LAST MAD THROB OF
RED JUST AS IT TURNS GREEN, THE ULTIMATE
SHRIEK OF ORANGE CALLING UPON ALL THE
BLUES OF HEAVEN FOR RELIEF OR FOR SUPPORT;
THESE GEORGIA O'KEEFFE IS ABLE TO USE. IN
HER CANVASES EACH COLOUR ALMOST REGAINS
THE FUN IT MUST HAVE FELT WITHIN ITSELF, ON
FORMING THE FIRST RAIN-BOW.

CHARLES DEMUTH

LIST OF PAINTINGS

THE SHELTON, NEW YORK NO. I
THE SHELTON, NEW YORK NO. II
THE SHELTON, NEW YORK NO. III
THE SHELTON, NEW YORK NO. IV
STREET, NEW YORK NO. I
STREET, NEW YORK NO. II
EAST RIVER FROM THE SHELTON NO. I
EAST RIVER FROM THE SHELTON NO. II
EAST RIVER FROM THE SHELTON NO. III
THE DARK IRIS NO. I
THE DARK IRIS NO. II
THE DARK IRIS NO. III
WHITE CALLA LILY NO. I
WHITE CALLA LILY NO. II
WHITE CALLA LILY NO. III
YELLOW CALLA LILY NO. I
YELLOW CALLA LILY NO. II
BLACK PETUNIA & WHITE MORNING-GLORY I
BLACK PETUNIA & WHITE MORNING-GLORY II
BLACK PETUNIA & WHITE MORNING-GLORY III
RED CANNA NO. I
RED CANNA NO. II
BLACK PANSY & FORGET-ME-NOTS
L. K.—WHITE CALLA & ROSES
FLOWERS FROM GEORGE
THE SEA SHELL & OLD SHINGLE NOS. 1-7
LIGHT BLUE SEA—MAINE
THE SEA-SHELL NOS. 1-6
THE SIDE OF THE BARN, NO. I
THE SIDE OF THE BARN, NO. II
THE OLD MAPLE, LAKE GEORGE
THE RED MAPLE, LAKE GEORGE
THE WHITE BIRCH, LAKE GEORGE
ABSTRACTION NO. I
ABSTRACTION NO. II
ABSTRACTION NO. III

THE ANDERSON GALLERIES BUILDING
489 PARK AVENUE, NEW YORK

Demuth's Introduction to the catalogue for Georgia O'Keeffe's
January 11-February 27, 1927, exhibition at The Intimate Gallery.

GEORGIA O'KEEFFE PAINTINGS, 1928

The Intimate Gallery: Room 303

"ACROSS THE FINAL SURFACE,—THE TOUCH-
ABLE BLOOM IF IT WERE A PEACH,—OF ANY
FINE PAINTING IS WRITTEN FOR THOSE WHO
DARE TO REAL THAT WHICH THE PAINTER
KNEW, THAT WHICH HE HOPED TO FIND OUT,
OR, THAT WHICH HE WHATEVER."

CHARLES DEMUTH.

FEBRUARY 4—MARCH 17
1929

LIST OF PAINTINGS

EAST RIVER FROM THE SHELTON NO. VI
EAST RIVER FROM THE SHELTON NO. VII
RITZ TOWER, NIGHT
CALLA LILIES WITH RED ANEMONE
CALLA LILIES ON RED
CALLA LILY ON RED
CALLA LILY ON GRAY
A ROSE ON BLUE
RED CANNA NO. I—1928
RED CANNA NO. II—1928
RED CANNA NO. III—1928
RED POPPY NO. V
RED POPPY NO. VI
RED BARN, WISCONSIN
PINK BLEEDING-HEART
WAVE—NIGHT
SHELL NO. I
SHELL NO. II
SHELL NO. III
SEA-BEAN
ABSTRACTION NO. I
ABSTRACTION NO. II
ABSTRACTION NO. III
ABSTRACTION NO. IV
ABSTRACTION NO. V
ABSTRACTION NO. VI
LEAVES, PINK ON YELLOW
YELLOW LEAVES
YELLOW HICKORY LEAVES WITH DAISY
FADED AND BLACK LEAVES
DARK LEAVES
CHESTNUT TREE, AUTUMN
PLUMS IN DISH
RED PEPPER, GREEN GRAPES
A CHRISTMAS PRESENT

THE ANDERSON GALLERIES BUILDING
489 PARK AVENUE, NEW YORK

Demuth's Introduction to the catalogue for Georgia O'Keeffe's
February 4-March 17, 1929, exhibition at The Intimate Gallery.

Although, as stated above, Stieglitz was never Demuth's financial guarantor, the photographer and his wife functioned as supporters of their friend's morale. Any artist needs spiritual sustenance and encouragement from knowledgeable people, and it was in this realm that Stieglitz and O'Keeffe meant most to Demuth professionally. Because he respected their judgment and integrity, they were able to provide him with meaningful appreciation. In a letter dated August 20, 1968, Miss O'Keeffe expressed this contribution in the following way:

He [Stieglitz] had a remarkable way of giving people faith in themselves. . . .

As I think about the relationship between Demuth and Stieglitz I rather think that Stieglitz was probably a bit of a steadying hand on his shoulder. They had a faith in common that neither found too often elsewhere.[14]

[14] Georgia O'Keeffe to the author.

Premature Death

Toward the close of his life Demuth found it difficult to paint during the summer. In the fall he would report to Stieglitz the accomplishments of the preceding season, and his reports were invariably rueful. In a letter to Stieglitz dated October 30, 1927, he confided:

≈ Must say the summer didn't add much to my work. Tried some watercolours several weeks ago—they were terrible—the field is [yielded] to Marin.

Almost a year later, on August 6, 1928, he wrote to the same correspondent:

≈ My work . . . has been going, but going very strangely this summer. They—the paintings—have a strange, inner strange look about them. They look sometimes like I think my own things do or should, and then again when I look at them they seem to look very different & strange with a strange strangeness. Really I can't tell—you'll see them unless they look too strange some morning and I do away with them; only remembering the summer of '28 without any work to help me remember some terrible days.
Am sending you some money. . . .
I think this, after reading it over . . . is pretty bad. . . . I think

my critical sense is failing, too—still, I let you have it. Perhaps what it's all about could not be gotten into words anyway! However, someone quite recently told me that my much discussed "Peggy Bacon" [his foreword to her exhibition catalogue] had two or three sentences of purest English.

Give my love to O'Keeffe and love for you.

During the long, hot summers Demuth, who was tied to Lancaster by the requirements of his diabetic regimen, yearned to get away and experience again the festive mood of his beloved Provincetown or the sophisticated environment of Paris. In a letter he wrote Stieglitz in July, 1927, he said:

I would love to go somewhere—where I don't know—any place is almost impossible. . . . I'm really all right here, but at times I almost wish I could "go in for"—hysterics; but all I can go in for is another picture.

In a letter he wrote Stieglitz the following month, on August 15, 1927, Demuth disclosed that he had gotten away and gone to Beverly, Massachusetts, near Boston, for ten days. It was in this letter the artist spoke of having been greatly impressed by the Washington Allston paintings he saw in the Boston Museum.

The following summer, in a letter to Stieglitz dated June 4, 1928, which was written on blue stationery carrying the letterhead One Hundred and Eighteen East King Street, Lancaster, Pennsylvania, Demuth wistfully reiterated his desire to get away from Lancaster for a while:

It's almost time for you to be going [to Lake George], I suppose. I wish that I could too, go to the sea, some place on the Mad Cape—Cape Cod. This morning I got from there a lot of wild pink orchids. . . .

I'll stay here and work—I don't see anything else—I like a few places and a few people, but I see them seldom. Perhaps I wouldn't work at all if I did. Still, I don't like most of my work—and maybe that's what keeps me working. . . .

Off did [for] me a beautiful frame for my yellow flowers—I can use it on some others; expensive, but still . . .

Will send you some money for the Marin, soon. Hope the lake is as always.

In 1930 Darrell Larsen came to Lancaster to teach drama at Franklin and Marshall College, and he and Demuth became close friends. Larsen recalled that during the period he knew the artist, which was from 1930 until his death in 1935, regularly every evening Demuth would take a walk in the course of which he would limp down East King Street one and a half blocks to the city square, then go two blocks north along North Queen Street until he reached the entrance to the Brunswick Hotel, from which point (after pausing for a while to watch people come and go) he would amble back to the old Demuth home down Duke Street. According to Larsen, during the thirties he and Demuth went to drinking parties together in Lancaster "at least twice a week," frequently at the home of Jack and Blanche Steinman;[1] after each of which events Augusta Demuth would help her son return to his strict regimen of special diet and rest.

In the October 12, 1930, letter which was written on Hotel Brevoort stationery and mailed to Stieglitz at his Lake George home, Demuth said:

Just couldn't write you before. Was not very well part of the summer, and then too something else happened to me which almost finished me in another direction. So, all in all, my summer was one of the worst. However!!—here I am again back in New York, not much changed.

This was the summer that, along with Larsen, the artist visited the Steinmans in 'Sconset on Nantucket Island, occupying the

1 Interview with Darrell Larsen.

guesthouse across the street from the Steinman summer home; and the period when at least one of the pornographic watercolors of sailors cavorting on the beach was produced.

It was sometime during this same year, 1930, that Demuth's old Philadelphia friend George Biddle stopped by to see him in Lancaster. While Biddle was there, Demuth related to him the details concerning Pascin's death, which had evidently just occurred—how the talented Spanish Jew from Bulgaria who had become an American citizen just before his death had tried first to hang himself in his studio and, unsuccessful in this attempt, had then slashed his wrists and "very slowly bled to death." Demuth, who was exceedingly impressionable, was evidently deeply affected by Pascin's suicide—just as, at an earlier time, he had been by that of Holliday.

As his letters to Stieglitz show, during the twenties Demuth was seized by a great longing to return to Cape Cod. In the summer of 1930, the same summer that he and Larsen visited the Steinmans on Nantucket, he was able to get to Provincetown for a while with his old Lancaster friends Frank and Elsie Everts, who were driving to the Cape in their car. Mrs. Everts recalled that on the way "my husband, Frank, and I" sat in the front of the car, "Tommy and Demuth, in the back."[2] The fourth individual in the car was Tommy Farrar, the decorator who managed the Newport Theatre (established in 1929 in Stanford White's famous Newport Casino) and who married Beatrice Locher after her divorce. The Evertses were familiar with the area since they owned a thirty-eight-foot boat which they docked at Newport, and while en route the four friends stopped to eat at the Casino. For Demuth it was a long-postponed return to a way of life and an environment he loved.

Four years later, in the summer of 1934, Demuth again escaped from the stay-at-home pattern of his declining years and spent the entire season on the Cape. The Evertses had taken a cottage—The

[2] Interview with Mrs. Everts, 1956.

Sunbeam—in Provincetown for the summer and Demuth had a room in this cottage, which was situated at the water a long way "up along"; that is, at the northern end of Commercial Street. Because the cottage was built out over the bay, the front porch gave one the sensation of being on the deck of a boat, and the whole structure was involved in the life of the water—the sound of water, the effects of sunlight on water, and the push and pull connected with the ebb and flow of the tide. On the north side of the cottage a wooden stairway with a handrail led up from the water to a side entrance which was designed for persons who arrived by boat.

Demuth experienced no diabetic attacks this summer, a result of the Evertses' regular schedule and Mrs. Everts' conscientious preparation of his food according to the special requirements of his diet. Elsie did the baking herself, she said: "We had fish or shell-fish every day for lunch, and some different kind of meat—meat roast—for dinner." She baked two pies every day, preparing the dough for the crust without salt. Years later she recalled that "Charlie would help prepare vegetables," and once "Demuth himself made home-made fresh vegetable beef soup," one of Lancaster County's favorite dishes. He declared that "for once he was going to have it as he liked, with more of one kind of vegetable than the other."[3]

Twice a week the Evertses and Demuth gave a dinner party, at which time they hired a woman from the village to help in the kitchen. In turn, the three Lancaster friends were invited out to various social events in the homes and studios of artist friends. Once a week they ate together in one of Provincetown's colorful restaurants.

Every morning after breakfast the three went shopping together. And every day after lunch, in fair weather, Demuth went out on the beach beside The Sunbeam to sketch the United States fleet, which was based at Provincetown that summer. Mrs. Everts recalled that there were as many as fifty-four different kinds of

---

[3] Mrs. Everts to the author, May 28, 1956.

ships in the fleet, and that Demuth was fascinated by the sight. He had always loved boats—their decks, funnels, masts, and rigging. This last summer on the Cape he would sit at night watching the ships' searchlights play across the harbor in constantly moving, crisscross patterns so like the rays the Futurists used in their paintings as a device for the breaking up of light.

Elsie said that Demuth felt quite well during the summer of 1934 in Provincetown, that he seemed "just as always." He appeared not to have been aware of the final approach of death. But Demuth's works are a reliable mirror of the state of his health, and the sketchbook containing figurative paintings he produced this summer reveals not the artist whose genius had burst into flower in 1916–21 and 1930–33 but, instead, a dying man whose rare talent had drained away. Stiff, awkward, and curiously static, the pathetic 1934 sketchbook serves only to demonstrate that at this time the artist's creative powers were depleted and about to cease. Demuth must have realized this himself since, though he lived on for over a year following this summer, he never painted again.

At the close of the 1934 season in Provincetown, Demuth returned to Lancaster and remained at home thereafter, except for his usual train trips to Philadelphia and New York. The radically altered handwriting of an undated note he sent Stieglitz suggests that it must have been written about this time. This note, which contained a curious message regarding the large Mayan stone toad Mrs. Demuth eventually willed to Dr. Barnes, read:

> My Dear M. Stieglitz:
> You will get by express, sometime today, the toad which Hartley has spoken to you about, and which I would like you to have for a month or two. You will like it, I think.

The penmanship in this note is almost illegible, very different from the artist's ordinarily clear script.

In spite of rapidly diminishing vitality, Demuth proceeded with plans for the future. His health had been so good while he was in Provincetown with the Evertses that Augusta Demuth gave her approval to the artist's plan for visiting Paris in the fall of 1935 with Elsie and Frank. Demuth intended to make some illustrations (in all likelihood for Proust's *À la Recherche du Temps Perdu*), and felt that he had to go to Paris to do these properly.

Because of his closeness to the French author in life history and fundamental nature, Demuth had never been able to shake off the experience of *Swann's Way*, *Within a Budding Grove*, *The Guermantes Way*, *Cities of the Plain*, *The Captive*, *The Sweet Cheat Gone*, and *The Past Recaptured*, which he had begun to read in the summer of 1927. In her article about Demuth which appeared in *Creative Art* in 1931, Rita Wellman reported: "He thinks it would be wonderful for him to illustrate an edition of Marcel Proust. So do I."[4]

And much later, in a letter dated May 28, 1956, Elsie Everts wrote:

> Charlie, my late husband and myself were going to go to Paris in the fall of 1935. Charlie was going to do illustrations for a privately published book [to be] put out by Jack Chrysler, and he said he would be unable to do the illustrations unless he was in Paris. . . . His mother, Mrs. Demuth, said he could go if we went along and saw that he ate properly.[5]

But Demuth never saw Paris again. On October 23, 1935, he died unexpectedly, without any warning beyond the fact that, according to Larsen, he suffered from swollen legs for several weeks before his death, a condition about which the artist was worried, since it is considered to be indicative of heart trouble.

There are several theories regarding exactly how Demuth died. And since both Mrs. Demuth and the attending physician died long ago, proof concerning the exact nature of the artist's death may never come to light—a situation which would have delighted the man who so loved the mystery resident in hidden truth.

[4] Rita Wellman, "Pen Portraits," *Creative Art*, Vol. IX (December, 1931), 483–84.
[5] Mrs. Everts to the author, May 28, 1956.

According to Locher and Weyand, the artist died in the old Demuth home in Lancaster in the little upstairs bedroom which faced his mother's garden, of either influenza or the grippe complicated by pneumonia.[6] But Locher was in New York at the time and probably knew only what a grief-stricken Augusta Demuth told him.

Dr. Williams, who was not there either, wrote in his *Autobiography*: "[Demuth] was careless [about taking insulin] and died ... while on his way home to Lancaster, either from lack of insulin or an overdose; I was never able to get the answer."[7]

It is well known that Demuth sometimes stubbornly refused to give himself the life-sustaining insulin, and this fact lends credence to Dr. Williams' version. But his report suggests that Demuth may have suffered a diabetic seizure while he was a passenger on a train, probably during the three-hour trip between New York and Lancaster. This would have been a dreadful experience—a matter of possibly an hour or more in the throes of diabetic shock with no relief.

Demuth's first cousin, Christopher Demuth, who operates the family tobacco shop next door to 118 East King Street, said that though the artist did once undergo diabetic shock while on a train, this did not occur at the time of his death. Christopher said: "Charles went into a diabetic coma and died at home here. His doctor was Dr. Miller, who is gone now himself. He died a natural death from diabetes. He was ready to die."[8]

Probably the most authentic version of Demuth's death is that provided by Mrs. Everts, whose husband Frank, a close friend of the artist, occupied an office near the Demuth home. Elsie said: "He [Demuth] would get bull-headed sometimes and refuse to take the insulin injections. That's how he died."[9]

Demuth underwent unusually severe shock, so extreme that his mother called Dr. Miller, who, after examining Demuth, said, "Let

[6] Interview with Richard Weyand.
[7] Williams, *Autobiography*, 152.
[8] Interview with Christopher Demuth.
[9] Interview with Mrs. Everts, 1956.

COLOR PLATE I *The Circus.* 1917. Watercolor, 8 x 10⅝ in. (mat opening). The Columbus Gallery of Fine Arts, Columbus, Ohio: The Ferdinand Howald Collection.

COLOR PLATE II *At a House in Harley Street*. Illustration #1 for Henry James's *The Turn of the Screw*. 1918. Watercolor, 8 x 11 in. Collection of the Museum of Modern Art, New York: Gift of Mrs. John D. Rockefeller, Jr.

COLOR PLATE III *Roofs and Steeple*. 1921. Watercolor, 14¼ x 10⅜ in. Collection of the Brooklyn Museum.

COLOR PLATE IV   *Poster Portrait: Charles Duncan.* c. 1925. Oil or Gouache, 19¾ x 23¼ in. Courtesy of the Yale University Art Gallery: Gift of Georgia O'Keeffe for the Alfred Stieglitz Archive, Collection of American Literature, Yale University Library.

COLOR PLATE V–A   *Poster Portrait: John Marin.* c. 1925. Oil, 27⅜ x 33¾ in. Gift of Georgia O'Keeffe for the Alfred Stieglitz Archive, Collection of American Literature, Yale University Library, published through the courtesy of the Yale University Art Gallery.

COLOR PLATE V–B   Jasper Johns, *Three Flags.* 1958. Encaustic on canvas, 30⅞ x 45½ x 5 in. Collection of Mr. and Mrs. Burton Tremaine, Meriden, Connecticut.

COLOR PLATE V–A

COLOR PLATE V–B

COLOR PLATE VI *Poster Portrait: Longhi on Broadway* (*Hommage to Eugene O'Neill*). 1927. Oil on composition board, 34 x 27 in. Collection of the William H. Lane Foundation, Leominster, Massachusetts.

COLOR PLATE VII *Buildings, Lancaster.* 1930. Oil on composition board, 24 x 20 in. Collection of the Whitney Museum of American Art, New York: Anonymous Gift.

COLOR PLATE VIII *"After All . . . ."* 1933. Oil on composition board, 36 x 30 in. Collection of the Norton Gallery and School of Art, West Palm Beach, Florida.

him rest." The artist lay down to rest according to the physician's instructions, and Mrs. Demuth went to take a nap before the evening meal. A little later, "when she went in to see him around five, she saw it was the end."

Whatever the circumstances, it was on October 23, 1935, that Demuth died, fifteen days before his fifty-second birthday. He was buried in the old Demuth plot in the Lancaster Cemetery beside the large horizontal gravestone, itself almost buried in the weeds, on which are engraved the names of his father, his mother, and himself. It is a wild, tree-shaded section of the cemetery crowded with centuries-old, half-sunken stones, over which sometimes the sun sets in an orange sky.

The presence of Demuth in the old house in Lancaster did not terminate with his death for the reason that Augusta Demuth lived on for eight years after her son died. A tall, stately woman with a beautiful face and a clear voice like a bell, Mrs. Demuth had worn mourning (black clothing, including a sailor hat with a ribbon-edged veil so long it fell all the way to her waist in the back) ever since her husband's death in 1911. Following Charles's death in 1935 she had double reason to wear mourning. As Elsie said: "He was all she had. Her grief must have been terrible to bear."

One day in 1943 when, as had been her lifelong custom, Mrs. Demuth went to Lancaster's Central Market early in the morning to select her foodstuffs at the neat, well-provisioned stalls of the Plain people, she was struck by an automobile and suffered a broken hip. She died two weeks later at eighty-seven.

Mother Demuth, as she was called, never returned to 118 East King Street after setting out for market on that day. After her death, relatives and friends discovered the touching perpetuation of Demuth's life in his personal effects, meticulously preserved by his mother just as he had left them eight years before. Demuth's rubbers were on the floor and his expensive coats on the rack in the front hall. Throughout the house all of the artist's possessions had been retained in perfect order exactly as he had left them,

175

even "down to the special tray for his diabetic syringe, with a white towel or napkin over it, which she [Mrs. Demuth] changed every week until her accident."[10]

So, in a sense, it was not until Augusta Demuth died that Demuth died. Perhaps that is always the way with a child and his mother, but this relationship had been unusually close. In so carefully preserving the tangible evidences of Charles's existence, Mother Demuth must have felt much like Hartley did when, shortly after the artist's death, he wrote in his magnificent ten-page tribute, "Farewell, Charles":

Charles has only just gone, rest his winsome bones; I will proceed to the period of twenty-three years ago, the place is Paris, the time is nineteen twelve-thirteen, and the hour of the first meeting a certain déjeuner at the Restaurant Thomas, on the Boulevard Montparnasse. . . .

At all events, at a certain déjeuner, the restaurant was crowded, and for the purpose of regaling Charles's memory as if he were here, and how do we know he isn't, for I am sure all of my friends are around a corner somewhere, and so my sense of mourning for physical losses never lasts very long. . . .

I shall recall to Charles, perhaps more to give a setting for his own entrance . . . I shall recall to him the day he ambled up to our table. . . .[11]

Demuth himself left evidence of having sensed his immortality, possibly more acutely than anyone else, in the words he wrote pertinent to one of his own literary compositions:

Perhaps this is not a story, at all, and yet I think it is. Is life ever definite in its answer? Is the story ever really finished? We can, all of us, imagine things to come after the end of a story, be the story our own or that of some other.[12]

10 Mrs. Everts to the author, May 28, 1956.
11 Hartley, "Farewell, Charles," 552–54.
12 Weyand Scrapbook No. I, 88.

Epilogue

Demuth the Highly Respected Ancestor of Pop: His Works Mined by Indiana, Johns, Warhol, and Others

The most obvious Demuth influence as we near the three-quarter mark of the century resides in the five New Realist works by Robert Indiana (Plate 31) and one New Realist work by Jasper Johns (Plate 30–b) which are derived from *I Saw the Figure 5 in Gold* (Plate 30–a). In the catalogue for the 1966 Demuth exhibition at William Penn Memorial Museum in Harrisburg, Pennsylvania, New York critic Emily Genauer called these Indiana paintings "homages" to Demuth, but commented: "Demuth, I think, would not be amused. . . . No artist could be altogether pleased that a younger artist's tribute . . . should win such renown as, in certain areas, to exceed his own." Miss Genauer went on to point out that, on the other hand, Demuth himself had placed Henry James in a comparable position—had excelled the New England author in the great illustrations he created for *The Turn of the Screw* and *The Beast in the Jungle*.

According to Miss Genauer:

Several younger artists . . . queried on and acknowledging the considerable influence Demuth has had on them, say it stems chiefly from their admiration for his precise forms, carefully disciplined composi-

177

tions, and fresh color. . . . They also respond to his sharp identification with the world of visual reality.[1]

No doubt Indiana's initial interest in *I Saw the Figure 5 in Gold* was triggered by his enthusiastic reaction to the dramatic major configuration in this Demuth painting, a motif consisting of three numerals five situated one inside the other in a recessive manner, the farthest being laid in gold leaf. As early as 1960, Johns made use of this same central motif in his work *The Large Black Five.* Three years later Indiana produced his five paintings which are derived from Demuth's great poster portrait of Dr. Williams. Indiana himself enumerated these paintings in a letter he wrote the author on December 11, 1968:

All of my paintings, and they number five, based on Demuth's *I Saw the Figure 5 in Gold* are listed here in the order of execution and completion:

1. *The Demuth American Dream No. 5* 1963 . . . .
2. *X–5* 1963 . . . .
3. *The Demuth Five* 1963 . . . .
4. *The Small Demuth Five* 1963 . . . .
5. *The Figure 5* 1963 . . . .

It is the last painting, *The Figure 5,* which hung in the White House for a few years beginning in the fall of 1965, but was removed this spring to hang in the National Collection of Fine Arts Gallery in Washington where it is now on extended loan. That is the Smithsonian's beautiful new (old) museum at Eighth and G Streets which used to be the Patent Office Building.[2]

In the particular Indiana version which is titled *The Demuth Five* the artist retained much of Demuth's original design, including the color, used ambiguously in the poster portrait to suggest both a fire engine racing noisily through the streets of New York and Dr. Williams' powerful, egotistical personality. In this work Indiana placed the already given central motif against a series of geometric shapes (a star, a pentagon, a circle, a diamond) and added

[1] Emily Genauer, text for *Charles Demuth of Lancaster,* catalogue.
[2] Robert Indiana to the author.

the words "HOG," "EAT," "USA," "ERR," and "DIE" between the points of the star. (These four three-letter words and one abbreviation together comprise a curiously succinct summation of Pop: the endomorphic love of food, patriotism, and existentialism.) The end product is unique, the result of a brave new vision honestly, simply, and aggressively declared on a grandiose scale with emphasis laid on bare, existential fact. Completely absent are the equivocations and deliberate uncertainties, subtleties, and nuances resident in such baroque technical traits as value gradation coupled with lost edges, flickering lights, vibrating surfaces, and sudden recessions into depth. In a sense, the Indiana works seem to be a culmination of Demuth's own development.

Indiana has also been influenced by *Love, Love, Love* (Plates 32–a and 32–b), Demuth's poster portrait of Gertrude Stein. In the aforementioned letter written on December 11, 1968, Indiana stated: "There are many, many LOVES [by Indiana]." It will be recalled that at the close of a letter Demuth wrote the Stieglitzes April 21, 1923, he said: "Love—yes, I send you both that. It is all we really have, after all." So that, in his philosophy, also, Demuth seems to have anticipated the art and flower children of the 1960's.

Another Pop work which appears to be derived from Demuth is Andy Warhol's *Flowers* (1965) (Plate 10–b). The source for this painting, a large work eighty-two inches high, is said to have been a photograph taken from a Kodak journal, and the tall grasses in the background may very well have come from such an origin. But the important part of *Flowers*, the four blossoms, appears to be derived from Demuth's 1915 watercolor *Pansies #1* (Plate 10–a), which was reproduced in the Andrew Carnduff Ritchie monograph published in 1950 in connection with the Museum of Modern Art's Demuth retrospective. In this book Ritchie wrote: "Demuth's greatest flower pieces have often a disturbingly sinister quality. . . ." And: "In some mysterious way the whole effect is one of sinister suggestion . . . not the innocent blossoms one was led to expect."[3]

[3] Ritchie, *Charles Demuth*, 10.

179

Demuth was a great admirer of Watteau. He read and illustrated Pater's imaginary portrait of Watteau, *A Prince of Court Painters*. Strangely, in an article about Warhol which appeared in *Art News* in 1966, David Antin wrote the following regarding Warhol's *Flowers*:

The flowers are shaped like baggy-pants comedians . . . and somehow they resemble . . . Watteau's traveling players. It is practically impossible to say what the object of the pathos in *Flowers* is. Warhol manipulates an almost impossible pathos. It is, in a sense, the images themselves, their awkwardness, their insubstantiality, their unnaturalness. Watteau's comedians are also awkward, insubstantial and unnatural.[4]

Demuth was an ardent student of Watteau. Warhol appears to be an ardent student of Demuth. The critical difference is that Demuth did not copy Watteau's paintings, but absorbed the spirit of Watteau and translated it into some of his early flower and figure paintings, such as *Pansies #1* and *Flora and the Governess* (1918) (End Papers).

More than once in his writings Demuth made reference to what he termed "a moment," by which he meant the aesthetic experience. In an essay describing the way he and other young painters spent their days in New York during the second decade of the century, he related:

The forenoon had been this and that. The afternoon dragged through an exhibition or two, a saloon or two—some art talk.
Then . . . we found ourselves at Fisk's direction, in a place, a gallery.
. . .
May we see the new Picasso?
It was brought into the room. A Picasso.
That was a moment. . . .[5]

It is the aesthetic experience the current Park Place Group is trying to evoke, as explained by Dean Fleming in his statement: "We want to make people realize that what they see has a trans-

[4] David Antin, "Warhol: the Silver Tenement," *Art News*, Vol. LXV, No. 4 (Summer, 1966), 58. Hereafter cited as "Warhol."
[5] Demuth, "Between Four and Five," No. 47 (July, 1914), *Camera Work*, 32.

lucent nature and a multiplicity and that they themselves are capable of this change inside their own psyches; and the experience of that change can be ecstatic."[6]

Though Demuth's and Fleming's moment of change is primarily a matter of the experience of form, there is a connection between this and the fluctuating ambiguity which Johns describes as the magical metamorphosis of a common into an uncommon object, the "moment in which one identifies a thing precisely, and . . . the slipping away of that moment."[7] In a *Life* magazine article titled "Art or not, it's food for thought," Tomkins suggested that at least some Pop art works are not art but exist instead "somewhere in the no man's land between art and life"—a fascinating concept because it stakes out the subjective area (be it prairie, foothills, or abyss) which lies between the territory of the layman and that of the creative mind. For Pop artist Johns, Pop also exists on an imaginary border line between the nonillusory and the illusory, between the real beer can and the imaginary one.

Both the idea of change inherent in the time concept of a moment and the factor of ambiguity are peculiarly baroque. And the latter factor is present in strength in the early Mannerist-Expressionist works of Demuth. His flower paintings are frequently fraught with sinister, unwholesome overtones, reminding one of Nolde's flower paintings and Baudelaire's *Fleurs du Mal*. His illustrations, all of them executed noncommercially for literary masterpieces which tend to be concerned with either implied homosexuality or evil women who delight in ruining men's lives, outdo their texts in the insertion of morbid, macabre content. Even some of the 1916–17 Cubist-influenced landscapes painted in Bermuda possess tree limbs subtly suggestive of human limbs. The artist used the well-known phallic sculpture by Brancusi, *Mlle. Pogany*, as the central motif for his *Illustration for McAlmon's Distinguished Air*, which was excluded from the Museum

[6] David Bourdon, "E=MC² à Go-Go," *Art News*, Vol. LXIV, No. 9 (January, 1966), 25.
[7] "Catcher of the Eye," *Time*, Vol. LXXXIV, No. 23 (December 4, 1964), 84.

181

of Modern Art's 1950 Demuth retrospective as being "too controversial."

Ambiguous sexual content, understated and subtle in Demuth, appears with casual, un-self-conscious overtness in such Pop works as Claes Oldenburg's *Quadruple Sketch of a Dormeyer Mixer* (1965) and Warhol's Happening *The Exploding Plastic Inevitable*. In the latter event, Warhol's painting of Indiana entitled *Eat* appears on the left, his painting *Banana* on the right, and "a beautiful female impersonator in full dress lies on a couch while [Gerard] Malanga, this time well-dressed in 19th century Viennese gentility, with another actor, looks on significantly. (Freud and Breuer? An abortion?)"[8]

To those who are acquainted with Demuth's works, the above description recalls his poster portrait of the female impersonator Bert Savoy, titled *Calla Lilies* (1929). And the Happenings of the sixties are seen to relate in an uncanny way to Demuth's illustrations for the Wedekind plays *Erdgeist* and *Die Büchse der Pandora*.[9] In the Wedekind illustrations the speeches of the various characters are placed inside small balloons, just as they are in Roy Lichtenstein's cartoon paintings (see Plate 19–b). In the *Earth-Spirit* illustration *The Animal Tamer Presents Lulu* (1918) (Plate 19–a) the figures of a man attired like a ringmaster and a young woman dressed like a clown are depicted standing in front of a tent which bears the sign "MLLE. LULU." The animal tamer (a caricature of Wedekind himself), who is sporting dark curls and the traditional ringmaster costume consisting of top boots, white

---

[8] Antin, "Warhol," *Art News*, Vol. LXV, No. 4 (Summer, 1966), 59.

[9] Demuth's illustrations for *Erdgeist* seem now to have been four in number, as follows:

   #1. *The Animal Tamer Presents Lulu*. Prologue.
   #2. *"No, No O God! . . ."* Act III.
   #3. *Lulu and Alva Schön in the Lunch Scene*. Act IV.
   #4. *Interior with Group of People around Red-headed Woman*. Act IV.

His illustrations for *Die Büchse der Pandora* seem to have been three:

   #1. *Lulu and Alva Schön*. Act I.
   #2. *The Ladies Will Pardon Hy Mouth's Being Full*. Act II.
   #3. *The Death of the Countess Geschwitz*. Act III.

riding breeches, and dress coat with tails, presents a nonchalant, foppish appearance. In one hand he flourishes a whip, in the other a revolver, and he appears to be making a dramatic entrance to the sound of fanfares. Lulu is depicted standing demurely on a small box, like a trained animal, and between the two figures appears the head of a man in the audience who leers at the scene with evil eye. According to the speeches written inside the balloons, Lulu announces herself by saying: "Your bride is here!" While the animal tamer commands: "Hop, Charlie, march!" The corresponding Wedekind text reads:

> *She was created to incite to sin*
> *To lure, seduce, corrupt, drop poison in,—*
> *To murder, without being once suspected.*
> . . . .
>
> *Hop, Charlie, march! Carry her to her cage. . . .*[10]

In the illustration for *Pandora's Box* called *The Ladies Will Pardon My Mouth's Being Full* (1918) (Plate 22), three standing figures are depicted: at center, an acrobat wearing a costume consisting of black tights, green shirt, and red star-patterned belt; on the left, a woman attired in a blue military uniform; and on the right, a woman gowned in a décolleté white evening dress with train. In the conversational balloons emerging from the figures' mouths appear, reading from left to right, the speeches: "How?" "Goodnight, children," and "The ladies will pardon my mouth's being full."

The last speech, when considered in relation to the art of the sixties, brings vividly to mind the strange emphasis in Pop art on the subject of food. This theme relates directly to the endomorphic category of psychosomatic medicine. Not only has Warhol made much of this theme with his *Eat, Banana,* and much publicized Campbell soup cans; Wayne Thiebaud has become famous for his still lifes of delicatessen items—pies, cakes, and other "frosted delights"; and Oldenburg, in addition to his *Floorburger*

[10] Ritchie, *Charles Demuth,* 49. This quotation is from the Prologue, Act I of Franz Wedekind's *Erdgeist.*

and *Dual Hamburger*, has constructed a ten-foot-high work entitled *Spilling Bag of Shoestring Potatoes* (1965).

There is common interest in the witty title here. Duchamp liked such titles as *Why Not Sneeze?* (1921), and Demuth's titles include *Many Brave Hearts Are Asleep in the Deep* (1916), *From the Garden of the Château* (1921 or 1925), and *Nospmas M. Egap Nospmas M.* (1921). The first of these Demuth works is a vaudeville piece depicting two men singing onstage; the château is the Demuth home in Lancaster; while *Nospmas M.* (meaning Monsieur Sampson) is an industrial landscape. This kind of wit is not very different from that expressed in Johns's *Painted Bronze* (1960), a three-dimensional work in which two larger-than-life beer cans, one empty and the other fashioned of solid bronze and both capable of being lifted, sit side by side.

One of Demuth's witty titles, *My Egypt* (1927), refers to the huge columnlike grain elevators of John W. Eshleman and Sons, which stand near the center of downtown Lancaster. The elevators function as a single monumental object in the painting, hieratic in its frontal placement on the format. This device (which the artist repeated in the recessive numerals five of *I Saw the Figure 5 in Gold* [1928] and the whisky bottle used as the central motif in *Longhi on Broadway* [c. 1927] [Color Plate VI], his poster portrait of O'Neill) has greatly influenced Pop artists, who habitually favor the large, central motif.

The grain elevators of *My Egypt*, the fire engine of *I Saw the Figure 5*, and the Broadway theme of *Longhi* are all related to the American idea. Demuth was concerned about America, where he sensed a philistine lack of sympathy for art, and he stressed this theme in such of his titles as *Scene with American Flag* (c. 1916), *In Vaudeville: Columbia* (1919) (Plate 24), and "*. . . and the Home of the Brave*" (1931). In his *Poster Portrait: John Marin* (c. 1925) (Color Plate V–a) the words "MARIN" and "PLAY" appear along with a red arrow and two white stars against a red, white, and blue striped ground. Historically, these works lie behind the flag paintings of Johns and the patriotic billboard-influenced paintings of Robert Rauschenberg, who strives to prove that the United States is a beautiful, not an ugly, land.

Demuth produced many industrial paintings which bear witness to the fact that he, too, found beauty in the American scene. One of these, his 1921 oil *Business* (Plate 25–a), anticipates the existentialist philosophy characteristic of the art of the sixties. He entertained an aristocratic disdain for the workaday world and the laborer victimized by an industrial society, and this attitude is reflected in *Business* in the rows of monotonously repeated windowpanes which pattern a close-up view of a factory wall. On the panes are lettered the numerals one through nine and abbreviations for the days of the week—in summation, a visual protest against the monotony of lives spent behind this wall. One hears the existentialist "Why? Why am I trapped in the deadening routine of daily living?" Thus, *Business* foreshadows the existentialist trend in theater during the sixties, where repetitive speech patterns occur in plays where there is little plot and where little happens, suggestive of "eternal repetitions in human behavior." Similarly, *Business* anticipates the way the Happenings of the sixties possess no end and no beginning, only a monotonous middle—such Pop manifestations as Warhol's repetitious portraits of Sidney Janis (Plate 25–b), Indiana, Marilyn Monroe, and Elizabeth Taylor; and such sounds as the Voice of Nico in Warhol's Happening *The Exploding Plastic Inevitable* singing: "Let me be your mirruh! Let me be your mirruh! Let me be your mirruh!"

Still another factor in Demuth which seems to have affected the New Realism is his frequent use of a pristine, immaculate, antiseptic white ground. It was notably in his watercolor still lifes that he habitually placed exquisitely delineated positive objects (peaches, eggplant, striped kitchen towels) against a luminous, unpainted ground. This device has reappeared during the sixties in the works of Californian Thiebaud, who employs pure white grounds behind relieflike human figures as means toward the psychological and technical isolation of his subjects.

Demuth's Influence on Optical and Hard-Edge Art

Op artists, who rose in large numbers, even in groups, on an international level during the decade of the sixties, practice a cool, rational approach to art which is diametrically opposed to Abstract-Expressionist emotional involvement. In their revival of objectivity and psychical distance (both classical traits) the New Idealists are the inheritors of Albers, Mondrian, Malevich, and, before them, of such Renaissance masters as Jan Van Eyck, Paolo Uccello, and Piero della Francesca. In America, Op artists are successors of an early twentieth-century group of painters whom critics saddled with the unfortunate label, Precisionist.[11]

The so-called Precisionists (or Cubist-Realists) included such artists as Sheeler, Spencer, O'Keeffe, Preston Dickinson, Schamberg, and Demuth, all of whom worked for at least a time in a classical manner involving hard edges, closed color, exactitude, extreme clarity, and a deliberate approach applied to the American industrial scene. In the severity of their technique they approached the machine-directed purism of Le Corbusier and Ozenfant. And it was this classical technique Op artists continued, inheriting it by way of Albers.

The major concern Op painters have displayed with such factors as optical illusion, retinal response, and the after-image finds no antecedent in Demuth or any of the Cubist-Realists; indeed, it stems more from science than from art and correspondingly evokes a nonart response outside the realm of the aesthetic experience of form.

The excellent Hard-Edge painter George Ortman, in his 1957

---

[11] "Precisionist" is an unnecessarily narrow label; the term "Cubist-Realist" coined by Milton W. Brown strikes a more accurate note. Throughout the ages, classical art has been characteristically to some degree precise, since it involves clarity allied to linear emphasis and closed color. For as sensitive and perceptive an artist as Demuth to be placed permanently in a Precisionist or Immaculate category would be, to say the least, imprecise. The term is particularly unjust in Demuth's case, since the body of his work is strongly informed with feeling. His important early figure pieces and illustrations were Mannerist-Expressionist paintings characterized by lack of clarity, hot color, immediacy, and psychology-imbued emotional effects.

work *Journey of a Young Man,* used a series of symbols to celebrate the life cycle. Demuth used this concept in three of his still lifes: *Youth and Old Age* (1925), in which large, warm-hued blossoms situated at the base of a pyramidal composition progress toward small, cool-hued flowers at the top; *Corn and Peaches* (1929), in which three ears of sweet corn symbolize three stages of life; and *Poppies* (1929), which depicts four stages in the life of a flower.

Decadence in the Art of the Sixties.

From Braque's and Picasso's 1912 *collages* it had been only a step to Duchamp's ready-mades. These included his 1913 *Bicycle Wheel,* his 1917 mounted urinal entitled *Fountain,* and his *Why Not Sneeze?* (1921), which consisted of a bird cage holding "sugar lumps" fashioned out of marble, a thermometer, and a cuttlebone. After the great wave of Abstract-Expressionism had receded, it was only another step from Duchamp's ready-mades and that other Dadaist Kurt Schwitters' environmental *Merzbau,* a totally designed studio interior, to New Realist Johns's whimsical beer cans, Warhol's aggressive soup cans, and Edward Kienholz' Los Angeles beanery. From the crass soup cans of Warhol and the depressing *Bed* of Rauschenberg, it could be only one more step to the utter dethronement of painting as an art. Hilton Kramer was thinking along these lines when he reported as follows from Venice regarding the 1966 *Biennale*: "This entire *Biennale* may be described as one long giggle over the dismal and destructive spirit that has overtaken so much of the art of our time."[12]

In view of twentieth-century decline in the art of painting, its digression by stages toward what will hopefully prove to be only temporary eclipse, it should be stated that in spite of his considerable influence on the art of the middle of the century, Demuth was never antiart in his thinking. He was never a Dadaist but instead reacted negatively toward Dada and its mockery of art.

[12] Hilton Kramer, "Death in Venice, With Giggles," *New York Times.*

Were Demuth alive today, he would in all likelihood be repelled by the vulgarity and lack of taste resident in Pop art. A man who loved elegance, distinction, and refinement of all kinds and who possessed a passion for understatement, Demuth would have felt uneasy about the raising of banal everyday objects to the level of icons and would have found the Happenings of the sixties lacking in subtlety and upsetting to his sensibilities. Like most important artists, Demuth was an ectomorph, not an endomorph, and would have found Pop emphasis on food ridiculous and repulsive. (The emphases on patriotism and existentialism he would have understood—also, the wit.)

Demuth would have recognized a few of the New Realists and New Idealists as fellow artists—Johns and Ortman, for instance, and Rauschenberg. But he would have felt that, as usual, there existed a dearth of men who were truly knowledgeable about pictorial form. Demuth would have laughed with Warhol, but privately he would have felt disdain when Warhol said: "Paintings are too hard. The things I want to show are mechanical. Machines have less problems. I'd like to be a machine, wouldn't you?"[13]

The more than one thousand paintings and drawings which Demuth produced over a period of two decades were complicated labors of love. He worked hard to produce them, against great odds.

[13] "Pop Art—Cult of the Commonplace," *Time*, Vol. LXXXI, No. 18 (May 3, 1963), 72.

Chronology

1883   November 8: Born at 109 North Lime Street, Lancaster, Pa.

1887   Became permanently lame as the result of a hip injury.

1889   Ferdinand Demuth moved his family from the North Lime Street address to 118 East King Street, next door to the family tobacco shop, the residence at this address having been just vacated by Charles Demuth's last remaining great-aunt.

1895   July and August: Wrote letters and cards home to Lancaster from Atlantic City which are dated July 27 and August 2.

1896   Painted what may have been his earliest watercolor, a landscape with a windmill.

1899–1900   September: Entered Franklin and Marshall Academy, a preparatory school in Lancaster.

1900–1901   The artist's second year at Franklin and Marshall Academy. Studied china painting with Miss Letty Purple of Columbia, Pennsylvania, and did some pyrography.
March 31: Was confirmed at the Evangelical Lutheran Church of the Holy Trinity, situated in the

same block as the Demuth home, by the Reverend John E. Whittaker.

June: Was graduated from Franklin and Marshall Academy.

1901–1902   Fall: Probably entered Drexel Institute in Philadelphia, commencing his formal training in art.

1903–1904   October 13–May 25: Attended Drexel Institute.

1904–1905   September 26–June 6: Attended Drexel Institute. Met William Carlos Williams this year at Mrs. Chain's boardinghouse on Locust Street in Philadelphia.

November 8: Is reported to have been in Paris on this, his twenty-first birthday.

April 20: First registered at the Pennsylvania Academy of the Fine Arts.

Summer: Attended the School of Industrial Art in Philadelphia, where he was encouraged by Mrs. Mary Andrade, an instructor at this school, to continue his studies at the Pennsylvania Academy.

1906–1907   October 13–May 3: The artist's second year at the Pennsylvania Academy, when he studied with Anshutz, Chase, Breckenridge, and McCarter.

July 26–August 19: Attended Darby School, the Pennsylvania Academy's summer camp at Fort Washington, Pennsylvania, where he continued to study under Anshutz and Breckenridge.

Late summer: After Darby School closed, the artist visited New York briefly.

1907–1908   September 21: Received his passport, #40695, in Lancaster.

October 4: Sailed for his second visit to Europe.

October 30: Was staying in Paris with Lawrence Fellows, an old Philadelphia friend, at 9 rue de la Chaumière.

November 8: Sent a cable to Mrs. Louise Haas Michaelis of Lancaster on her wedding day.

December 10–December 25: Was still living in Paris, at 113 Notre Dame des Champs.

December 12: Wrote a letter to his Grandmother Demuth in Lancaster saying he intended to go to Berlin during the Christmas holidays to be with his cousin, Pauline Cooper, who was studying music in that city.

February 2: His address was 35 rue Delambre, Paris.

March 21: Was at sea on his way back to the States.

April and May: Was enrolled at the Pennsylvania Academy.

April 29–early May: Painted a portrait of Louise Haas Michaelis as a class problem.

Summer: Sketched and painted in New Hope, Pennsylvania, along with Clive Weed, a student friend. While in New Hope courted divorcée Emmasita Register (Mrs. Charles) Corson.

1908–1909 Fall through spring: The artist's third year at the Pennsylvania Academy. His address: 216½ Walnut Street, Philadelphia.

Summer: Was in Lancaster.

1909–10 Fall and winter: The artist's fourth year at the Pennsylvania Academy. His address: 136 North Seventeenth Street, Philadelphia.

November: First met Robert Locher.

Summer: Was on Monhegan Island in Maine.

1910–11 Fall through spring: The artist's fifth year at the Pennsylvania Academy. His address: 908 Filbert Street.

Summer: Sketched and painted in Lambertville, New Jersey.

1911–12 Ferdinand Demuth died in 1911 at the age of fifty-four, and the artist remained at home in Lancaster with his mother during the academic year 1911–12. Summer: Sketched and painted in Lambertville, New Jersey, and New Hope, Pennsylvania.

1912–13 November 10–December 15: First exhibited his work, in the Pennsylvania Academy's annual watercolor exhibition in Philadelphia.

November 23–December 13: Exhibited a self-portrait in the Loan Exhibition of Historical and Contemporary Portraits presented at the Woolworth Building in Lancaster.

December: Left for his third and most extended European visit, during which he became acquainted with *Les Fauves* and such Americans as Marsden Hartley and Gertrude Stein.

December 11: His address: 7 rue Bréa, Paris.

December 25: Spent Christmas in Paris, producing the drawing *Paris: the Night before Christmas* on Christmas Eve.

Winter: Attended the Académie Moderne in the late afternoons and evenings, drawing from three-minute poses.

April: Attended a dance recital given by Isadora Duncan.

Summer: Attended a performance by Diaghilev's Ballet Russe de Monte Carlo at Le Théâtre des Champs-Élysées. During this period abroad met Edward Fisk, traveled to Cornwall with Cornwallis, a painter friend, and went to Étretat to paint the rocky seashore.

1913–14 Fall through spring: Studied in Paris at the Académie Colarossi and the Académie Julien. Was in Berlin with Arnold Rönnebeck for a time.

December: *The Glebe*, published in New York by Albert and Charles Boni, devoted a complete issue to Demuth's one-act play, *The Azure Adder*.

Spring: Returned to the States.

Summer: Went to Provincetown on the Cape, where along with Helene Iungerich he organized an exhibition of Living Japanese Prints. Was in Provincetown when World War I began.

September: Returned to Lancaster from the Cape.

1914–15 Fall through spring: Divided his time between Lancaster and New York. During this year made some pastels (later destroyed), using the New York skyline as subject matter. Also painted *The Drinkers* and *At Marshall's*, among the first of his mature figure pieces.

October–November: Exhibited for the first time in a commercial gallery when Watercolors by Charles Demuth, a one-man show, was presented at the Daniel Gallery in New York.

Summer: Was in Provincetown with Edward Fisk. Contributed to end-of-the-summer shows on the Cape.

August 2: Signed an indenture, County of Barnstable, Massachusetts.

1915–16 Fall through spring: Still dividing his time between Lancaster and New York, rented an apartment on Washington Square South (45 Washington Square). During this year he made his single illustration for Zola's *L'Assommoir* and began his series of vaudeville pieces. And during this year Duchamp, Picabia, and Gleizes arrived in New York from France.

October 30–November 9: The artist's second one-man show, Watercolors by Charles Demuth, was presented at the Daniel Gallery.

Summer: Was in Provincetown.

1916–17 Fall until spring: Was in Bermuda, probably with Hartley, where both men experimented with Cubism.

December: The artist's third one-man show, Watercolors by Charles Demuth, was presented at the Daniel Gallery.

April 10–May 6: Was represented in the first annual exhibition of Société Anonyme, Inc.

May: The second number of *The Blind Man*, a review edited by Marcel Duchamp, appeared carrying a contribution by Demuth.

Summer: Was at Gloucester and at home in Lancaster, painting Cubist-influenced landscapes of the type begun in Bermuda.

1917–18　Fall through spring: Divided his time between Lancaster and New York. During this year produced *The Circus*, more vaudeville pieces, and more of his fish series which were painted at the Aquarium in Battery Park.

November–December: The artist's fourth exhibition at the Daniel Gallery, Watercolors by Charles Demuth and Oils by Edward Fisk, was presented.

May–October: Was in Provincetown.

1918–19　Fall through spring: Painted in Lancaster, with intermittent visits to New York and Philadelphia. During this year produced his illustrations for Henry James's *The Turn of the Screw* and more vaudeville pieces. He was suffering from a "chronic illness" at this time.

November–December: The artist's fifth show at the Daniel Gallery, Recent Drawings in Watercolor by Charles Demuth, was presented.

Summer: Painted in New England. *Back-drop of East Lynne* and *Gloucester* (or *Mackerel 35 Cents a Pound*) were both painted in 1919.

1919–20　Fall through spring: Painted in Lancaster, with intermittent visits to New York and Philadelphia. In 1919 produced the last of his illustrations, those for Henry James's *The Beast in the Jungle*. Experi-

194

mented with tempera and began his architectural-industrial landscapes. In 1920 produced *After Sir Christopher Wren, Lancaster, Machinery* (or *For W. Carlos W.*), *Modern Conveniences, and New England.*

Summer: Was in Provincetown where, during July and August, he began to suffer acute diabetic attacks.

1920–21 Fall through spring: Though at times completely incapacitated by diabetic attacks, he continued his pattern of wintering in Lancaster combined with weekly visits to New York and Philadelphia.

December: The artist's sixth exhibition at the Daniel Gallery, Arrangements of the American Landscape Forms, was shown.

Summer: May have been in Provincetown during June or July.

June 28. A passport permitting travel in England and France was mailed to him in Lancaster.

July 27: He obtained British and French visas in Philadelphia.

August: Sailed to Europe for the fourth and last time.

August 12: Mailed a letter to his mother from Southampton, where his passport was stamped on this day.

August 15 (?): Arrived in France.

1921–22 October 3: Left the American Hospital, Neuilly-sur-Seine, where he had been hospitalized for a week.

October 10: Obtained a receipt from Leonce Rosenberg, proprietor of L'Effort Moderne, for two watercolors entitled *Views of the City.*

October 29: His French visa was stamped, and he received a police identity card, his address at the time being 43 Raspail.

November 12: Left France, his passport being

stamped at Le Havre by the American Consulate on this date.

November 19: Landed in New York.

The artist probably painted the architectural-industrial landscapes *Aucassin and Nicolletta* and *Incense of a New Church*, both dated 1921, before leaving for Europe; *Rue du Singe Qui Pêche* while he was in Paris; and *Paquebot Paris* in Lancaster after his return.

Spring and summer: The artist and his mother went to Dr. Allen's Physiatric Institute in Morristown, New Jersey, where, following initial starvation treatment, insulin injections were begun. Met Alexander Lieberman at Morristown.

1922–23   Accomplished only a few paintings this year, all watercolor still lifes.

December: The artist's seventh exhibition at the Daniel Gallery, Recent Paintings by Charles Demuth, was presented.

Mid-March into May: Second period of confinement at Morristown.

1923–24   November-December: The artist's eighth and last exhibition at the Daniel Gallery, Watercolors by Charles Demuth, was presented.

Produced the first of his *hommages*, those dedicated to Dove and O'Keeffe, in 1924.

1924–25   March 9–28: Appeared in the exhibition Seven Americans arranged by Alfred Stieglitz in The Intimate Gallery at the Anderson Galleries, along with Marin, O'Keeffe, Dove, Hartley, Stieglitz, and Paul Strand. Painted numerous watercolor still lifes during this year; and probably at this time, his *hommages* for Duncan and Marin (c. 1925).

1925–26   April 5–May 2: Recent Paintings by Charles Demuth, a one-man show presented at Stieglitz' Intimate Gallery.

1926–27   October 11: Was awarded a silver medal for his watercolor *Plums* (1925), on exhibition in a show related to Philadelphia's Sesquicentennial Exposition. November 23: Was awarded the Dana Watercolor Medal for *Roses* (1920 or 1926), on display in the PAOFA's 24th Annual Philadelphia Watercolor Exhibition.

Produced some of the watercolor still lifes belonging to his eggplant series; and painted his well-known oil *My Egypt* (1927).

Summer: Spent ten days in Beverly, Massachusetts, during the month of August.

1927–28   Winter: Helped design the stage set for a Chekhov play produced by the Lancaster Dramatic Club.

Produced two more of his *hommages*: *I Saw the Figure 5 in Gold* (1928), dedicated to William Carlos Williams, and *Longhi on Broadway* (c. 1928), dedicated to Eugene O'Neill.

1928–29   October 18–December 9: Exhibited in the 27th International Exhibition at the Carnegie Institute, Pittsburgh, Pennsylvania.

April 29–May 18: *Charles Demuth—Five Paintings*, a one-man show presented at Stieglitz' Intimate Gallery.

Summer: Went to Atlantic City with Edith Gregor Halpert to attend the first municipal art show in America, which was staged by Mrs. Halpert.

1929–30   December 13–January 12: Was represented in the exhibition *Paintings by 19 Living Americans* at the Museum of Modern Art.

April–May: Participated in a group exhibition of the work of O'Keeffe, Demuth, Marin, Hartley, Dove (Retrospective) at An American Place.

June–September: Was represented in the Museum of Modern Art's Summer Exhibition: Retrospective.
Summer: Along with Darrell Larsen, visited Jack and Blanche Steinman at 'Sconset on Nantucket Island, residing in the Steinman guesthouse while there. Also went to Provincetown this summer. Probably the time when the pornographic watercolors were painted.

1930–31 March 16–30: Was represented in Seven Masters of Water Color, at New York's Downtown Gallery.
April: Paintings by Charles Demuth, a one-man show presented at Stieglitz' An American Place.
May: Was represented in Group Show (Impromptu Exhibition of Selected Paintings): Marin, Hartley, O'Keeffe, Dove, Demuth at An American Place.
In 1930 painted his controversial "illustration" for Robert McAlmon's *Distinguished Air*.

1931–32 May 20–June 14: Was represented in Impromptu Exhibition of Selected Paintings (Dove, Demuth, Marin, O'Keeffe, Hartley) at An American Place.

1932–33 October 31–January 31: Was represented in the exhibition American Paintings and Sculpture (1862–1932) at the Museum of Modern Art.
November 22–January 5: Was represented in the Whitney Museum's First Biennial Exhibition of Contemporary American Painting.

1933–34 May 12–October 12: Was represented in the 19th International Biennial Art Exhibition at Venice.
Summer: Was in Provincetown, where he stayed with Frank and Elsie Everts in their cottage, The Sunbeam. Produced his 1934 sketchbook of figurative paintings.

1934–35 Spent the year at home in Lancaster.

1935 October 23: Died at 118 East King Street in Lancaster from the effects of diabetes.

Catalogue of Works
Mentioned in the Text

In the listing of dimensions below, height precedes width.
Data relating to the illustrations have not been repeated here
but appear with the reproductions. See List of Illustrations.

1912

Bartender at Brevoort. c. 1912. Watercolor, 8 3/8 x 5 3/8 in.
Unsigned and undated. Edgar Kaufmann, Jr., purchased from
Durlacher Bros., October 17, 1956.

The Conestoga, Winter. 1912. Watercolor. Signed in l.l.: *C.
Demuth.* The Coleman Art Gallery, Philadelphia, Pennsylvania.

Paris: the Night before Christmas. 1912. Ink drawing with watercolor, 10 5/8 x 7 1/4 in. Unsigned, but inscribed in l.l.: *Paris—
la nuit devant Noël—1912.* Edwin C. Wilson, Washington,
D.C., purchased at Parke-Bernet auction, October 16, 1957, #8
in catalogue.

1914

The Bay, Provincetown. c. 1914. Watercolor, 10 x 13 3/4 in.
Signed vertically in l.l.: *C. Demuth.* The Toledo Museum of
Art, Toledo, Ohio, purchased from C. W. Kraushaar Galleries,
1938. (There are three early Demuth watercolors and one early
oil on academy board entitled *The Bay.*)

1915

At Marshall's. 1915. Watercolor, 7 7/8 x 10 1/8 in. Signed, dated, and inscribed in l.l.: *C. Demuth/At Marshall's—1915.* Carl Van Vechten, New York, N. Y. (deceased).

The Drinkers (or *Chez Ritz*). 1915. Watercolor, 10 3/4 x 8 1/4 in. Signed, dated, and inscribed in l.l.: *C. Demuth/1915/Chez Ritz.* The Columbus Gallery of Fine Arts, Columbus, Ohio, Gift of Ferdinand Howald, April 23, 1931.

Dunes. 1915. Watercolor, 11 3/8 x 15 15/16 in. Signed and dated in l.l.: *C. Demuth/1915.* The Columbus Gallery of Fine Arts, Columbus, Ohio, Gift of Ferdinand Howald, April 23, 1931.

Flower Piece. 1915. Watercolor, 18 x 11 1/2 in. Signed in l.r. along base: *Demuth.* Lawrence Art Museum, Williams College, Williamstown, Massachusetts, Bequest of Miss Susan Watts Street, 1956.

Scene after Georges Stabs Himself with the Scissors (2nd version). Illustration No. 8 for Zola, *Nana* (Chapter XIII). 1915–16. Watercolor, 8 x 10 (or 7 3/4 x 12 3/4) in. Unsigned and undated. Purchased at Parke-Bernet auction, February 5, 1958, #56 in catalogue.

Waiters at the Brevoort (or *Two Figures at Café Table*). c. 1915. Watercolor, 6 x 8 3/4 in. Unsigned and undated. Mr. and Mrs. Nelson Goodman, Schwenksville, Pennsylvania, acquired by exchange from Robert Locher, May 24, 1955, in return for *Man on Dock* (c. 1916).

1916

Illustration for Zola's L'Assommoir. 1916. Watercolor, 8 x 10 1/2 in. Signed and dated in l.l.: *C. Demuth. 1916—.* Inscribed in l.r.: *"La Debutante's Mon—la—d'—lle's."* [Illegible.] The Philadelphia Museum of Art, Philadelphia, Pennsylvania, Gift of A. E. Gallatin, 1952.

"Many Brave Hearts Are Asleep in the Deep . . . ." 1916. Watercolor, 13 x 8 in. Signed and dated in l.l.: *C. Demuth. 1916—.* Miss Mary Mullen, The Barnes Foundation, Merion, Pennsylvania.

Negro Girl Dancer. 1916. Watercolor, 12 7/8 x 7 7/8 in. Unsigned and undated. Robert Laurent, Brooklyn, New York, purchased from the Daniel Gallery (?).

Negro Jazz Band. 1916. Watercolor, 13 x 7 7/8 in. Signed and dated in u.l.: *C. Demuth—/1916.* Private Philadelphia collection, purchased at Parke-Bernet auction, January 19, 1955. Formerly owned by Henry McBride.

The Nut, Pre-Volstead Days. 1916. Watercolor, 10 9/16 x 7 13/16 in. Signed and dated in l.l.: *C. Demuth. 1916.* The Columbus Gallery of Fine Arts, Columbus, Ohio, Gift of Ferdinand Howald, April 23, 1931.

Our Little Mary (or *Our Mary in "As You Like It"*). c. 1916. Oil, 23 1/2 x 19 1/2 in. Unsigned and undated. Miss Georgia O'Keeffe, Abiquiu, New Mexico, Demuth Bequest, 1935.

Scene after Georges Stabs Himself with the Scissors (1st version). Illustration No. 7 for Zola, *Nana* (Chapter XIII). 1916. Watercolor, 8 1/2 x 10 3/4 in. (sight). Signed and dated in u.r.: *C. Demuth. 1916.* The Barnes Foundation, Merion, Pennsylvania.

Scene with American Flag. c. 1916. Watercolor, 8 1/2 x 11 in. Signed in l.l.: *C. Demuth.* Mr. and Mrs. Nelson Goodman, Schwenksville, Pennsylvania, purchased from Robert Locher, March 22, 1956.

The Shine. 1916. Watercolor, 7 3/4 x 10 1/4 in. Signed, dated and inscribed in l.l.: *C. Demuth. /—1916./ The Shine.* The Museum of Modern Art, New York, Gift of James W. Barney, 1934.

Spring. c. 1916. Oil, 21 3/4 x 23 3/4 in. Unsigned and undated. C. Philip Boyer, Boyer Gallery, Philadelphia, Pennsylvania.

1917

Bermuda #1 (Tree and Houses). c. 1917. Watercolor, 10 x 13 7/8 in. Signed and inscribed at l.c.: *C. D./Bermuda.* The Metropolitan Museum of Art, New York, Bequest of Alfred Stieglitz, 1949.

Bermuda #2 (The Schooner). 1917. Watercolor, 10 x 13 7/8 in.

Signed and dated in l.l.: *C. Demuth/1917*. The Metropolitan Museum of Art, New York, Bequest of Alfred Stieglitz, 1949.

Bermuda #3 (The Tower). 1917. Watercolor, 10 x 14 in. Signed and dated in l.l.: *C. Demuth, 1917*. The Art Institute of Chicago, Chicago, Illinois, Gift of Miss Georgia O'Keeffe, 1949.

Bermuda #4. 1917. Watercolor, 9 5/8 x 13 11/16 in. Signed and dated in l.l.: *C. Demuth, 1917*. The Metropolitan Museum of Art, New York, Bequest of Alfred Stieglitz, 1949.

Bermuda: Houses. 1917. Watercolor, c. 8 x c. 14 in. Signed and dated in l.l.: *C. Demuth/1917–*. The Barnes Foundation, Merion, Pennsylvania.

Eight O'Clock–Evening. 1917. Watercolor, 8 x 10 3/8 in. Signed, dated, and inscribed at c. base: *–8 o'clock–/C. Demuth. 1917–*. Wadsworth Atheneum, Hartford, Connecticut, Gift of George J. Dyer, 1951.

Eight O'Clock–Morning #1. 1917. Watercolor, 7 7/8 x 10 1/8 in. Signed diagonally in l.l.: *C. Demuth, 1917*. The Museum of Modern Art, New York, Gift of Mrs. John D. Rockefeller, Jr., 1935.

Eight O'Clock–Morning #2. 1917. Watercolor, 7 7/8 x 10 3/16 in. Signed, dated, and inscribed: *C. Demuth 1917–8 o'clock*. Wadsworth Atheneum, Hartford, Connecticut, acquired in 1958.

Landscape. c. 1917. Watercolor, 9 11/16 x 13 9/16 in. (sight). Signed in l.l.: *C. Demuth*. The Columbus Gallery of Fine Arts, Columbus, Ohio, Gift of Ferdinand Howald, April 23, 1931.

1918

Pink Lady Slippers. 1918. Watercolor, 16 1/2 x 10 in. Signed and dated in l.l.: *C. Demuth 1918*. Mrs. William Carlos Williams, Rutherford, New Jersey.

A Prince of Court Painters #2. Illustration for the section on Watteau in Pater, *Imaginary Portraits*. c. 1918. Watercolor, c. 11 x c. 8 in. Signature unknown. Sold by Alanson Hartpence of the Daniel Gallery, 1925 or 1926. Formerly owned by Polly Holliday.

Provincetown. 1918. Watercolor, 13 1/4 x 9 1/2 in. Signed and dated in l.l.: *C. Demuth 1918.* Christopher Demuth, Lancaster, Pennsylvania, Gift of Robert Locher, May 23, 1943.

Red Chimneys. 1918. Watercolor, 9 3/4 x 13 3/4 in. Signed and dated in l.l.: *C. Demuth./1918–.* The Phillips Memorial Gallery, Washington, D.C., acquired from the Montross Gallery.

1919

At "The Golden Swan" Sometimes Called "Hell Hole." 1919. Watercolor, 8 1/4 x 10 3/4 in. Signed and dated in l.l.: *C. Demuth–1919–.* Inscribed in l.r.: *At "The/Golden Swan"/ Sometimes called "Hell Hole."* Herbert S. Levy, Lancaster, Pennsylvania.

Back-drop of East Lynne. 1919. Tempera on cardboard, 19 7/8 x 15 7/8 in. Signed and dated in l.l.: *C. Demuth–/Gloucester./ 1919–.* The University of Nebraska Art Galleries, Lincoln, Nebraska, purchased from Kraushaar Galleries, 1946.

Box of Tricks. 1919. Tempera on board, 19 1/2 x 15 1/4 in. Signed and dated in l.l.: *C. Demuth–/1919–Gloucester.* The Philadelphia Museum of Art, Philadelphia, Pennsylvania, purchased from Morton R. Goldsmith.

Cottage Window. c. 1919. Tempera on thick yellow board, 15 7/8 x 11 7/8 in. (back of board). Signed in u.l. on reverse: *Charles Demuth.* The Columbus Gallery of Fine Arts, Columbus, Ohio, Gift of Ferdinand Howald, April 23, 1931.

Gloucester (or *Mackerel 35 Cents a Pound*). 1919. Crayon, transparent watercolor and tempera on rough paperboard, 16 x 20 in. Signed, dated, and inscribed in l.l.: *C. Demuth–/Gloucester '19.* Inscribed on reverse: *MACKEREL 35 CENTS A POUND, C.D. 1919.* The Museum of Art, Rhode Island School of Design, Providence, Rhode Island, purchased from Mrs. Cornelius J. Sullivan (her gallery) through the Jesse Metcalf Fund, October, 1939.

In the Key of Blue. c. 1919–20. Tempera on paper, 19 1/2 x 15 1/2 in. Signed in l.l.: *C. Demuth.* The Museum of Modern Art, New York, Gift of Mrs. John D. Rockefeller, Jr., 1935.

The Primrose. c. 1919. Tempera on thick yellow board, 15 3/4 x 11 11/16 in. (sight). Unsigned and undated. The Columbus Gallery of Fine Arts, Columbus, Ohio, Gift of Ferdinand Howald, April 23, 1931.

Sails (or *Sailboats,* or *The Love Letter*). 1919. Tempera, 15 3/8 x 19 3/8 in. (sight). Signed and dated in l.l.: *C. Demuth 1919.* The Santa Barbara Museum of Art, Santa Barbara, California.

A Sky after El Greco. 1919. Tempera, 20 x 16 in. Signed and dated in l.l.: *C. Demuth./1919.* Arizona State College, Tempe, Arizona, Collection of American Art.

1920

After Sir Christopher Wren (or *New England*). 1920. Tempera on paperboard, 23 7/8 x 20 in. Signed and dated in l.l.: *C. Demuth 1920.* The Worcester Art Museum, Worcester, Massachusetts, Anonymous Loan.

End of the Parade—Coatesville, Pa. (or *Milltown*). 1920. Tempera on board, 19 1/2 x 15 1/2 in. Signed and dated in l.r.: *C. D./—1920—/Coatsville* [*sic*],/*Pa.* Mrs. William Carlos Williams, Rutherford, New Jersey, purchased from the Daniel Gallery.

In the Province #1 (or *Roofs*). 1920. Tempera, 28 x 24 in. Signed, dated, and inscribed: *Demuth—1920 Lancaster Pa.* Inscribed on reverse: *C. Demuth, Lancaster, Pa.* John McAndrew, Wellesley, Massachusetts, purchased from the Downtown Gallery, 1955 or 1956.

Lancaster (or *Gloucester*). 1920. Tempera and pencil on paper, 23 3/8 x 19 1/2 in. Signed, dated, and inscribed in l.l.: *C. Demuth./1920—/Lancaster/Pa.* The Philadelphia Museum of Art, Philadelphia, Pennsylvania, Gift of Louise and Walter Arensberg, 1952.

Machinery (or *For W. Carlos W.*). 1920. Tempera and pencil on cardboard, 24 x 19 7/8 in. Signed, dated, and inscribed in

l.l.: *C. Demuth 1920—Lancaster, Pa./For W. Carlos W.* Inscribed on reverse: *"For W. Carlos W." Lancaster, Pa. C.D.
1920.* The Metropolitan Museum of Art, New York, Bequest
of Alfred Stieglitz, 1949.

The Tower (or *After Sir Christopher Wren*). c. 1920. Tempera
on pasteboard, 23 1/2 x 19 5/16 in. Unsigned and undated. The
Columbus Gallery of Fine Arts, Columbus, Ohio, Gift of Ferdinand Howald, April 23, 1931.

1921

Aucassin and Nicolletta. 1921. Oil on canvas, 23 3/8 x 19 3/8
in. Signed and dated on reverse: *C. Demuth—/1921.* The Columbus Gallery of Fine Arts, Columbus, Ohio, Gift of Ferdinand Howald, April 23, 1931.

August Lilies. 1921. Watercolor, 11 3/4 x 17 7/8 in. (sight). Signed,
dated, and inscribed in l.l.: *C.D.* [illegible word]/*1921—.* The
Whitney Museum of American Art, New York, purchased
from Kraushaar Galleries, March 2, 1931.

From the Garden of the Château. 1921 (or 1925). Oil, 25 x 20 in.
Signed and dated vertically in l.l.: *C. Demuth/1921* [or 1925].
William H. Bender, Jr., National Life Insurance Co., New
York. Formerly owned by the Whitney Museum of American
Art. "Badly damaged while on tour in South America in 1941
under the auspices of the Coordinator of Inter-American Affairs. Total damage paid to Museum. Painting taken by Insurance Company to be restored." (Quotation from Weyand files
of Demuthiana.)

Modern Conveniences. 1921. Oil on Canvas, 25 7/8 x 21 1/8 in.
(back of stretcher bars). Signed and dated vertically in l.l.:
C. Demuth, 1921. The Columbus Gallery of Fine Arts, Columbus, Ohio, Gift of Ferdinand Howald, April 23, 1931.

Nospmas M. Egap Nospmas M. 1921. Oil, 24 x 20 in. Signed,
dated, and inscribed on reverse: *C. Demuth, Lancaster, Pa.
1921 "Nospmas M. Egiap [sic] Nospmas M."* Mrs. Edith
Gregor Halpert, New York (deceased).

Paquebot Paris. c. 1921. Oil on canvas, 24 3/4 x 19 7/8 in. (back of stretcher bars). Unsigned and undated. The Columbus Gallery of Fine Arts, Columbus, Ohio, Gift of Ferdinand Howald, April 23, 1931.

Rue du Singe Qui Pêche. 1921. Tempera on cardboard, 21 x 16 1/4 in. Signed, dated, and inscribed in l.r.: *C.D./Paris./1921.* Mr. and Mrs. Bernard Heineman, Jr., New York, purchased from the Downtown Gallery c. 1951. (A nearly identical 1921 watercolor titled *Hotel* [19 1/2 x 14 1/2 in., signed *Demuth* in the l.l.] is owned by D. E. Weiss of Chicago, Illinois. This work is not listed in either Weyand's or the author's catalogue of Demuth works, but may be one of the two watercolors called "Views of the City" sold to L'Effort Moderne in Paris October 10, 1921.)

Welcome to Our City. 1921. Oil, 24 1/2 x 19 5/8 in. Signed and dated in l.l.: *C. Demuth 1921.* Max Miller, Miami Beach, Florida, purchased from the Downtown Gallery, c. 1952.

1922

Eggplant and Peppers. 1922. Watercolor, 9 3/4 x 13 3/4 in. (sight). Signed and dated in l.r.: *C. Demuth, 1922.* Fisk University, Nashville, Tennessee, Bequest of Alfred Stieglitz, 1949.

Fruit No. 1. 1922. Watercolor, 9 5/16 x 12 7/8 in. (sight). Signed and dated diagonally in l.l. near c.: *C. Demuth—/1922—.* The Columbus Gallery of Fine Arts, Columbus, Ohio, Gift of Ferdinand Howald, April 23, 1931.

Fruit No. 2. 1922. Watercolor, 9 3/8 x 12 15/16 in. (sight). Signed and dated diagonally in l.r.: *C. Demuth./1922—.* The Columbus Gallery of Fine Arts, Columbus, Ohio, Gift of Ferdinand Howald, April 23, 1931.

Still Life No. 2. 1922. Watercolor, 9 5/8 x 12 5/8 in. (sight). Signed and dated in l.r.: *C. Demuth./1922.* The Columbus Gallery of Fine Arts, Columbus, Ohio, Gift of Ferdinand Howald, April 23, 1931.

Tuberoses. 1922. Watercolor, 13 1/2 x 11 1/2 in. Signed and dated

in l.l.: *C. Demuth. 1922.* Mrs. William Carlos Williams, Rutherford, New Jersey.

Yellow Calla Lily Leaves. 1922. Watercolor, 19 7/8 x 13 7/8 in.
Signed and dated at r.c.: *Charles Demuth '22.* Yale Univer-
sity Art Gallery, New Haven, Connecticut, Gift of Philip L.
Goodwin, 1937.

1923

Amaryllis (or *Flower Study*). c. 1923. Watercolor, 17 1/2 x 11
3/4 in. Unsigned and undated. The Cleveland Museum of Art,
Cleveland, Ohio, Hinman B. Hurlbut Collection.

Flower Study No. 1. 1923. Watercolor, 18 1/8 x 12 in. Signed
and dated in l.l.: *C. Demuth—/1923.* The Art Institute of Chicago, Chicago, Illinois, Gift of Annie Swan Coburn in memory
of Olivia Shaler Swan, 1933.

White Lilacs. 1923. Watercolor and pencil, 13 3/4 x 9 3/4 in.
Signed and dated in l.r.: *C. Demuth 1923.* Mrs. James H. Beal,
Pittsburgh, Pennsylvania, purchased from Durlacher Brothers,
June 15, 1954.

1924

Mme. Delaunois. 1924. Pencil drawing with watercolor, 11 x 8
1/2 in. Signed and dated in l.l.: *Demuth—1924.* Inscribed at c.
base: *Mme. Delaunois—.* Inscribed in u.l.: *League of/Composers
—/Nov. 30th.* Inscribed in u.r.: *Myosotis d'Amour/Florette—/
Stravinsky—.* Purchased at Parke-Bernet auction October 16,
1957, #29 in catalogue.

Poster Portrait: Arthur G. Dove. c. 1924. Oil on board, 20 x 24 in.
Unsigned and undated. Inscribed on reverse: *For Helen with
love from Demuth.* Alfred Stieglitz Archive, Collection of
American Literature, Yale University Library, Gift of Georgia
O'Keeffe.

1925

Youth and Old Age (or *Flowers*). 1925. Watercolor, 17 1/2 x
11 5/8 in. Signed, dated, and inscribed near c. of r. edge: *Aug.—
C. Demuth, 1925—/Lancaster, Pa.—* Inscribed in l.r.: *Youth and*

Old Age. Inscribed in u.l.: *Black-Eyed Susans.* The Museum of Fine Arts, Boston, Massachusetts, purchased through the Frederick Brown Fund, 1940.

1926

Carrots and Apples. 1926. Watercolor, 13 3/4 x 19 3/4 in. Signed, dated, and inscribed in u.r.: *C. Demuth—Lancaster, Pa./1926—.* George H. Fitch, New York.

1927

Poster Portrait: Calla Lilies (Hommage to Bert Savoy). 1927. Oil on composition board, 42 1/8 x 48 (or 40 5/8 x 46 3/4) in. Unsigned and undated (?). Fisk University, Nashville, Tennessee, Gift of Georgia O'Keeffe, 1949.

1928

Daffodils. 1928. Watercolor, 17 11/16 x 11 5/8 in. Signed and dated diagonally at c. base: *C. Demuth 1928—.* John S. Newberry, Jr., Grosse Pointe Farms, Michigan.

1929

Calla Lilies. 1929. Watercolor, 13 11/16 x 19 11/16 in. Signed, dated, and inscribed at l.c.: *C. Demuth,/Lancaster, Pa./1929—.* The Lawrence Art Museum, Williams College, Williamstown, Massachusetts, Bequest of Miss Susan Watts Street, 1956.

Corn and Peaches. 1929. Watercolor, 13 3/4 x 19 3/4 in. Unsigned and undated. The Museum of Modern Art, New York, Gift of Mrs. John D. Rockefeller, Jr., 1935.

Design for a Broadway Poster (unfinished). 1929. Not *Longhi on Broadway* (1927), since the two works were exhibited simultaneously at the Intimate Gallery in the 1929 show, Charles Demuth—Five Paintings. Mentioned in Demuth-Stieglitz letters, Collection of American Literature, Yale University Library, p. 83.

Green Pears. 1929. Watercolor, 13 1/2 x 19 1/2 in. Signed and dated at l.c.: *C. Demuth—/'29—.* Philip L. Goodwin, New York (deceased).

Red Cabbages, Rhubarb and Orange. 1929. Watercolor, 14 x 19 7/8 in. Signed, dated, and inscribed along rhubarb stalk: *Lancaster Pa., C. Demuth '29*. The Metropolitan Museum of Art, New York, Bequest of Alfred Stieglitz, 1949.

Red Poppies. 1929. Watercolor, 14 x 20 in. Signed and dated in l.r.: *1929/C. Demuth*. Mrs. Edith Gregor Halpert, New York (deceased).

1930

Illustration for McAlmon's Distinguished Air. 1930. Watercolor, 16 x 12 in. Signed and dated on diagonal line at c.: *C. Demuth, 1930*. Inscribed in l.l.: *For/"Distinguished/Air."—by/Robert/McAlmon*. Sold at Parke-Bernet auction October 16, 1957, #51 in catalogue.

Waiting (or *Ventilators, 1930*). 1930. Tempera on academy board, 15 3/4 x 20 in. Signed, dated and inscribed in l.l.: *C. Demuth 1930 Lan Pa*. Signed, dated, and inscribed on reverse in the artist's hand: *"Waiting" Lancaster Pa. 1930 C. Demuth November*. The Art Institute of Chicago, Chicago, Illinois, Bequest of Alfred Stieglitz, 1949.

1931

". . . and the Home of the Brave." 1931. Oil on composition board, 30 x 24 in. Signed and dated at c. base: *C.D. 1931*. Signed, dated and, inscribed on reverse: *"—and the home of the brave"* C. *Demuth, 1931, Lancaster, Pa.* The Art Institute of Chicago, Chicago, Illinois, Gift of Miss Georgia O'Keeffe, 1948.

Buildings Abstraction—Lancaster, 1931. c. 1931–32. Oil on canvas, 27 7/8 x 23 5/8 in. Unsigned and undated. The Detroit Institute of Arts, Detroit, Michigan, purchased from the Downtown Gallery (?) after March, 1950.

Chimney and Water Tower. 1931. Oil on composition board, 30 x 23 7/8 in. Signed and dated in l.r.: *C.D. '31*. The National Gallery of Art, Washington, D.C., Alfred Stieglitz Collection, on Loan from Miss Georgia O'Keeffe, 1949 on.

1934

The 1934 sketchbook made in Provincetown included the following twelve watercolors.

1. *Bathers, Provincetown.* 1934. 8 1/2 x 11 in. Signed and dated in l.l.: *C. Demuth 1934.* Robert H. Tannahill, Grosse Pointe Farms, Michigan.

2. *Beach Study #3, Provincetown.* 1934. 8 1/2 x 11 in. Signed and dated in l.l.: *Demuth '34.* Dartmouth College, Hanover, New Hampshire, Gift of Mrs. John D. Rockefeller, Jr.

3. *Child on Beach, Provincetown.* 1934. 8 1/2 x 11 in. Signed and dated in l.l.: *C. Demuth, 1934.* Miss Heather Jane Smith, Gift of Richard W. C. Weyand, June 12, 1956.

4. *Figures on Beach #1, Provincetown.* 1934. 8 3/8 x 11 in. Signed and dated in l.l.: *C. Demuth '34.* Downtown Gallery, New York, purchased from Durlacher Brothers, November 1, 1954.

5. *Figures on Beach #2, Provincetown.* 1934. 8 1/2 x 11 in. Signed and dated in l.l.: *C. Demuth '34.* Alan H. Temple, Scarsdale, New York, purchased at Parke-Bernet auction, February 5, 1958, #39 in catalogue.

6. *Girl Reclining on Beach, Provincetown.* 1934. 8 1/2 x 11 in. Unsigned and undated. Mr. and Mrs. Gerald S. Lestz, Lancaster, Pennsylvania, purchased at Parke-Bernet auction, February 5, 1958, #77A in catalogue.

7. *Group on Beach #3, Provincetown.* 1934. 8 1/2 x 11 in. Signed and dated in l.l.: *C. Demuth '34.* Mr. and Mrs. Leonard B. Schlosser, New York, purchased at Parke-Bernet auction, February 5, 1958, #2 in catalogue.

8. *Man and Woman, Provincetown* (or *Beach Study #2*, or *Two Figures*). 1934. 10 5/8 x 8 1/4 in. Signed and dated in l.l.: *C. Demuth '34.* Mr. and Mrs. Sam Cantey III, Fort Worth, Texas, purchased from M. Knoedler & Co., November 21, 1950.

9. *Man in Bathing Suit on Beach, Provincetown.* 1934. 11 x 8 1/2 in. Unsigned and undated. Mr. and Mrs. Gerald S. Lestz,

Lancaster, Pennsylvania, purchased at Parke-Bernet auction, February 5, 1958, #77B in catalogue.

10. *Man with Newsboy, Provincetown.* 1934. 11 x 8 1/2 in. Signed and dated in l.l.: *C. Demuth '34.* Downtown Gallery, New York, purchased from Durlacher Brothers, November 14, 1956.

11. *Pink Dress, Provincetown.* 1934. 8 x 10 1/2 in. Signed and dated in l.l.: *C. Demuth '34.* The Museum of Fine Arts, Springfield, Massachusetts, purchased from Kraushaar Galleries through the Horace P. Wright Fund, January, 1949.

12. *Women on Beach, Provincetown.* 1934. 8 1/2 x 11 in. Unsigned and undated. Miss Louise Schayek, New York, purchased at Parke-Bernet auction, October 16, 1957, #73 in catalogue.

NOTE: *The author's total catalogue of Demuth works, which lists 747 paintings and 327 drawings, each with description and provenance, is on file in the Main Library of Ohio State University, Columbus, Ohio.*

Bibliography

Personal Interviews

Interviews with:

Miss Louetta Bowman in Lancaster, Pennsylvania, January 13, 1956.

Charles Daniel in New York, January 27, 1956.

Stuart Davis in New York, January 20, 1956.

Christopher Demuth in Lancaster, Pennsylvania, August 29, 1958.

Marcel Duchamp in New York, January 21, 1956.

Elsie (Mrs. Frank J.) Everts in Lancaster, Pennsylvania, January 12, 1956; also, August 26–September 1, 1958, during which time the author was a guest in Mrs. Everts' home in Lancaster.

Edith Gregor (Mrs. Samuel) Halpert in New York, January 26, 1956.

Darrell Larsen in Lancaster, Pennsylvania, August 28, 1958.

Robert Locher in Lancaster, Pennsylvania, January 5–18, 1956.

Henry McBride in New York, January 23, 1956.

Miss Susan Watts Street in New York, January 21, 1956.

Carl Van Vechten in New York, January 23, 1956.

Abraham Walkowitz in New York, January 27, 1956.

Richard W. C. Weyand in Lancaster, Pennsylvania, January 5–18, 1956.

Dr. William Carlos Williams in Rutherford, New Jersey, January 26, 1956.

Questionnaires

Replies to a Demuth Questionnaire were received from:

George Biddle, Marcel Duchamp, Henry McBride, Abraham
Walkowitz, and William Carlos Williams.

Letters

Charles Demuth to Mrs. Ferdinand A. Demuth:
  August 12, 1921, October 15, 1921, October 17, 1921, and Novem-
  ber 7, 1921. Weyand Scrapbooks.
Charles Demuth to Gertrude Stein:
  September 6, 1921, December 26, 1922, and several undated notes.
  Stein Collection, Collection of American Literature, Yale Univer-
  sity Library.
Charles Demuth to Alfred Stieglitz:
  August 13, 1921, October 10, 1921, October 13, 1921, November
  29, 1921, July 30, 1922, December (?), 1922, January 29, 1923,
  March 12, 1923, April 16, 1923, April 21, 1923, May 2, 1923, September 4, 1923, July (?), 1927, August 15, 1927, October 30,
  1927, February 5, 1928 (or 1929), June 4, 1928, June 18, 1928,
  August 6, 1928, April 8, 1929, October 16, 1929, January 28,
  1930, October 12, 1930, and September 10, 1931. Also, an undated
  last (?) note. Stieglitz Collection, Collection of American Liter-
  ature, Yale University Library.
Charles Demuth to William Carlos Williams:
  September 17, 1907, October 13, 1921, June 9, 1922, and October
  16, 1922 (telegram). On microfilm in the Poetry Collection,
  Lockwood Memorial Library, University of Buffalo.
Elsie (Mrs. Frank J.) Everts to Emily Farnham:
  April 15, 1956, May 28, 1956, February 25, 1957, and January 20,
  1958. Collection of the author.
Robert Indiana to Emily Farnham:
  December 11, 1968. Collection of the author.
Alexander Lieberman to Richard Weyand:
  October 5, 1940. Weyand Scrapbook No. I, 73.
Georgia O'Keeffe to Emily Farnham:
  August 20, 1968. Collection of the author.
Charles Sheeler to Emily Farnham:
  March 31, 1956. Collection of the author.
Alfred Stieglitz to Charles Demuth:
  January 28, 1930, and one undated letter. Stieglitz Collection, Col-
  lection of American Literature, Yale University Library.

Unpublished Material by Charles Demuth

"Among Friends," MS of a one-act play with only the scene given. Weyand Scrapbook No. 1, p. 80.

"Fantastic Lovers, a Pantomime after Paul Verlaine," MS of a play. Weyand Scrapbook No. I. pp. 85–87.

"In Black and White," MS of a short story. Weyand Scrapbook No. I, pp. 87–89.

"In the Fields," MS of a poem. Weyand Scrapbook No. I, p. 92.

Introduction to catalogue for Georgia O'Keeffe exhibition, An American Place (New York), January 18–February 27, 1931.

"Painting, a Play," MS of a play.

"A Pantomime with Words," MS of a play, decorated by Robert Locher.

"The Voyage Was Almost Over," MS of a short story. Weyand Scrapbook No. I, 90–92.

"You Must Come Over," MS of a play. Weyand Scrapbook No. I, pp. 82–83.

Published Material by Charles Demuth

"Aaron Eshleman, Artist," *Lancaster County Historical Society Papers*, Vol. XVI, No. 8 (Lancaster, Pennsylvania, Lancaster County Historical Society, October, 1912), 247–50.

"Across a Greco Is Written," *Creative Art*, Vol. V (September 29, 1929), 629–34, illustrated.

"The Azure Adder," *The Glebe*, Vol. I, No. 3 (December, 1913), complete issue. (Published by Albert and Charles Boni.)

"Between Four and Five," *Camera Work*, No. 47 (July, 1914), 32. Written in response to Stieglitz' request for a reply to the question: What is "291"?

"Brief Reply by Charles Demuth to the Question: Can a Photograph Have the Significance of Art?" *Manuscripts*, No. 4 (December, 1922), 4.

"Confessions: Replies to a Questionnaire," *The Little Review*, Vol. XII, No. 2 (May, 1929), 30–31, with portrait.

"Filling a Page, a Pantomime with Words," *Rogue*, Vol. I, No. 2 (April 1, 1915), 13–14, illustrated.

"For Richard Mutt," a poem, *The Blind Man*, No. 2 (May, 1917), 6. Edited by Marcel Duchamp and published by Beatrice Wood.

Contributions by E. Satie, C. Demuth, W. C. Arensberg, L. Eilshemius, G. Buffet, A. Stieglitz, and others.

Introduction to catalogue for Georgia O'Keeffe exhibition, The Intimate Gallery (New York), February 4–March 17, 1929.

Introduction to "Georgia O'Keeffe Paintings," The Intimate Gallery
(New York), exhibition catalogue (folder), 1926. Reprinted in
The Philadelphia Museum Bulletin (Philadelphia, Pennsylvania),
40 (May, 1945), 78–80, illustrated.

"Lighthouses and Fog," in *America and Alfred Stieglitz*, a collective
portrait edited by Waldo Frank and others. New York, The Literary Guild, 1934, p. 246.

"Lighthouses and Fog," *Stieglitz Memorial Portfolio*, 1864–1946 (New
York, Twice a Year Press, 1947), p. 12.

"Peggy Bacon," The Intimate Gallery (New York), foreword to exhibition catalogue (folder), 1928.

Catalogues, Papers, Brochures

Brightbill, Ruth. "Wine of the Country," unpublished term paper on
the master's degree level, Columbia University, 1947.

Clifford, Henry, and Zigrosser, Carl. "History of an American—Alfred Stieglitz: '291' and After," Philadelphia Museum of Art (Philadelphia, Pennsylvania), catalogue, 1944.

Foltz, Josephine Kieffer. "An Appreciation of Charles Demuth," bro-
chure written in connection with Demuth Memorial Exhibition,
Franklin and Marshall College (Lancaster, Pennsylvania), 1941.
Weyand Scrapbook No. II, 115.

Genauer, Emily. Text for *Charles Demuth of Lancaster*, William
Penn Memorial Museum (Harrisburg, Pennsylvania), catalogue,
1966.

Henderson, Helen W. "Charles Demuth," paper read before the
Junior League of Lancaster, Pennsylvania, November 10, 1947.
Weyand Scrapbook No. II, 158–61.

Henderson, Helen W. Information Regarding Charles Demuth,
Weyand Scrapbook No. I, 69.

Lancaster County Historical Society (Lancaster, Pennsylvania), Loan
Exhibition of Historical and Contemporary Portraits Illustrating
the Evolution of Portraiture in Lancaster County, catalogue, 1912.

Malone, Mrs. John E. "Charles Demuth," *Lancaster County Histori-*

cal Society Papers, Vol. LII, No. 1 (Lancaster, Pennsylvania: Lancaster County Historical Society, 1948), 1–18, illustrated.

McBride, Henry. Foreword, "Charles Demuth, Artist," Whitney Museum of American Art (New York), Demuth Memorial Exhibition, catalogue, 1937–38.

The Pennsylvania Academy of the Fine Arts (Philadelphia, Pennsylvania), 150th Anniversary Exhibition, catalogue, 1955. Sections: Henderson, Helen W., "Thomas Pollock Anshutz," 105–106 and Ingersoll, R. Sturgis, "Henry Bainbridge McCarter," 95–99.

Newspaper Articles

"Cape Cod Is an Artistic Haven" (name of Provincetown newspaper unknown), August 15 (no year [c. 1914?]). Weyand Scrapbook No. II, 180.

"Charles Demuth Honored in the World of Art" (name of newspaper unknown), September 27, 1919. Weyand Scrapbook No. II, 197.

"Charles Demuth a Successful Cubist" (name of newspaper unknown; n.d.). Contains reference to and quotations from Henry McBride article in the *New York Evening Sun*. Weyand Scrapbook No. II, 179.

Lancaster (Pennsylvania) *New Era*. "207-Year-Old City Building Sold," March 28, 1957, p. 9.

"Mother and Two Artists Share Demuth Estate" (name of New York newspaper unknown), January 30, 1936. Weyand Scrapbook No. III, 220.

New York Evening Sun. October 30, 1914 (no headline). Weyand Scrapbook No. III, 220.

———. Henry McBride, "Works of Charles Demuth Shown in Daniel Galleries" (n.d.). Weyand Scrapbook No. III, 227.

New York Globe and Commercial Advertiser. H. C. Nelson, "Art and Artists," November 30, 1917, p. 12.

New York Herald. "Art of Painter, Etcher and Sculptor Fills the Galleries," October 26, 1914, p. 6.

New York Herald Tribune. Carlyle Burrows, "Pioneers of Modern Painting: American Artists and Chagall," April 14, 1946, Sec. 5, p. 7.

New York Sun. Henry McBride, "News and Reviews: Charles Demuth Displays His Beautiful Landscapes at Daniel's," December 5, 1920. Weyand Scrapbook No. II, 182.

———. Henry McBride, "An Underground Search for Higher Moralities," November 25, 1917, Sec. 5, p. 12.

New York Times. "Alfred Stieglitz Dies Here at 82," July 14, 1946. Weyand Scrapbook, No. II, 142.

———. Newton Arvin, "Henry James: Autobiography," April 29, 1956, Sec. 7, p. 1.

———. Edward Dahlberg, "Beautiful Failures," January 15, 1967, Book Review sec., pp. 4, 36–41, illustrated.

———. Hilton Kramer, "Death in Venice, With Giggles," June 26, 1966, Sec. 2, p. D 21.

———. Stuart Preston, "Among Current Shows," April 11, 1954, Sec. 2, p. 9.

New York Tribune. "Random Impressions in Current Exhibitions," December 24, 1922, Sec. 5, pp. 7–8.

Philadelphia Evening Bulletin. "Charles Demuth's Painting Reproduced in Living Flowers at Art Museum," April 18, 1933. Weyand Scrapbook No. III, 214.

Philadelphia Inquirer. November 1, 1914, Sec. 2, p. 2.

———. Helen W. Henderson, "Art and Artists Pass in Review," (n.d.). Weyand Scrapbook No. III, 204.

———. Helen W. Henderson, "Art and Artists Pass in Review," December 1, 1918, Feature sec., p. 8.

———. Helen W. Henderson, "Charles Demuth," in column "Art and Artists Pass in Review" (n.d. except 1947). Weyand Scrapbook No. II, 158–59.

"Play by Local Author, 'The Azure Adder,' from Pen of Charles Demuth, Appears in New York Periodical" (name of Lancaster, Pennsylvania, newspaper unknown; n.d.). Weyand Scrapbook No. III, 194.

Periodicals

Antin, David. "Warhol: the Silver Tenement," *Art News*, Vol. LXV, No. 4 (Summer, 1966), 47–49+, illustrated.

Bourdon, David. "E=MC² à Go-Go," *Art News*, Vol. LXIV, No. 9 (January, 1966), 22–25+, illustrated.

"Catcher of the Eye," *Time*, Vol. LXXXIV, No. 23 (December 4, 1964), 84–87, illustrated.

Faison, S. Lane, Jr. "Fact and Art in Charles Demuth," *Magazine of Art*, Vol. XLIII, No. 4 (April, 1950), 122–28.

Farnham, Emily. "Charles Demuth's Bermuda Landscapes," *Art Journal*, Vol. XXV, No. 2 (Winter, 1965–66), 130–37, illustrated.

Goodrich, Lloyd. "The Decade of the Armory Show," *Art in America*, Vol. LI, No. 1 (February, 1963), 60–63, illustrated.

Judkins, Winthrop Otis. "Towards a Reinterpretation of Cubism," *Art Bulletin*, Vol. XXX (December, 1948), 270–78.

Lane, James W. "Notes from New York: Memorial Exhibition at the Whitney Museum," *Apollo*, Vol. XXVII (February, 1938), 96–98, illustrated.

Lee, Alwyn. "Poets: the Second Chance," *Time*, Vol. LXXXIX, No. 22 (June 2, 1967), 67–74, illustrated.

McBride, Henry. "Watercolours by Charles Demuth," *Creative Art*, Vol. V (September 29, 1929), 635.

"Pop Art—Cult of the Commonplace," *Time*, Vol. LXXXI, No. 18 (May 3, 1963), 69–72, illustrated.

Seiberling, Dorothy. "Horizons of a Pioneer," *Life*, Vol. LXIV, No. 9 (March 1, 1968), 40–53, illustrated.

Smith, Jacob Getlar. "The Watercolors of Charles Demuth," *American Artist*, Vol. XIX, No. 5 (May, 1955), 26–31, illustrated.

Tomkins, Calvin. "Profiles: Not Seen and/or Less Seen," *New Yorker*, Vol. XL, No. 51 (February 6, 1965), 37–39.

Van Vechten, Carl. "Charles Demuth and Florine Stettheimer in Pastiches et Pistaches," *Reviewer* (Richmond, Virginia), Vol. II, No. 4 (February, 1922), 269–70.

"Watercolors at Daniels [*sic*]" (name of magazine unknown, n.d. [c. 1914?]). Weyand Scrapbook No. II, 148.

Wellman, Rita. "Pen Portraits: Charles Demuth, Artist," *Creative Art*, Vol. IX (December, 1931), 483–84, portrait.

Wright, Willard Huntington. "Modern Art," *International Studio*, Vol. LX, No. 239 (January, 1918), 98.

Monographs

Duchamp, Marcel. "A Tribute to the Artist," short article in Andrew Carnduff Ritchie, *Charles Demuth* (New York, Museum of Modern Art, 1950), p. 17.

Gallatin, Albert E. *Charles Demuth.* New York, William Edwin Rudge, 1927.

Murrell, William. *Charles Demuth*. One of American Artists Series. New York, Whitney Museum of American Art, 1931.

Ritchie, Andrew Carnduff. *Charles Demuth*. New York, Museum of Modern Art, 1950.

Weyand, Richard W. C. Scrapbooks Nos. I, II, III, IV. Demuth memorabilia, including newspaper and magazine clippings, photographs, letters, and other items. Compiled in the Demuth home in Lancaster, Pennsylvania, over a period of approximately ten years. Destined for the Collection of American Literature, Yale University Library.

Works Containing Sections on Demuth

Geldzahler, Henry. *American Painting in the Twentieth Century*. New York, The Metropolitan Museum of Art, 1965, pp. 133–38.

Hartley, Marsden. "Farewell, Charles, an Outline in Portraiture of Charles Demuth—Painter," in *The New Caravan*. Edited by Alfred Kreymborg, Lewis Mumford, and Paul Rosenfeld. New York, W. W. Norton & Co., Inc., 1936, pp. 552–62.

Lee, Sherman E. "A Critical Survey of American Water-color Painting." Unpublished Ph.D. dissertation, Western Reserve University, 1941.

Mellquist, Jerome. *The Emergence of an American Art*. New York, Charles Scribner's Sons, 1942, pp. 336–40.

Soby, James Thrall. *Contemporary Painters*. New York, Museum of Modern Art, 1948. pp. 9–15, illustrated.

Williams, William Carlos. *The Autobiography of William Carlos Williams*. New York, Random House, 1951, Chapter 26.

Books and Other Secondary Sources

Beckett, Samuel. *Proust*. New York, Grove Press, Inc., 1931.

Biddle, George. *Adolphe Borie*. Washington, D.C., American Federation of Arts, 1937.

———. *An American Artist's Story*. Boston, Little, Brown & Co., 1939.

Boulton, Agnes. *Part of a Long Story*. Garden City, N.Y., Doubleday & Co., Inc., 1958.

Brown, Milton W. *American Painting from the Armory Show to the Depression*. Princeton, Princeton University Press, 1955.

Frank, Waldo, and others, eds. *America and Alfred Stieglitz, a Collective Portrait*. New York, Literary Guild, 1934.

Giedion, Sigfried. *Space, Time and Architecture*. Cambridge, Mass., Harvard University Press, 1954.

Hapgood, Hutchins. *A Victorian in the Modern World*. New York, Harcourt, Brace & Co., 1939.

Hartley, Marsden. *Adventures in the Arts*. New York, Boni & Liveright, 1921.

Johnson, James Weldon. *Black Manhattan*. New York, Alfred A. Knopf, 1930.

Janis, Sidney. *Abstract and Surrealist Art in America*. New York, Reynal & Hitchcock, 1944. Braque quotation from "Testimony against Gertrude Stein," *Transition*, 1934–35.

Larkin, Oliver. *Art and Life in America*. New York, Rinehart & Co., Inc., 1950.

Malraux, André. *Museum without Walls*, Vol. I of *The Psychology of Art*. Translated by Stuart Gilbert. New York, Pantheon Books, 1949–50.

McBride, Henry. *Florine Stettheimer*. New York, Museum of Modern Art, 1946.

McCausland, Elizabeth. *Marsden Hartley*. Minneapolis, University of Minnesota Press, 1952.

Pater, Walter. *Imaginary Portraits*. London, Macmillan & Co., Ltd., 1922.

Raynal, Maurice, and others. *From Picasso to Surrealism*, Vol. III of *History of Modern Painting*. Geneva, Albert Skira, 1950.

Stein, Gertrude. *The Autobiography of Alice B. Toklas*. New York, Random House, 1933.

Tomkins, Calvin, and the Editors of Time-Life Books. *The World of Marcel Duchamp*. Time-Life Library of Art. New York, Time Incorporated, 1966.

Wedekind, Frank. *Tragedies of Sex*. Translation and introduction by Samuel A. Eliot, Jr. New York, Boni and Liveright, Inc., 1923.

Williams, William Carlos. *Sour Grapes*. Boston, The Four Seas Co., 1921.

Yutang, Lin. *The Importance of Living*. New York, Reynal & Hitchcock, 1937.

Index

C Demuth — "Flora"